SPEEDWAY
THE PRE-WAR YEARS

SPEEDWAY
THE PRE-WAR YEARS

ROBERT BAMFORD
ASSISTED BY
DAVE STALLWORTHY

TEMPUS

First published 2003

Tempus Publishing Ltd
The Mill, Brimscombe Port
Stroud, Gloucestershire GL5 2QG
www.tempus-publishing.com

© Robert Bamford and Dave Stallworthy, 2003

The right of Robert Bamford and Dave Stallworthy to be identified
as the Authors of this work has been asserted in accordance with the
Copyrights, Designs and Patents Act 1988.

All rights reserved. No part of this book may be reprinted
or reproduced or utilised in any form or by any electronic,
mechanical or other means, now known or hereafter invented,
including photocopying and recording, or in any information
storage or retrieval system, without the permission in writing
from the Publishers.

British Library Cataloguing in Publication Data.
A catalogue record for this book is available from the British Library.

ISBN 0 7524 2749 0,
Typesetting and origination by Tempus Publishing.
Printed in Great Britain by Midway Colour Print, Wiltshire.

CONTENTS

Introduction	7
1. Prelude	9
2. Dirt-Track Racing Arrives in Britain	17
3. Developments	28
4. The League Years	40
5. Test Matches	117
6. Star Championship and World Finals	150
7. The Riders	174

INTRODUCTION

Welcome to this story of pre-war speedway, which Robert and I trust you will enjoy. When reading on, you will encounter the words that tell the wonderful tale of a trip down memory lane, and you will be able to get inside what dirt-track racing was really like in the early years. To make all this possible, Robert Bamford, who has brought out many splendid speedway books, came on the scene to produce this marvellous volume. As well as adding details on the Star and World Championships, Test matches and rider pen pictures, Robert has also included all the necessary statistics, showing league tables and cup winners in order to further augment this nostalgic trip.

With a lot of information from the time still remaining somewhat blurred and sketchy, an awful lot of hard work and research has gone into this publication. As such, Robert and I are very grateful to numerous people who have helped along the way, in particular, Trevor James, Barry Stephenson and Mike Terran with information on results and league tables. John Warner from Orpington has also been of immeasurable assistance, not only with the checking of results, but also with vital pieces of additional information which has helped to greatly enhance the finished publication. The fabulous *Speedway Researcher* and its many contributors was also a great source of information to this end, as were various other magazines, namely *Speedway World*, *Speedway Echo*, *Speedway News*, *Speedway Star*, *On the Track*, *The Motor Cycle* and *Broadsider*. Mention must also be made here of the excellent series of *Speedway Archives* publications by Peter Jackson, which have proved to be an invaluable point of reference.

Meanwhile, grateful thanks go to good friends John Jarvis and Glynn Shailes, who were on hand to help as ever, and also provided added impetus and enthusiasm when the project appeared to be losing direction. Much gratitude is extended to Derek Copson too, for supplying information on early motorcycle races at Bristol and Cheltenham, which has helped to further augment the story.

Thanks are also due to John Burroughs, a good friend of the late Lionel Crossley, who gave us permission to use extracts from Lionel's unpublished book entitled *Speedway or who started all this anyway?* Lionel, of course, was very much involved in speedway, right up to his latter years, producing a fabulous book on Crystal Palace Speedway, and as well as being involved with the Iwade training track, he was also timekeeper at several tracks, including Hackney and Wimbledon.

Rare photographs have been reproduced in this volume, and for these illustrations we are very grateful again to John Warner for wading through his extensive collection, as well as the amazing Geoff Parker, who has also been of great assistance in several previous publications. Acknowledgement is made to the known photographers of the time, these being Bachan, Bass, T.H. Everitt, H. Kellett and R.G. Nichols, as well as other unknown image aces. Rare programme covers have also been reproduced to further enhance the book, and for these we are very appreciative of the help offered again by Geoff Parker, as well as Ian Somerville up in Scotland.

Dave Stallworthy
October 2003

1
PRELUDE

Right from the invention of the first practical motorcycles in 1885, riders and machines have been in constant competition regarding speed, distance between breakdowns and fuel consumption.

Endurance runs and trials were fairly regularly promoted, the results often being headline news. Motorcycles performed heroics during the First World War, and large numbers of dispatch riders became hooked on the new two-wheeled motor sport after hostilities ceased. All forms of motorized sport took the public fancy in a very big way during those inter-war years. The concern here is one brand only – 'Dirt-track racing' or, as it subsequently became known, 'Speedway'. Indeed, the term 'Speedway' was coined in Australia, and subsequently became a kind of trademark for a company known as International Speedways Ltd. This was formed by promoter A.J. Hunting, whose impressive rider base included Frank Arthur, Hilary Buchanan, Billy Lamont, Frank Pearce and Dicky Smythe. There was also a rival company, who unsurprisingly incorporated the term in their title, namely Dirt-Track Speedways Ltd, which was under the management of Jimmy Baxter, and they had the likes of Paddy Dean, Billy Galloway, Geoffrey 'Buzz' Hibberd and Keith McKay on their books.

Not much documentary evidence now exists regarding dirt-track racing in those far off days. Very few people still alive today can cast their minds back so far; any that can must be upwards of eighty years in age. One that could and did, however, was the venerable John S. Hoskins, the pioneer Australian promoter, who sadly passed on in April 1987, at the ripe old age of 95. To him must go the accolade for first presenting dirt-track racing at the West Maitland Electric Light Carnival on 15 December 1923, when the programme for the event was intriguingly titled 'Electric Light Sports'.

Prior to this in Britain, there were some loose surfaced events, as well as some on concrete, but all were of an impromptu or amateur nature, although they did prove popular and exciting for spectators nonetheless. The first motorcycle race in Bristol is known to have been staged in May 1903 at the Bristol Post Office Sports Ground. Sadly, an accident caused the deaths of S. Gover (aged fourteen) and F. Marks (aged four), plus injuries to many others, when two riders collided in the final and went into the nearby spectators. Also in June 1903, the Cheltenham Wheelers Club held races at the Athletic Ground, when Burt Yates of Coventry covered a mile in a track

Billy 'Cyclone' Lamont.

record time of 1 min 46⅘ sec from a flying start. Racing is known to have taken place on a loose surfaced oval circuit at Portman Road, Ipswich in July 1904, and later on, there was motorcycle racing at a track in Roundhay Park, Leeds during 1920. Canning Town in London's East End had a concrete track on the Isle of Dogs, whilst Brooklands attracted large crowds of spectators in the years immediately following the First World War, when speeds of more than 100mph were recorded at the three-mile banked Weybridge circuit.

It is also worth recalling the board-racing that took place in America. Between 1908 and 1925, Jack Prince was responsible for constructing most of the all-wood banked race tracks, which took the country by storm. The first of these circular motordromes was built at Playa Del Rey in California and was one mile in circumference. Prince was something of an engineering wizard and with the help of locally recruited carpenters, he could erect a track in a matter of weeks. The riders reached speeds of up to 70mph on these circuits and the machines used included Indian, Reading-Standard, Merkel and Thor. Other motordromes were constructed of varying lengths at Cleveland, Chicago, New Jersey, Atlanta, Pennsylvania, Salt Lake City, Georgia, Illinois, Nebraska and Omaha, to name but a few of the many venues.

The amazing Jake De Rosier enjoyed a highly successful career, winning a huge total of over 900 races, beginning on the velodrom cycle circuits at the age of seventeen, prior to moving on to the board-racing scene. Mounted on an Indian, the

Canadian broke record after record between 1909-10, winning hundreds of events across the country. He travelled to Britain in 1911, firstly appearing in the London to Edinburgh road trial and scooping the gold medal. The brilliant racer also took part in the TT races on the Isle of Man, but he was unfortunately disqualified, having received roadside assistance following an accident. De Rosier then practised at the famous Brooklands circuit, near London, establishing a then world record time of 87.38mph for one mile. A week later, he competed in a match race series against Charlie Collier. After taking victory in the first contest over $5\frac{1}{2}$ miles, the Canadian suffered a burst tyre in the second race over $13\frac{1}{2}$ miles, with Collier going on to an untroubled success. In the final and deciding race over 27 miles, the riders kept the crowd on their toes by trading places over the first few laps, before De Rosier pulled away to win after Collier had encountered ignition problems. Before returning home, the Canadian had another blast around Brooklands, re-breaking his own world record and clocking 88.23mph for one mile.

In February 1912, Jake De Rosier appeared at the newly-opened Los Angeles Stadium Motordrome. Unfortunately, while racing flat out, rival Charlie Balke lost control and careered across the track, hitting De Rosier and bringing him down in a horrifying smash. Balke suffered only minor injuries, but unfortunately De Rosier was left lying unconscious with a badly broken thigh. He only just survived the subsequent operation, which had to be paid for and took a huge chunk out of his savings. Sadly, another operation was required several months later and what remained of De Rosier's money had soon disappeared, along with all his trophies, which were sold to raise funds. His condition deteriorated and a year after the accident he entered hospital in Springfield, where he endured another lengthy operation. Unfortunately, there was no improvement and Jake De Rosier died on 25 February at the age of just 33.

America staged factory sponsored meetings as early as 1911, on earth and clay surfaced race tracks at the popular State and Country Fairs. These continued at regular intervals until the late 1920s. The factories concerned were Indian, Harley Davidson, American X, Excelsior and a few smaller marques. Large numbers of spectators flocked to these impromptu meetings. Races were frequently of five or ten miles duration, and quite a few illustrious names appeared, including Eddie Brinck, Joe Petrali, Jim Davies, John Vance, Maldwyn Jones, Paul Anderson, Lloyd 'Sprouts' Elder and many others. These were all solo riders, but a few sidecar exponents also caught the eye, though they didn't achieve the notoriety of those previously mentioned. Most of the machines used were the big 1000cc side valve motors, capable of quite high speeds for the time. These huge monsters reigned supreme for a number of years until a maximum engine size of 500cc was imposed for loose-surface racing in 1924.

On one of these huge monsters, Maldwyn Jones (1000cc Excelsior) adopted a new and exciting style of negotiating the left-hand loose surfaced bends. Instead of braking for the turns, he actually opened the throttle wider, thereby promoting massive rear wheel slides. By persevering, he soon discovered that this method also determined his direction of travel without losing much speed. He is generally

The one and only Lloyd 'Sprouts' Elder. In his day he was sensational and the first-ever American superstar.

thought to have been the originator of the pendulum or power slide. This occurred around 1921, and subsequently many of his American contemporaries followed suit. We know it now as broadsiding, the very essence of modern speedway racing. Indeed, where would our beloved sport be without it?

Whilst all this was evolving, European racing was progressing in a somewhat different direction, predominantly road racing in France, Germany, Italy, England and the Isle of Man. Hill climbs were also very popular, as were trials and cross country runs. Although not really racing as such, these events did foster a competitive spirit amongst the keen and ardent clubmen of the day. This augered well for the future of motorcycle competition in Britain which was shortly to follow.

Basically, the various forms of motorcycle sport were originally in the hands of private owners. These soon banded together to form clubs, and the clubs then became affiliated to the Auto Cycle Union (ACU), who in turn became the national organizing body that we recognize today in this country. Committees were introduced to look after the various branches of motorcycle sport. The same kind of evolution was also taking place at the same time in most other countries, culminating in a world supreme body known nowadays as the FIM (Fédération Internationale Motorcycliste). Thus, the ACU in England soon got its own division for speedway, responsible for rules, regulations and the proper running of the sport. This took a little time, and indeed improvements and alterations are still being implemented, even to the present day under the auspices of the Speedway Control Board (SCB).

PRELUDE

The British Speedway Promoters' Association (BSPA) also have a considerable say in domestic speedway, since they are primarily concerned with financing the sport. The Speedway Riders' Association (SRA) came into being at a later date to safeguard the riders' interests as a sort of trade union. This aims to protect riders' pay and safeguard track conditions and insurance amongst other matters. Despite all this, disputes and anomalies do still occur, but usually they are short-lived and are quickly settled.

Popular hill climbs were regularly promoted at Shelsley Walsh in Worcestershire, Fingle Bridge in Devon, Post Hill near Leeds, Bobs Nob at Layhams Farm in Kent and Knatts Valley near Brands Hatch, also in Kent, Nailsworth Ladder in Gloucestershire and at numerous other hills, scars and edges up and down the country. Each venue had its own popular devotees, many of them subsequently transferring their attentions to the newly-emerging grass-track racing, which was introduced to the public at the Cambridgeshire Agricultural Show in 1923.

Dirt-track racing in Britain and Europe at this time was quite unknown, even though motorcycles were becoming increasingly popular as a means of transport. Some sand racing took place on the beaches at Southport, Ainsdale, Formby, Redcar, Pendine and other suitable sites at somewhat infrequent intervals. These were often quite well supported by spectators, and doubtlessly afforded the competitors some ideas on loose-surface racing. Very high speeds were often attained at these sand meetings, with some sprint events achieving 100mph or more.

As previously mentioned, the first real attempt at organized dirt-track racing took place in December 1923, at West Maitland in Australia under the auspices of Mr John S. Hoskins. This was a somewhat haphazard affair with up to a dozen assorted riders per race, put on as a climax to the Electric Light Carnival, which commemorated the installation of the town's new electricity supply. The event followed a day of sports, horse racing and general jubilation attended by a huge crowd.

A few of the original competitors at this meeting were Bill Crampton (Norton), Bill Cogan (Douglas), Les Upfold (Norton), George Ross (American X) and Andy Eyre (Harley). This meeting was held under lights, being the very first of such, and was a huge success. Two previous trial meetings, held in daylight, were run in order to guage spectator feelings, but were purely experimental. Johnnie Hoskins had actually ridden in an earlier 'try-out' to see if racing was feasible at the track, but this was in fact the only 'race' he ever took part in, after all he was in his thirties at the time.

Rules and regulations were non-existant at this meeting, but following some minor disputes, a few were quickly made up for future events. At least a start had been made, and the thousands of very voluble spectators loved it, clamouring for more, and soon. Regular meetings quickly followed, with better safety precautions for both competitors and spectators alike, with some hard and fast regulations then introduced. So great was the public acclaim that new tracks were soon opened at Perth and Adelaide, followed by Musselbrook, Cessnock, Singleton and Dungog later in 1924. Due to dust problems at some tracks, the original cinders were quickly substituted by red or yellow shale from local quarries. It was an immediate success, and we still use shale to this very day. Interestingly, machines of any size, make or shape had been permitted, but in 1924 a 500cc limit on engine size was proposed on the grounds of rider safety. Larger motors were then banned from solo racing.

Following his marriage to Audrey (an organist's daughter), Mr and Mrs Hoskins moved to Newcastle (New South Wales) and opened a new track there on 14 November 1925. A crowd of 40,000 turned up for the first meeting, but it was marred when a car went through the safety fence in the last race, killing one man, with another forty folk taken to hospital. Cars were immediately barred from the circuit, with bikes only permitted to race thereafter.

From this track emerged a lot of famous names, among them Billy Lamont, Charlie and Jimmy Datson, Paddy Dean and Ernie Buck. Most came to England in 1928-29, indeed Lamont, who acquired the nickname of 'Cyclone', raced here for a number of tracks right up to the Second World War, when he returned home. In the main, the remainder stayed for considerably less time, however, before returning to their native Australia.

A further track was opened by Johnnie Hoskins at Sydney Royal in July 1926, before he moved on to Claremont. Two meetings were staged at the latter venue in May 1927, prior to regular floodlit events which started on 10 September that year. Another promoter destined to become a legendary figure within the sport was the aforementioned A.J. Hunting and he was behind the opening of two tracks in Brisbane, firstly at the Exhibition Grounds on 16 October 1926 (when Vic Huxley took victory in the first-ever race), and subsequently at Davies Park in October 1927.

Thus, a brand new breed of public heroes emerged in Australia and included the aforementioned Lamont, Huxley and the Datson brothers, along with Frank Arthur, Sig Schlam, Ron Johnson, Tommy Benstead, Keith McKay, Roy Hindle and others. These were the original legendary pioneers of our present sport, with Frank Arthur and Vic Huxley taking their first rides at the Brisbane Exhibition Grounds in 1926, while Ron Johnson debuted at Claremont on 28 May 1927. Sig Schlam also made his first appearance at Claremont and it was a dream start too, as he won the Silver Gauntlet in the first meeting under floodlights in September 1927.

Shortly after this, several celebrated American riders reached Australia, amongst them Cecil Brown, Sprouts Elder, Art Pechar, Eddie Brinck and Ray Tauser. These swelled the competitors lists much to the delight of the ever increasing numbers of fans. The Americans brought with them the new-fangled power slide and they taught the idea to numerous Australian stars of the time. They were quick to learn and soon perfected the new art. This influx of riders to Australia soon spelled doom to a number of American tracks, very few of which prospered for much longer. In fact, very few remained solvent after 1926, and a period of depression ensued in the USA. Quite the reverse was happening in Australia, where a huge boom was starting. Almost every city and town sported its own dirt-track, where enormous crowds thronged the many stadia up and down the country.

Things went from strength to strength in Australia, so much so that the first recorded attempt to stage a World Championship took place at Newcastle in December 1926. The riders were mainly Australian, but three visiting Americans took part, together with a couple who had English nationality. A huge trophy was

PRELUDE

Frank 'The Wizard' Arthur.

put up for competition and some £750 in prize money, to be shared amongst the riders. History does not record who was the eventual winner, but a letter received in England some years later did recall that the trophy was still in the hands of Roy Hindle, a most promising rider of the time. Roy, unlike a lot of his contemporaries, never came to these shores to ride.

Back in England, by 1926, the Brooklands track at Weybridge in Surrey was drawing huge crowds to watch the exciting racing on the three-mile banked concrete track, where speeds often exceeded 100mph.

Meanwhile, the popular path race meetings commenced at Crystal Palace on a one-mile circuit of loose gravel. These came about as a result of the depression, which caused the trustees of Crystal Palace Light Car Club to look around for new means of attracting larger crowds through the turnstiles. They proved to be an immediate success, with more than 20,000 patrons attending the first meeting on 21 May 1927, and numbers increased steadily as the monthly summer promotions were staged. Many competitors at these meetings subsequently transferred their allegiance to speedway, which would eventually make a big impact in 1928. These were names such as Roger Frogley, Miss Fay Taylour, Joe Francis, Lew Lancaster, Triss Sharp, Gus Kuhn, Karl Pugh, Lionel Wills and many, many more. However, at this stage in 1926, dirt-track racing had still not made its debut in this country – in fact, very few people had even heard of it.

Following several successful path race meetings at the Palace circuit, one of the more illustrious riders of the time paid a business-cum-holiday trip to Australia. His name was Lionel Wills, a Cambridge undergraduate, heir to the family tobacco and shipping fortunes, and a very well-known amateur racing motorcyclist of the day. He attended several dirt-track meetings and was spellbound at what he saw. An introduction to Johnnie Hoskins eventually produced a few rides for Wills, who learned quickly without breaking any records. Numerous letters to friends back home urged that a start be made here with this new and exhilarating form of racing. The motorcycle and technical press were also informed and asked to take more interest.

2
DIRT-TRACK RACING ARRIVES IN BRITAIN

Upon Lionel Wills's return to England at the end of 1927, he quickly contacted London Motor Sports, who had been running the original Crystal Palace path race meetings. To say that Fred Mockford and his partner Cecil Smith were interested is an understatement, as they immediately impressed the Light Car Club trustees and Sir Henry Buckland, general manager at Crystal Palace, with a scheme to lay a custom-built track in the spacious grounds. Richard Crittall & Co. quickly drew up plans to construct a banked cinder track of 600 yards at the Penge end of the grounds, around the old football pitch that had hosted the FA Cup final between 1895 and 1914. The pitch at the time was actually being used by the Corinthians amateur club for weekly matches.

Whilst the construction work was in progress, others had been persuaded by Wills's enthusiastic letters to jump the gun and present meetings of an exploratory nature in 1927. At Camberley, Surrey, on heathland overlooked by the Military College, the local motor club staged what was then billed as the 'First British dirt-track meeting' on 7 May. To all intents and purposes it actually amounted to a form of sand-track racing, conducted in a clockwise manner on a quarter-mile circuit. However, the surface and direction proved no handicap to C. Harman, who powered to victory in the 350cc class, the 500cc class and the sidecar event, while Miss Fay Taylour was also successful, taking victory in the unlimited class.

The following month on 25 June, under the organization of Harrison Gill, the South Manchester Motor Club staged a meeting on a 600-yard cinder track at Dodd's Farm, Droylsden. Here, the racing took place in the proper anti-clockwise direction, and Ron Cave took the plaudits by winning the 350cc class, the 600cc class and the sidecar competition.

That same year, a crude form of cinder-track racing took place on a quarter mile track at the rear of a public house on the Wellingborough to Kettering road, 'The Half Way House'. Here, the local iron works dumped tons of ash and clinker, which the Leicester Query Club members graded into a form of dirt-track. Members of the club could practise and try their prowess at the new form of racing. Riders such as Cyril 'Squib' Burton and Fred Wilkinson among others, who later found fame on the Midland speedway circuits, were regulars at this impromptu venue, which lasted for about two years. It was one of the very first in this country, although never open to the general public – it appears to have no name, only a location!

An attempt to stage a meeting at High Beech in Epping Forest on 9 November 1927, was thwarted by the ACU ruling body, as it contravened the Lord's Day Observance Society regulations concerning meetings on the Sabbath, other than purely club functions. That proved to only be a temporary setback, however, as ACU approval was granted for the Ilford Motorcycle and Light Car Club to stage a meeting at High Beech, for club members only, on 19 February 1928. This prompted great interest and riders from all over the country applied for membership so that they could ride in the event. The meeting had been widely advertised in the local and motorcycling press, and the promoter Jack Hill-Bailey, along with his wife, brother and a few loyal helpers, reckoned they might get a crowd of around 3,000 spectators!

The great day dawned, marking the official beginning of ACU approved dirt-track racing in this country and is therefore a milestone in the history of the wonderful sport. All the roads into and around Epping Forest were soon clogged up as people arrived in droves. They travelled by foot, bicycle, motorcycle, car, bus, charabanc, lorry and even steam wagon. Set in a clearing at the rear of the King's Oak Hotel, the entrance was via two huge wooden gates at the north side of the hotel, where it was proposed to sell admission tickets for the princely sum of one shilling. These all went in a few minutes and further efforts to collect money were soon abandoned, with literally thousands of folk getting in for free. From the gates, the intrigued spectators proceeded down a short tree-lined avenue to a huge oak tree of enormous girth – 'The King's Oak'. Beyond was the track, which became variously known as 'King's Oak' or 'High Beech', due to the many beech trees that surrounded the circuit. These formed a convenient vantage point for hundreds of spectators, while others were herded behind a stout rope, mounted on stakes. The track had no safety fence and spectators were also permitted to the infield, thus the races were run through an avenue of excited fans. Clearly, this was not an ideal situation, but could not be obviated on the day.

Anyway, the early races, which were chiefly for English riders who braked heavily for the corners, were exciting and very unpredictable. Machines were of almost any make and size, some even had headlamps still fitted, but at least a start had been made in this country, and what a beginning it proved to be too. Mounted on a Coventry Eagle, Fred Ralph was the first winner in the Ilford Novice event, clocking a time of 2 minutes 10 seconds. Other competitors on the day included Billy Galloway, Alf Medcalf, Reg Pointer, Ivor Creek, Colin Watson, Hugh Smythe, Rube 'Sonny' Wilson and Alf Foulds. Later on, and with the thronging crowd tense with excitement, three track aces gave a demonstration of the new art of broadsiding, namely Australian duo Hilary Buchanan and Keith McKay, plus New Zealander Stewie St George. Whereas previous English riders had used brakes prior to cornering, these fellows had no brakes, and actually opened the throttle even wider. This caused massive real wheel sliding and huge waves of damp black cinders to be showered on the luckless patrons viewing from the bends. The huge crowd were simply spellbound and cheered the three masterful exponents on their way. If this was dirt-track racing, then those present simply loved it and clamoured for more.

Stewie St George.

During the afternoon session, Mr A.J. Hunting, head of the International Speedways party in England and the man who had started the sport in Brisbane, arrived at the track and was shocked at what he saw. Being accustomed to well prepared and organized tracks, he quickly gave instructions for improvements, modifications and safety regulation changes before a second meeting could take place.

The huge public acclaim for this new sporting spectacle resulted in many new tracks springing up in various parts of the country. Following the official start at High Beech, the next track to open was a half-mile circuit at Audenshaw in South Manchester on 3 March. Here, an attendance of around 15,000 witnessed H. Mitchell take victory in the Unlimited final, and this was something of a surprise as the field also included star riders like Billy Galloway and Harold 'Ginger' Lees. Indeed, Galloway and fellow Australian Keith McKay give breathtaking demonstrations of broadsiding during the proceedings, much to the delight of the appreciative audience.

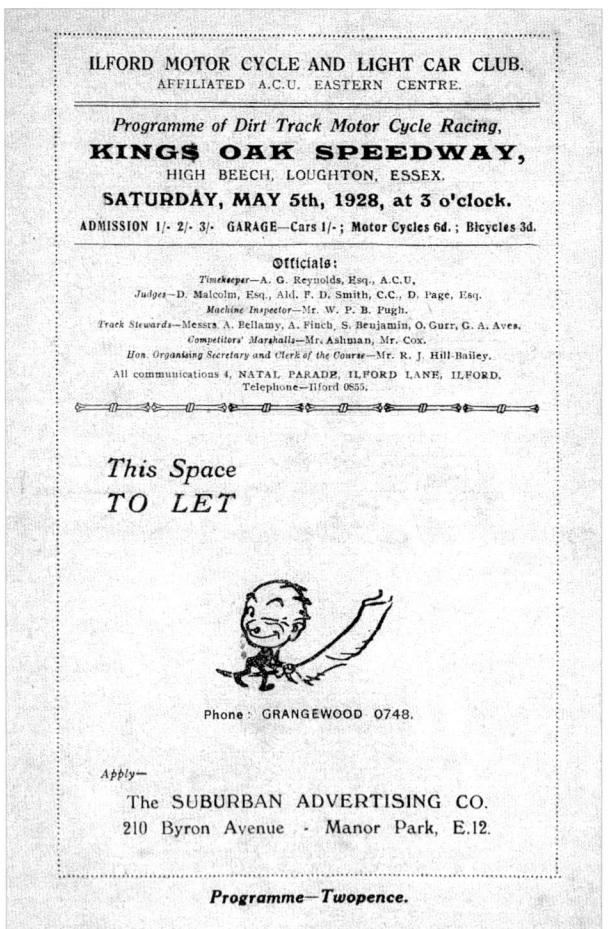

Ultra-rare High Beech programme from 5 May 1928.

Then, on 7 April, Brooklands TT rider Frank Longman put on a meeting at Greenford Driving Park, near Ealing, where Billy Galloway became the first overseas rider to win an event. At 930 yards in length, the genuine cinder track certainly served up some high-speed racing, and with races staged over five laps, the competitors covered a total distance of nearly three miles!

On Easter Monday 9 April, High Beech re-opened after extensive alterations, with a crowd of 17,000 present to watch the racing. A wooden safety fence had been erected around the outer periphery of the track, no spectators were to be admitted to the infield at all, and a fenced off pits area was provided for the competitors. In view of the original haphazard starting arrangements, a new referee's box on stilts was installed above the start line, with sufficient room to also accommodate the timekeeper. The stands were refurbished and spectator facilities were greatly improved upon. Thus the second meeting at the venue was run in better organized circumstances than the chaotic conditions which existed at the February meeting.

DIRT-TRACK RACING ARRIVES IN BRITAIN

That same Easter Monday saw dirt-track racing staged for the first time at Post Hill, Pudsey, near Leeds. The day was also significant as the sport took its bow in Scotland, at the Nelson Athletic Grounds, situated off Gallowgate in Glasgow. As more tracks opened up, crowds were generally large and enthusiastic, with the sport catching on in a big way. Described as being half grass and half cinders, Bradford (Shelf Moor) staged its opening meeting on 15 April and six days later, a track opened at the Highfield Road Sports Ground in Blackpool. Soon after these first meetings, the rest of the overseas riders arrived, with Jimmy Baxter hoping to use them at his new West Ham Stadium, which was under construction. Completion delays forced Baxter to open a track at another venue, so on 28 April, Celtic Park in Glasgow, staged its first meeting, where a crowd of 3,500 saw Stewie St George win both the Opening Handicap and the Golden Gauntlet from a field which also included Sprouts Elder and Keith McKay.

An opening meeting was held at Thrum Hall Cricket Ground in Halifax on 2 May. Thanks to the positioning of acetylene flares on the inside of the circuit, dirt-track fans at the Yorkshire venue witnessed the first meeting to be held under artificial lighting in this country. Three days later, Stamford Bridge welcomed supporters of the new sport for the first time, with Roger Frogley taking victory in the Senior Handicap event, held under the floodlights of Chelsea FC. On 19 May, another five new circuits welcomed supporters for the first time, as Marine Gardens in Edinburgh staged its first public meeting, while in the pouring rain, Crystal Palace opened under the guidance of Fred Mockford and Cecil Smith. The track was originally planned to be 600 yards in length, but after receiving instruction from Johnnie Hoskins, this had been significantly reduced to 441 yards for the opener, before being subsequently altered to 449 yards the following year. A further three circuits were opened on 19 May, with London's White City staging a star-studded event, featuring Billy Lamont and Frank Arthur. Mansfield (Park Hall) also staged its first meeting, as did a second Bradford venue at Fronby Avenue, although this was described as being a mixture of soil and loose cinders.

Carntyne Greyhound Stadium in Glasgow held an opening meeting on 25 May, when a meagre attendance of 600 witnessed Jimmy Pinkerton triumph in the 350cc class, while George Cumming claimed victory in the Unlimited category. The track at Carntyne was actually laid by one Jack Nixon-Browne, who was the son of a director of the Scottish Greyhound Racing Co. Ltd. Significantly, Nixon-Browne later went into politics, taking a seat in the House of Commons as MP for Glasgow Craighton. He rose to become a Minister of State in the Scottish Office and was one of the MPs who, in the 1950s, spoke out against the crippling Entertainment Tax that was levied on speedway at the time. Later in life, he was elevated to the House of Lords as Lord Craighton, and became the only member of the Veteran Speedway Riders' Association with a peerage.

On 28 May, Wimbledon opened at Plough Lane in South London, and the following day Harringay staged its first meeting, as did Barnsley (Lundwood). Then, Wolverhampton (Monmore Green) became the twentieth track in operation, when opened on 30 May. The following month saw another three tracks start up, these being

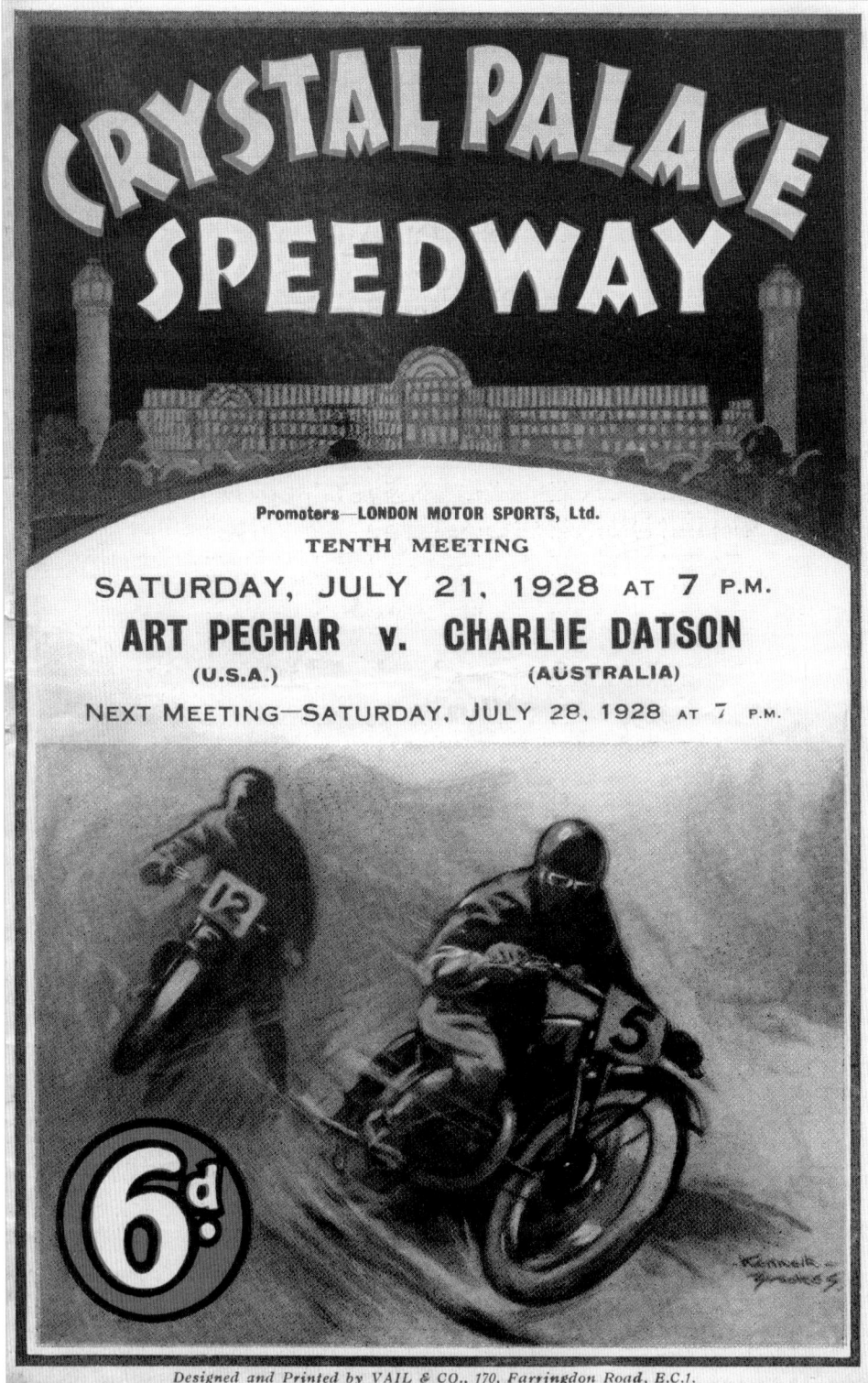

White City, Manchester (16 June), Brighton (23 June) and White City, Glasgow (29 June). The Greenfield Autodrome became the third venue to open in Bradford on 7 July, when Alec Hill was victorious in the Championship Belt. Five days later, the Alexander Sports Stadium in Perry Barr, Birmingham saw its first dirt-track action, and on 14 July, Lea Bridge in east London opened its doors for the first time.

After previously being used purely for practice, Chalton, near Horndean in Hampshire staged its first meeting on 15 July, followed by a track at Foleshill in Coventry six days later. Two further venues opened on 28 July, at Belle Vue (Kirkmanshulme Lane), Manchester, and West Ham (Custom House) finally staged its first meeting after the delayed stadium construction.

Tracks were mushrooming and there was no let up as further circuits opened at Birmingham (Hall Green) and Huddersfield (Quarmby Stadium) on 3 and 4 August respectively. Also on 4 August, the first staging of the sport in Swindon took place at the Autodrome, situated to the rear of the Duke of Edinburgh Hotel in Gorse Hill. Walter Hobbs, the chairman of the Swindon Sports Club Ltd, was the main driving force behind the project, which staged meetings in conjunction with the North Wiltshire Motorcycle and Light Car Club.

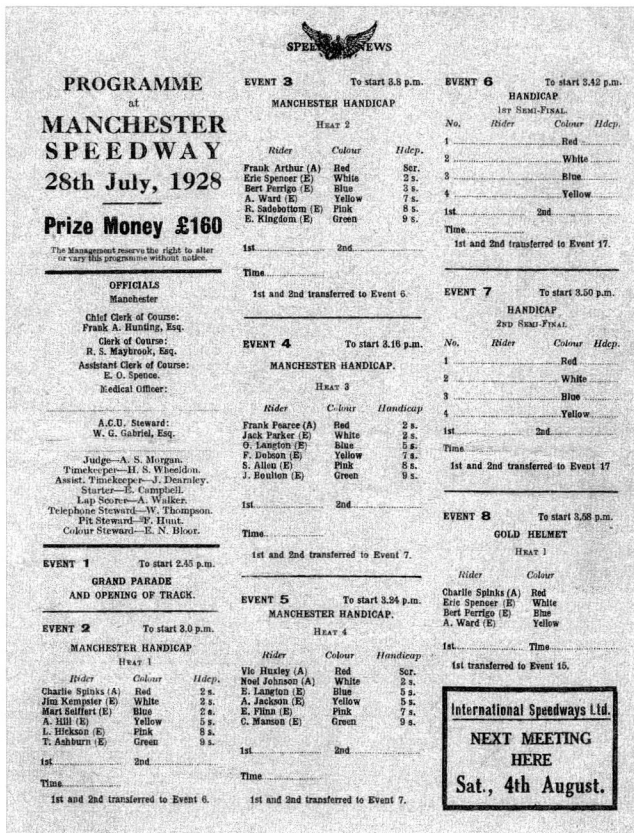

Opposite: Crystal Palace programme from 21 July 1928.

Right: The programme from the first-ever meeting at Belle Vue (Kirkmanshulme Lane) on 28 July 1928.

Rare Marine Gardens, Edinburgh programme from 29 September 1928.

Further tracks then opened at Birmingham (Motordrome), Rochdale (The Athletic Grounds), Bolton (possibly the first British track to have a red shale surface) and Middlesbrough. On 25 August, Bristol staged its first dirt-track meeting at Knowle Stadium, where TT rider Len Parker took victory in the Golden Helmet – the first of what became many successes for the ace racer who reigned supreme at the venue. Another August opening took place at Liverpool on the same day as Bristol, when a crowd of some 10,000 packed into the Stanley Park Greyhound Stadium to catch their first glimpse of the sport. Finally, Salford opened under floodlights on 27 August, when a crowd estimated at around 20,000, witnessed Eric Langton take victory in both the 'A' Grade final and the City Hall Cup.

Six more venues started in September, these were at Leicester (Stadium), Blackpool (Greyhound Stadium), Eastbourne, Dublin (Harold's Cross Greyhound Stadium), Belfast and Coventry's new track at Brandon. The sport arrived at Banister Court Stadium, Southampton on 6 October and exactly a week later, Leeds (Fullerton Park, Elland Road) opened up. The final track to start-up in 1928 was at the White City Stadium, Cardiff, which actually presented its first meeting on

Boxing Day! It would be fair to say that London and the Provinces had caught the dirt-track bug, with some 49 venues operating in that historic first year.

Taking the total to the half-century mark, Kettering could be added to the list, although the circuit wasn't strictly conventional, being described as a mixture of ashes and lumpy soil. The track, known as Red House Speedway, was situated at Hannington, but floundered after only a couple of meetings due to the efforts of the Lord's Day Observance people. Tracks situated at Carlisle (Harraby Park Stadium), Hoddesdon, Newton Grange and Broxburn, near Livingston could also be tagged on, although these were used for training and trials purposes only.

This then was 1928, a time when the country was only just emerging from the depression caused by the General Strike of 1926, and the aftermath of the First World War. The Australian cracks who arrived during the summer, together with a few American aces, tutored many hundreds of English hopefuls, who were clamouring for places in the weekly programmes up and down the country. A few quickly reached stardom, such as Jack Barnett at High Beech, Roger Frogley at Crystal Palace, Gus Kuhn and Les Blakeborough at Stamford Bridge, plus Jim Kempster at Wimbledon. Several others also became popular heroes during the first season of

Arthur 'Buster' Frogley.

The legendary Fay Taylour, a star in her own right.

British speedway, including Harold 'Tiger' Stevenson, Jack Parker, Arthur 'Buster' Frogley, Eric Langton, Colin Watson, Squib Burton and George 'Clem' Beckett.

In those dim and distant days, a few females tried hard to carve a niche for themselves in what had hitherto been a male domain. Five or six of them soon became fairly well-known names in the 1928 programmes. The previously mentioned smiling Irish lass Fay Taylour turned up at an early practice session at Crystal Palace, only to be ordered away. Not to be deterred, however, she tucked her copper coloured curls inside her crash helmet and managed to get some training rides. She improved rapidly and was soon beating most of the other novices. Within weeks, she was regularly winning races against all but the top star riders. She proved herself to be quite a girl and eventually rode at most tracks in the country and also undertook trips to Germany, Denmark and even to Australia.

Another lady rider was the Yorkshire girl from Bedale, a butcher's daughter named Eva Askquith. Already a well-known northern hill climb and grass-track exponent, she took to the dirt-tracks via Leeds, York and other northern circuits. Frequent visits to London soon found her in match races with Fay Taylour, and they were pretty evenly matched. Both raced Douglas machines with great verve, contesting

Eva Askquith, a lady of considerable ability on a speedway bike.

many races against male opposition and were never disgraced. Other lady riders to catch the public eye were 'Sunny' Somerset, a name taken from a popular railway poster of the time by Johnnie Hoskins, which was the alias for Miss Vera Hole from the West Country. Babs Neild, a baby-faced girl whose efforts belied her looks, also became quite well known. Edith Foley, a trials rider and scrambler, was another to try dirt-track racing, but sadly the females' reign as queens of the cinders came to a sudden end following a mishap at Wimbledon in 1930. Unfortunately, a lady rider had her chest crushed in an accident and the ACU ruling body immediately banned all future speedway racing by females, although they were permitted to train or give interval demonstration rides only. All the girls campaigned long and hard to have the ban lifted, but to no avail. Fay Taylour was partly appeased by becoming a champion rider at Brooklands for a time, and later as a midget car driver on the speedway circuits, as well as attaining great success when driving cars in road races.

3
DEVELOPMENTS

In Europe, tracks suddenly opened in Germany (at Hamburg) and Holland (at Amsterdam), as well as the Buffalo Stadium in Paris. It wasn't long before Denmark was taking more than a passing interest in the sport and a few Danish names cropped up in English programmes, with both Kai Andersen and Walther Ryle appearing at Crystal Palace. Later on of course, there was Morian Hansen, who rode for Belle Vue in 1930, and went on to represent West Ham (1931 and 1933), Hackney Wick (1935 to 1937) and Bristol (1938), prior to finally settling in at Wembley until the outbreak of the Second World War in 1939.

A few South African riders also graced the scene in those early days, the chief amongst them being Keith Harvey, who thrilled the Stamford Bridge patrons from 1930 to 1932. Harvey later rode for a variety of other teams such as Nottingham (1933), West Ham (1933-34), Cardiff (1936), Birmingham (1937-38), Crystal Palace (1939), Norwich (1939) and New Cross (1946-47), before finally retiring when aged over fifty. Will Nicholas also got some rides at Crystal Palace in 1929, but he was sadly killed in a van accident on Salisbury Plain, when returning at night from Exeter. Joe Sarkis, a former South African Champion and a very popular TT rider, tried hard at West Ham, but soon returned home after finding the opposition a little too tough.

In this category also came Stanley Woods, the famous Irish TT rider. He tried his hand as a 'slant artist', but despite some success, he returned to road racing where he reigned supreme until the advent of war in 1939. A little later, Harold Daniel also tried his hand, but with little success.

Two Belgian cities opened dirt-tracks at Liège (Stad De Rocour) and Ghent. The attraction at both venues was billed as 'La Chute' or the slide. Riders from England, Denmark and Norway formed the riding staff at the circuits, which appeared to last for one season only. Both Belgium and France each figured very low in European speedway circles.

Spain also promoted a few meetings, which were largely staffed by English riders and avidly supported by the Spanish Royalty. A few Spaniards had a modicum of success, although speedway appears to have been a poor second to bullfighting then and would be even further down the pecking order nowadays.

A new track was also opened in Egypt of all places, near the famous Pyramids at Zamlek. Here, betting was permitted to the excitable Arab spectators. Gus Kuhn, Les

DEVELOPMENTS

Blakeborough and some Australian riders were involved; however, the wily locals soon rumbled that the racing was being rigged and that the betting wasn't entirely in their favour. Thus, the riders returned to England after only one short season, minus the fortunes they had anticipated. Poor Les Blakeborough contracted diphtheria and he died from the effects of it not long afterwards.

Poland took to speedway very early on, but records are very sketchy prior to 1948, with most documentation being lost during the war. The Hamburg track in Germany enjoyed a lot of notoriety, especially amongst English and Australian visitors. Miss Fay Taylour was a frequent and popular competitor until all female riders were barred in 1930. Adolf Hitler and his Nazi regime eventually brought the sport to an abrupt end in 1933. Scandinavian countries did have dirt-track racing, but it wasn't until after the Second World War that they began to emerge as speedway nations.

Some other foreign riders also came to England in the early days, such as Fritz Niemeck from Germany, who rode at Wimbledon for a time. Then there were three Frenchmen from Paris, namely Fernand Meynier, who appeared at Rochdale; Ive de Lathe, who raced in the second halves at Crystal Palace; and finally Charles Bellisent, who made appearances at West Ham among other tracks in the Metropolis. Bellisent proved to be very good during his sojourn in England, but French national service was to end his career prematurely.

Thus the scene was becoming truly international, with riders from New Zealand, Australia, South Africa, France, Germany and other European countries – even a couple of riders from Spain making appearances here. So great was the public following that some tracks cashed in on this wave of popular acclaim by operating twice per week. Stamford Bridge was one, Crystal Palace another. Here, the normal race day was Saturday afternoon, but summertime meetings on Wednesday evening were also promoted when daylight permitted – floodlighting not being available at the Palace track. With admission at just one shilling per adult (5p), there is little wonder that crowds everywhere were enormous. One daily London newspaper even offered free tickets to children of regular readers! These provided the holders with free admission to Crystal Palace on all days except Thursday, which was fireworks night. Naturally, these children continued as fans in their own right as they grew older.

An interview with a 1928 pioneer rider provided some interesting information to say the least. The man in question was a rider of some early repute who enjoyed his dirt-track racing immensely. He was a leg-trailer *par excellence*, who just loved to ride as near to the safety fence as possible. Of course, he fell frequently during his first year, but gradually curbed his bad habits. Since he always travelled a great deal further than any other rider, he seldom won his races, actually only tasting victory five or six times in the five years he raced. The crowd just loved the spectacle he provided and for entertainment value, he had few peers. In fact, supporters petitioned the management and demanded to see more of the mercurial little rider from Selhurst. As a result, each week he was paid extra money *not to win*. His job was to thrill and entertain the large crowds by showering as many patrons as possible with damp black cinders at each bend and how well he did it too. With great certainty, many a Crystal Palace supporter will have remembered Frank North as the best rider never to attain a team place.

Pseudonyms were fairly frequent in the early days, either to mask parental disapproval or because the civil service barred its members from professional speedway activities. Karl Pugh was one, Les Bottomley was another; however, the latter took his mother's maiden name and became an early English star with Stamford Bridge – better known as Les Blakeborough of course. A third was Basil Greathaust, alias Basil Dudley, who later was associated with Gordon Cobbold in making the early GC Special machines which graced several southern speedways in those far off days.

Spectators frequently exceeded 30,000 for ordinary meetings and the atmosphere was electric, though entirely free from hooliganism and crowd incident. These were indeed heady, halcyon days when motorcycles were very much more popular as transport, and great interest was shown in the machines used by the popular heroes of the time. Shirts, pullovers, ties and badges bearing the names and insignias of any one of many different makes of bike seen on the early dirt-tracks, were sported by the partisan fans of the day, so great was the interest and following.

In early 1928, no special dirt-track models were as yet announced by any manufacturer. Thus riders used sports versions of most of the popular makes with many modifications which were deemed necessary, and some which were most certainly not! One could often see as many as 16 or 20 different types of machine at a meeting; almost anything from AJS to Zenith was used, so long as it boasted a reasonably quick engine. Needless to say, successful makes were soon at a premium.

Several manufacturers quickly offered special dirt-track models in their catalogues, including P & P, Sunbeam, Scott and Harley Davidson. With prices ranging from around £60 to £120, and the fact that a young man's pay packet seldom exceeded £3 per week, it was easy to see that a new bike represented 20 to 40 weeks' wages for a budding rider. A few successful speedsters soon offered bikes of their own design like the Frogley Specials, and the GC Special as mentioned previously or the McEvoy.

Amongst other manufacturers offering specialized dirt-track machines were: AJS, Ariel, BSA, Calthorpe, Chater Lea, Cotton, Coventry Eagle, Coventry Victor, Cotton, DOT, Douglas, Dunelt, Husqvarna, Indian, James, New Imperial, Norton, OEC, P & M, Rayleigh, Royal Enfield, Rudge, Triumph, Velocette and Wallis.

Of all the manufacturers mentioned, only a handful continued to make their dirt-track models after 1930. Price, poor performance and general lack of appeal all contributed to the eventual demise of the remainder. However, five extra makes soon made an appearance on the scene, namely AJW, Acme, Excelsior, JAP and Rex. Very briefly, this then is how speedway machines evolved from the first custom-built models of 1928. Only a very small number of these originals are still in existance today, either in museums or private hands, and they are now worth considerable sums of money.

Approved crash helmets and safety-glass goggles, tight-fitting body belts and absorbent back protectors were all implemented as part of a campaign to boost rider safety. Considering the hazardous nature of the sport, it was just as well that a qualified doctor, St John Ambulance crew and other staff were insisted upon at all meetings under ACU jurisdiction. Track rakers, grader driver, pushers, pit staff, flag marshals, starting marshal, timekeeper, announcer, referee and a competent machine

Harry Shepherd, who played an important part in inventing the starting gate.

examiner were also demanded at all meetings since rider enthusiasm was sometimes at variance with rules and common sense.

Up to this point, an attempt has been made to present as accurately as possible a picture of how our favourite sport evolved from its humble and obscure origins, in some sort of chronological order. Other sporting functions in Britain also attracted very large crowds at this point in time, with Wembley attracting a full-house for the FA Cup final, while Test cricket matches against Australia were played before massive crowds. The Isle of Man TT races were held before huge attendances, emphasizing these were heady days indeed for the sensation-seeking, sports-minded populace who had endured five years of the First World War, its aftermath, the General Strike and long unemployment queues. They were now giving full vent to their feelings and money was just a shade more plentiful by 1928.

Radios were popular enough, but motor cars were as yet beyond the reach of most people, and television was unheard of. However, with many motorcycles registered for use on British roads, a period of bike madness ensued and the influx of speedway was an almost natural evolvement.

Mention was made earlier of the haphazard starting arrangements. Unfortunately, the new breed of racing machines were not easy to start. Being usually quite high compression engines, they had fixed gears (no gearbox), but were fitted with clutches. Thus, in order to fire up these brutes, a pusher was supplied on the start line, one per competitor. Not all pushers were equally athletic, nor possessed the same strength. At this stage of the sport's evolution, all races were started with dead engines (that is to say, not running).

Having dragged the machine backwards until the compression stroke was encountered, the clutch was operated. Rider and pusher would then run the bike forward as fast as possible, the rider jumping into the saddle and releasing the clutch at the same time. With luck the engine would fire and the rider was on his way. If not, the procedure would have to be repeated with consequent loss of time and much cursing and swearing!

This procedure was subsequently replaced by the equally dreaded rolling starts. Here, all the competitors rode around the track slowly and roughly in line with each other, prior to the starter dropping his flag to begin the race. Competitors would then accelerate as hard as they could. However, with human nature being what it is, coupled with exuberance and nervous tension, few races actually started with all the participants level. Re-run races were frequent and often frustrating, but had to be endured by the long-suffering supporters.

The next innovation was to begin races with engines running and clutches held in. When the starting marshal was satisfied that all competitors were level on the line, he dropped his flag and the race was on. Creeping and clutch drag did pose a few problems under this scheme, but nothing like the problems of push starting or rolling starts of previous years. Clutch starts were in vogue until something akin to the modern day came about as a result of disatisfaction by riders and fans alike. In 1933, illustrious promoter Fred Mockford teamed up with Crystal Palace stalwart Harry Shepherd to burn the midnight oil and develop an electric hand-operated set of tapes which stretched across the start line. This idea was much like the starting tapes employed at horse racing. Riders lined up at these tapes with engines running and clutches operated. When all were still, the starting marshal released the tapes by operating a trip switch on one of the poles that held the tapes and as they sped upwards, the race got underway. In ordinary circumstances, no rider gained much of a march on his opponents, but there were always the odd few who would practise various dodges in order to gain a yard advantage. Eventually, electrically operated gates were introduced, with tapes and an unseen referee in charge of the release button. Riders in grids one and four now watch the magnets at the foot of the poles holding the tapes, thereby gaining a fractional advantage over those who merely watch the tapes from the middle starting positions.

As a result of all the public acclaim, and the opening of so many new tracks, coupled with the ever growing numbers of riders all seeking fame and fortune, a great deal of experimenting took place. Originally, pump petrol was used, although a few companies did offer a slightly better and more expensive fuel. Most notably, Pratts provided their Ethyl fuel which was suitable for sports engines, Cleveland supplied Discol for fast motors and ROP supplied Benzol mixture which was quite popular in sporting and racing circles. The standard pump fuel of the day would only have been the equivalent of latter day two-star petrol and not suitable for racing engines at all.

However, a Benzol fuel could easily be augmented by the addition of neat Benzol obtainable from most gas works, and this caused a dramatic increase in brake-horsepower. Similarly, the Ethyl compounds could be increased in like manner and these sudden increases in power output also demanded larger and more robust big end bearings. It also necessitated a larger supply of oil which obviously required bigger oil pumps. Stronger valve springs were also needed to ensure proper closure of the faster moving valves, while compression ratios also had to be raised.

Chains and clutches also needed to be strengthened, carburettors also required modification and spark plugs needed copper electrodes for speedier heat conduction. All this took time and money, with some riders finding all the answers and prospering, while others never did.

'Dope' too, suddenly appeared and was used by a few top-line riders which necessitated even more engine modifications. Methanol, wood alcohol or later a nitro mixture was soon perfected and these required a higher compression ratio, which obviously produced a very potent motor indeed. A few riders also mixed their own 'brews', and guarded their secrets most jealously.

In view of the sudden increase in engine power, the usual mineral oils were found to be quite inadequate, so expensive castor base oils were introduced by Castrol, Duckhams, Pratts and a few lesser known marques. This alleviated a lot of the previous seizure problems, but increased the riders' outlay. Commercial alcohols soon became available in quantity and riders then tended to these in lieu of homemade 'brews'.

Tyres also underwent a period of standardization – gone was the knobbly style of trial riding days, as well as the oddities of rope or chain wrapped around the rear wheel to provide extra grip. Standard size rear wheels and standard type tyre tread were introduced. Approved fuel was supplied at tracks to obviate the homemade mixtures and all these changes helped.

Quantity production of factory made special dirt-track machines soon incorporated most of the foregoing improvements, but unfortunately resulted in shorter wheelbase machines. This led to a preponderance of the foot forward style of riding to the gradual exclusion of leg-trailing contemporaries. Track surfaces likewise underwent changes, with cinders gradually being superceded by red or yellow shale as a top dressing, particularly on new tracks.

Four-valve motors, downdraught carburettors, ultra-high compression ratios, super-charging and a whole range of weight reduction ideas were tried in an effort to make machines faster and thus provide riders with an edge over their fellow competitors. It was always thus and probably ever shall be.

Quite a number of second-half innovations were tried during the early years of British speedway. Some lasted, while others were quickly dropped after only one or two performances. These included cheetah racing and elephant parades at West Ham, cycle racing at various circuits and displays of vehicles using eccentric wheels. Horse racing took place at Crystal Palace and while this was both colourful and exciting, there was a betting ban in operation and a lot of interest was lost as a result.

Due to the popularity of sidecars as a mode of transport, and the enthusiasm in these chariots at grass-track events, it was almost a natural progression to include this type of racing on speedway circuits. A number of the English version of left-hand sidecar outfits performed regularly at local grass circuits up and down the country and a number of well-known names appeared. Thus, sidecar racing was fairly regularly promoted as a second-half attraction at a number of southern tracks. A British Sidecar Speedway Championship eventually evolved which created a great deal of interest, however, due to the shortage of competitors, the same names would frequently crop up at all tracks. The racing was fast, furious and exciting, with the most popular performers being Brian Ducker, Arthur Horton, Jack Surtees, Len Truett, Claude Sewell, Cyril Hayward, Gordon Norchi, Charlie Smith, Fred Brackpool, Bill Nethercott, Art Noterman, Jack Middleton, Harold Taylor and Eric Oliver. Sadly, their numbers were too few to provide regular diversified competition, but they certainly tried hard. The machines used by this group of drivers varied from AJS, Coventry Eagle, Matchless, Norton, Rudge, Scott, Triumph and Velocette.

Midget Car racing was also run at a number of tracks, mainly in the Metropolis, being particularly popular at Lea Bridge. The sport was also tried at several other venues including Belle Vue, Coventry, Edinburgh (Marine Gardens), Glasgow (White City) and Hanley, though generally speaking the number of regular drivers precluded much diversified competition, with the same names appearing far too often. Although the racing was exciting, the cars were expensive to race, as was the cost of transporting them around the country. Among others, some of the more illustrious and colourful drivers were Spike Rhiando, Eric Worswick, Vic Patterson, Ron Wills, Basil De Mattos, Frank Chiswell, Syd Plevin, Walter MacKereth, Charlie Pashley, Squib Burton and Jean Reville.

By the mid-1930s, the neater, slightly faster and safer style of foot-forward riding was ousting the leg-trailing of the earlier days. Many riders, however, persisted with the old style, including Max Grosskreutz, George Newton, Stan Greatrex and others, although it is fair to say that the most successful track stars were using the foot-forward style.

Very few speedway machines from the earlier era were still being made, in fact only Rudge, JAP and Excelsior were still producing in quantity. These continued for a time, but after the war, only JAP remained in any numbers until the Czechoslovakian ESO and Jawa took over. A few ex-riders also produced some machines, namely Erskine, Mattingly, Chipchase and North, but none of them sold in great quantities, good though they were.

The staple racing fare for the British public was league racing, Test matches, World Championship rounds and some amateur racing at tracks such as Barnet, Crayford, Dagenham, Eastbourne, Luton, Smallford (St Albans), Rye House and California. These provided a ready-made source of young riders, all keen to progress to the professional tracks. Not many senior circuits provided actual training, although in 1934, a reserve league of seven teams was inaugurated and won by West Ham, with Wembley in second place. Sadly, it only lasted one season before being dropped.

DEVELOPMENTS

The major tracks preferred to rely on the amatuer tracks for the instruction and training of juniors and there was no shortage of keen youngsters. In fact an amateur league was eventually started before the Second World War. This was run by the Amateur Dirt-track Riders' Association, under the guidance of Arthur Warwick, himself a one-time rider at Stamford Bridge from 1929 to 1932.

Looking at some of the amateur tracks a little more closely, Eastbourne remained open with a considerable following until the outbreak of the war. Indeed, it is still operating to this day as a much more plush stadium and a member of the current Elite League set-up. In between, at various times, were periods in the Third, Second and First Divisions. Pre-war, as an amateur circuit, matches were raced against any track that would send a team. They also hosted one of the oldest competitions in speedway, the Championship of Sussex, which was a most prestigious event.

Barnet boasted two circuits, the first of which was located at the bottom of Barnet Hill, two miles from the Great North Road. This track was only used for training purposes in 1929, subsequently closing after an appeal against a rating assessment failed. The other venue was situated on the Barnet bypass, and was originally a grass track, which was made into a dirt-track after the grass had worn away. Lots of well-known riders started their careers here – like Tommy Price, a post-war World Champion – before gravitating to professional status at other metropolitan tracks. Despite being in a very rural setting, when the lease expired early in 1937, factory development spelled doom to the circuit of which no trace now remains.

Much the same could be said of the long-defunct Smallford track, to the east of St Albans on the Hatfield Road, which staged its first meeting on 19 July 1936. Having later formed a team, they were to be one of the founder members of the Sunday Dirt-track League in 1938.

Crayford first staged amateur dirt-track events in 1931, and again from 1935 to 1937. Later on, the venue had two spells of Second Division/National League action from 1968 to 1970 and 1975 to 1983, prior to a more compact greyhound stadium being constructed on the site in 1986.

Dagenham appeared in 1932, as an amateur circuit on Ripple Road, close to the then gas works. From 1932 to 1935, team matches were ridden at the venue, with the home side competing under the name of Romford and promoted by Hawk Speedways. Open licence racing subsequently continued at the venue until the war, during which time Dagenham competed in Sunday Dirt-track League of 1938.

Beginning in 1934, Luton was run primarily as a schooling centre for Wembley, with Jim Kempster and Don Durant on hand to do the coaching. In 1935, team challenge matches were staged against among others Wembley, Wimbledon and Hackney, with Keith Harvey, Mike Erskine, Norman Trimmell and Jack Dalton being regular members of the Hatters side. Quite a few up-and-coming riders had their debut here, but the track sadly closed in 1936, following an injunction over noise levels.

Rochester staged trial events at the City Way Stadium in December 1931, but the first actual meeting didn't go ahead until 1 August 1932, when Alf Foulds won the Chatham Scratch event. Unfortunately, just one further meeting was held on 9 August 1932, after which the sport ceased at the stadium.

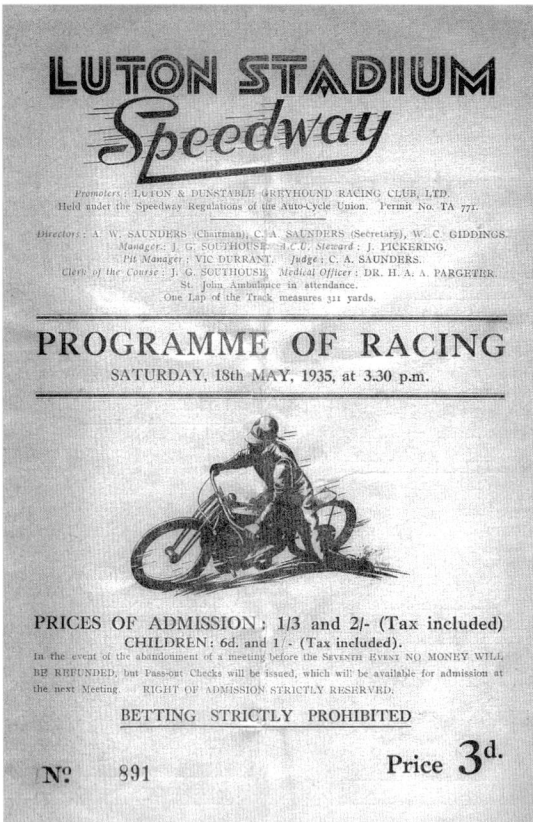

Opposite: The programme used for a meeting at California (Longmoor Speedway) on 19 September 1937.

Left: A very rare Luton programme dated 18 May 1935.

The original Rye House, situated at Hoddesdon Stadium on the bank of the river Lea, first opened for dirt-track operation in 1934, quickly becoming renowned for unearthing talented prospects. Training and open licence events continued to be staged until Rye House entered the Sunday Dirt-track League in 1938, under the promotion of Hackney Wick Speedway Motor Club. The circuit continued to run in 1939, with meetings subsequently held in 1940 under the title of Dick Case's Speedway, organized by Harringay Speedway Motorcycle & Light Car Club. The track was also used throughout 1941 and 1942, before the Harringay Speedway MC & LCC ran four meetings in 1943, with the gate receipts going towards the British Red Cross Prisoners of War Parcels Fund.

Longmoor Speedway at California-in-England, near Wokingham in Berkshire staged primitive-style Sunday afternoon events beginning on 28 May 1933. The track surface was described as being sandy, with the racing initially promoted by Reading Motorcycle Club. Lloyd Goffe is known to have started his speedway career at the venue in 1934, using an old big-port AJS machine. The 310-yard circuit continued to run throughout the remainder of the 1930s, hosting its final pre-war meeting on 20 August 1939, when Bill Newell won the California Cup.

076

Official Programme

Price 2d.

CHAMPIONSHIP MEETING
Motor Cycle
SPEEDWAY
RACING

California-in-England
Near WOKINGHAM

Sunday, Sept. 19th

THE TUDOR PRESS, OXFORD ROAD, READING

Bell End Speedway at Holbeach, near Spalding in Lincolnshire, was so called as locals reckoned it was the furthest place you could actually hear the church bells from! Originally this was predominantly a grass-track speedway venue, but with cinders on the bends. There are various conflicting reports about not only the track surface, but also the shape of the circuit. Meetings are known to have been staged in 1936 and 1937, but these were almost certainly grass-style speedway, with the first proper event subsequently run on 18 April 1938. Ten meetings are known to have been held that year, with mobile stands sometimes brought in to cater for the spectators. More events were run in 1939, the last of which saw Wilf Jay win the Bell End Laurels on 20 August.

Norwich is a venue that began life as a grass-speedway circuit on 18 August 1930, when future track ace Geoff Pymar was one of many interested spectators. Cinders were put down late in 1931, turning the circuit into a dirt-track, and the first such meeting went ahead on 13 September, when Norwich defeated Staines 33-26 in a challenge match. Open licence meetings continued until 1936, although only one event was held in each of the latter two years. In 1937, Peter McMahon took over the running of the track under the guise of Norwich Speedway Ltd, with Max Grosskreutz installed as speedway manager. Norwich Stars were subsequently born and entered the National League Division Two that year, with the first official meeting at the track going ahead on 1 May.

Aldershot opened up at Boxall's Lane on 3 July 1929, when Stan Lemon took victory in the Golden Armlet. This proved to be a short-lived dirt-track operation, however, with just eight meetings run that year, the last of which took place on 5 August. Thanks to the evidence supplied through rare programmes, the track is again known to have run in 1931, although details remain sketchy.

It seems likely that Ringwood held meetings at Matchams Park from 1937 to 1939, with the track situated at the rear of the present day stadium. Following the war, open licence events and training sessions were held during 1946 and 1947.

Portsmouth had two pre-war venues, the first of which was at the Wessex Stadium in Copnor Gardens. A track had initially been laid for a planned opening in September 1928, but this never materialized. Racing did commence in 1929, however, with the first event going ahead on 10 August, when Sprouts Elder took victory in the Golden Gauntlet. Sadly, only four meetings were held that year due to a bumpy track surface and a lack of suitable spectating facilities. The sport resumed in 1930, but ended abruptly in October that year when the City Council purchased the stadium and announced plans to build housing on the site, although they never actually did!

A second Portsmouth track appeared at the Greyhound & Sports Stadium in the Tipnor district. In 1935, Promoter Tom Bradbury-Pratt and a team of 50 men constructed a 300-yard circuit inside the existing greyhound course, but in the event it was to hold just one neutral meeting that year on 2 October. Due to a successful year, Harringay had run short of fixture space, so they ran their National League match against Hackney at the Hampshire venue, losing 32-35. A challenge match between Wembley and Wimbledon was scheduled a week later, but was cancelled after torrential rain had flooded the racing strip. There were no further meetings until 1937, when Albatross Motorcycle Club promoted just two events, the second of which proved to be the last staged at the stadium on 29 September.

Catford also tried the sport at two different circuits, the first apparently being the cricket ground in 1932, but details of this remain very hazy. The second venue was the Greyhound Stadium, with the circuit constructed inside the dog track. The initial dirt-track meeting at the floodlit arena went ahead on 1 September 1934, under the promotion of Tom Bradbury-Pratt, who advertised the track as 'The Sandown of Speedway Racing'. Unfortunately, that proved to be the only year the sport was held at the highly impressive stadium.

Staines Greyhound Stadium was mooted as a dirt-track venue in 1934, until prospective promoters Hawks Speedways were refused an ACU licence. Speedway was eventually held at the venue in 1938 and 1939, however, with the first year of activity including one of American Putt Mossmann's famous motor-cycle rodeo shows.

In the Irish Republic, only Harold's Cross Greyhound Grounds, situated three miles from the centre of Dublin, held any pre-war dirt-track racing. The racing strip was constructed around the pitch belonging to Transport Football Club, who were members of the League of Ireland. Just four meetings were staged at the venue, the first of which saw Jack Woods take victory in the Scratch Race final on 15 September 1928. The last such event was subsequently held on 12 October that year, when Stanley Woods was victorious in the Handicap final.

While on the subject of speedway in Ireland, it is interesting to note that very few Irish riders made the grade in speedway racing, the notable exceptions being Eric French, William 'Ginger' O'Beirne and Dom Perry. Looking at these three, French was the most successful, appearing in domestic racing for a number of seasons thus: Wimbledon (1939); New Cross (1946 to 1953); Wimbledon (1953); Wembley (1954 to 1956); Rayleigh (1957) and Poole (1958). Perry spent three years with Wimbledon from 1952 to 1954, briefly riding alongside Eric French in the middle year. Meanwhile, O'Beirne became quite a good rider, but was the least successful of the three as he never ventured beyond the shores of the Emerald Isle.

4
THE LEAGUE YEARS

1929

Handicap and scratch races had originally been the staple diet at the early meetings, with occasional match races for added interest involving the star riders. Golden Helmet, Golden Gauntlet and Golden Sash events amongst selected top names also added spice to programmes, particularly when some wealthy patron had sponsored such events. However, after a whole season of this kind of fare, promoters realized that something more was required in order to maintain public appeal. As a result of several discussions, team racing was introduced in 1929, following a few trials to assess public interest.

A Southern League of twelve teams was formed, with both Birmingham (Perry Barr Greyhound Stadium) and Wembley opening up to join forces with 10 tracks that had operated in 1928, namely Coventry (Brandon), Crystal Palace, Hall Green (Birmingham), Harringay, Lea Bridge, Southampton, Stamford Bridge, West Ham, White City (London) and Wimbledon. Matches were initially staged over six heats, but this was increased to nine races after a few weeks, with the earlier results allowed to stand. Meanwhile, the scoring system used throughout the campaign was: 1st place = 4 points; 2nd place = 2 points; 3rd place = 1 point.

Following a tight contest, the league was won with 34 points by Stamford Bridge, closely followed by Southampton on 32 points, and Coventry on 28. Unfortunately, there was one casualty along the way when Hall Green resigned after completing just seven fixtures, with their record being expunged from the table. Given the fact that stars of international repute were initially precluded from competing, the Southern League teams were represented by the following known riders over the course of the season:

BIRMINGHAM:
Ivan Anslow; Bill Ashcroft; George Britt; Joe Dallison; Joe Hassell; Arthur Johnson; Cyril Locke; Johnny Lloyd; Wally Lloyd; Tim Reid; Geoff Siddaway.

COVENTRY:
George Allbrook; John Deeley; P. Elwell; Wilmot Evans; Fred Farndon; Tom Farndon; 'Dilly' Gittins; Lew Lancaster; Cyril Lord; Stan Mauger; Norman Parker; Bert Perrigo; George Povey; Arthur Saunders; Arthur Sheene; Bill Stanley; Arthur 'Tiny' Tims; 'Bunny' Wilcox; Fred Wilkinson.

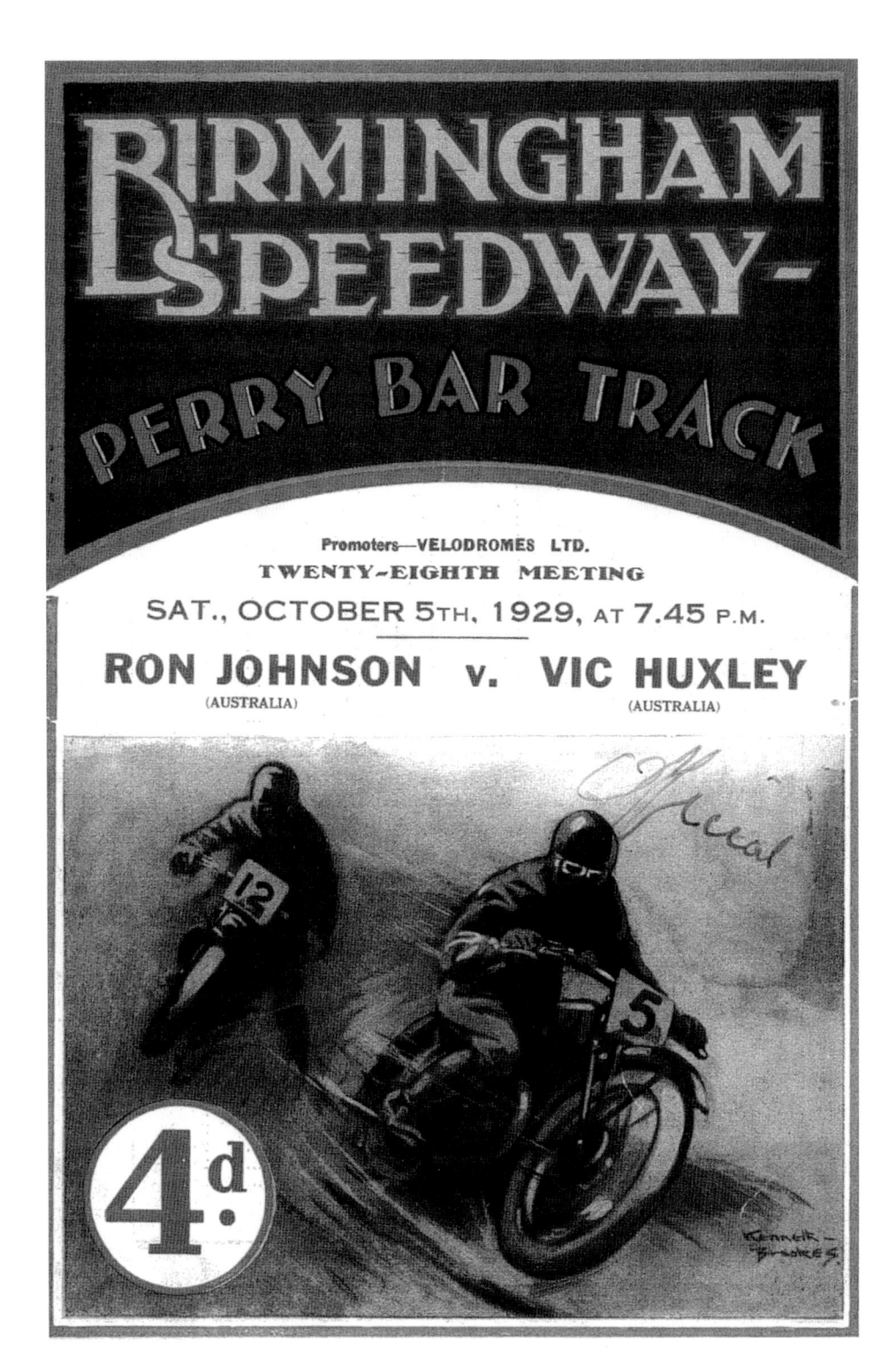

Rained-off Birmingham Speedway (Perry Barr) programme from 5 October 1929. Note the incorrect spelling of Perry Barr on the illustration.

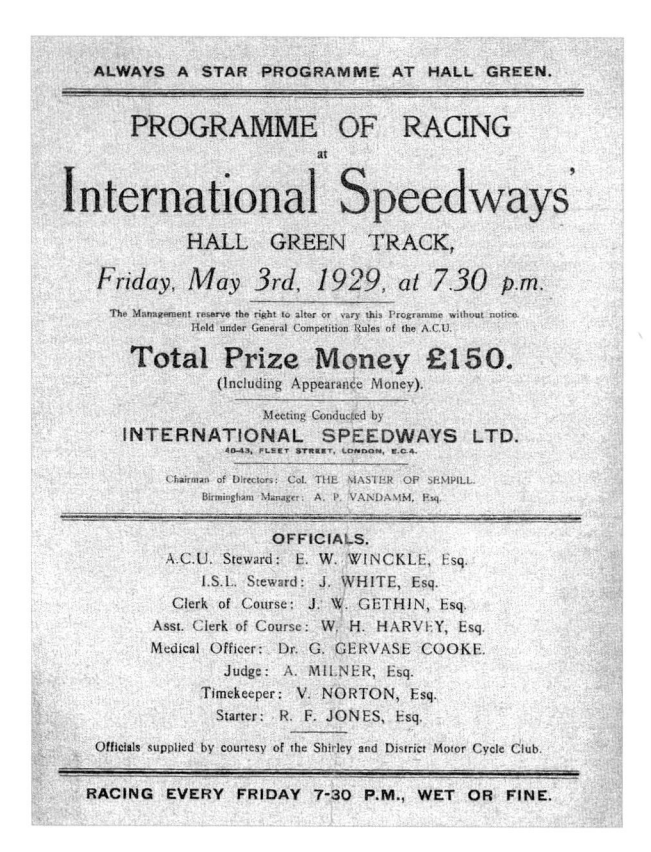

> **ALWAYS A STAR PROGRAMME AT HALL GREEN.**
>
> **PROGRAMME OF RACING**
> at
> ## International Speedways'
> HALL GREEN TRACK,
> Friday, May 3rd, 1929, at 7.30 p.m.
>
> The Management reserve the right to alter or vary this Programme without notice.
> Held under General Competition Rules of the A.C.U.
>
> **Total Prize Money £150.**
> (Including Appearance Money).
>
> Meeting Conducted by
> **INTERNATIONAL SPEEDWAYS LTD.**
> 40-43, FLEET STREET, LONDON, E.C.4.
>
> Chairman of Directors: Col. THE MASTER OF SEMPILL.
> Birmingham Manager: A. P. VANDAMM, Esq.
>
> **OFFICIALS.**
> A.C.U. Steward: E. W. WINCKLE, Esq.
> I.S.L. Steward: J. WHITE, Esq.
> Clerk of Course: J. W. GETHIN, Esq.
> Asst. Clerk of Course: W. H. HARVEY, Esq.
> Medical Officer: Dr. G. GERVASE COOKE.
> Judge: A. MILNER, Esq.
> Timekeeper: V. NORTON, Esq.
> Starter: R. F. JONES, Esq.
>
> Officials supplied by courtesy of the Shirley and District Motor Cycle Club.
>
> **RACING EVERY FRIDAY 7-30 P.M., WET OR FINE.**

Birmingham (Hall Green) programme dated 3 May 1929.

CRYSTAL PALACE:
Jack Barrett; Les Bowden; Bryan Donkin; Joe Francis; Wally Harris; George Lovick; Triss Sharp; Arthur Willimott.

HALL GREEN:
George Allbrook; Tommy Cross; Joe Dallison; Jimmy Gent; Arthur Johnson; Jack Lloyd; Johnny Lloyd; Wally Lloyd; Cyril Locke; Les Patrick; Arthur Sherlock; Bill Stanley; Cyril Taft; Harry Taft; Arthur 'Westy' Westwood; 'Bunny' Wilcox; Nev Wheeler.

HARRINGAY:
Leonard 'Dicky' Bird; Lou Burger; Bill Crouch; Will Dennis; Bert Gerrish; Noel Johnson; Jack Kidwell; Alf Medcalf; Ray Parsons; Reg Pointer; Eric Spencer; Stan Spencer.

LEA BRIDGE:
Frank Bond; Roy Dook; Doug Fairbairn; Stew Fairbairn; Alf Foulds; Allen Kilfoyle; A. Merrell; Howie Osment; Ernie Parry; Alec Slow; H. Standish; Jimmy Stevens.

Programme cover for a meeting at Stamford Bridge on 15 June 1929.

SOUTHAMPTON:
Cecil Barrow; Frank Bond; Cecil Bounds; Reg Bounds; Vic Collins; Tommy Cullis; Don Durant; Clarrie Eldridge; Jimmy Hayes; Eric Lister; Ernie Rickman; Col Stewart; Albert Wakerley.

STAMFORD BRIDGE:
Dick Bellamy; Les Blakeborough; Bert Bolt; Bill Bragg; Alan Day; Clem Dixon; Colin Ford; Gus Kuhn; Ernie Mayne; Nick Nicol; Wal Phillips; Fred Ralph; Arthur Warwick; Bill White.

WEMBLEY:
Charlie Briggs; Stan Catlett; Alf Chick; Vic Deale; Bert Fairweather; Arthur 'Buster' Frogley; H. Harris; Ron Hieatt; Vic Housley; Jack Jackson; Walter 'Nobby' Key; Jack Ormston; C. Pickwick; Len Reeve; Crawley Rous; Charlie Sticpewich; Ray Tauser; Harry Whitfield.

1929 Southern League Champions Stamford Bridge, featuring Les Blakeborough (top row, second left) and skipper Gus Kuhn (middle row, centre).

WEST HAM:
Jack Adams; Reg Bounds; Maurice Bradshaw; Ivor Creek; Frank Duckett; Don Durant; Geoffrey 'Buzz' Hibberd; Bruce McCallum; Les Maguire; Roger May; Harold 'Tiger' Stevenson; Col Stewart; Don Taylor; Wally Trumble; Arthur 'Bluey' Wilkinson; John 'Taffy' Williams.

WHITE CITY:
Leonard 'Dicky' Bird; Jack Bishop; Hilary Buchanan; Lou Burger; Larry Coffey; Clem Cort; Dudley Cox; Harold Crook; Cyril Emms; Frank 'Dank' Ewen; Del Forster; Syd Fuller; Eddie Green; Fred Hore; Alf Sawford; Mart Seiffert; Eric Spencer; Stan Spencer; Jimmy Stevens; Howard Traynor; Colin Watson.

WIMBLEDON:
Cecil Brown; Sid Chambers; Fred Cooper; Dudley Cox; Les Dearth; Bert Gerrish; Jim Kempster; Jack Kidwell; John Leete; Fred Osborne; Alf Sawford; Mart Seiffert; Eddie Slade-Jones; Jimmy Stevens; Alf Summersby; Rube 'Sonny' Wilson.

THE LEAGUE YEARS

Meanwhile, the sport had taken off in a big way up north, emphasized by the fact that 17 teams entered for the inaugural English Dirt-track League as it was called. Belle Vue moved from their Kirkmanshulme Lane venue to what was claimed to be Britain's first purpose-built dirt-track at Hyde Road, and were joined in the league by new tracks at Burnley, Long Eaton, Newcastle (Brough Park), Preston, Sheffield and Warrington. The rest of the participating sides had previously operated in 1928, these being Barnsley, Bolton, Halifax, Leeds (Fullerton Park), Leicester (Stadium), Liverpool, Middlesbrough, Rochdale, Salford and White City (Manchester).

To Barnsley went the distinction of staging the very first league match in Britain on 29 March, when visiting Leeds were victorious by 36 points to 26. The match was raced over nine heats, with a 4-2-1 scoring system, however, in an experiment with the race formula, the following week's meeting at the Lundwood venue saw Barnsley face Burnley over just four races. The home side again slipped to defeat by 11 points to 17, but this proved to be the one and only match raced over so few races, with the nine-heat format quickly reinstated for the rest of the season.

Unfortunately, this league was dogged with bad luck right from the start since Long Eaton never a raced an official match, instead staging only two open licence events. Bolton withdrew after just one fixture to be replaced by the newly-opened Hanley, however, they themselves pulled out after completing only five matches, although the Potteries outfit did continue with open licence meetings. On top of that, Burnley, Belle Vue, Warrington and White City (Manchester) failed to last the course, leaving but eleven sides at the end of the campaign and the league table in disarray with the fixtures incomplete. The reasons for the latter four not finishing the season were varied and extreme, with Burnley opting out due to a loss of capital, while Belle Vue stated that league racing wasn't popular enough. Warrington were expelled after completing 21 matches, and possibly the most bizarre exit was that of White City, who sat nicely on top of the table, yet still resigned in September following a dispute amongst the promoters. They did, however, continue to run open licence events for the remainder of the season.

Based on the results of the matches that were run in 1929, and with the exclusion of the records of those tracks who failed to last the course, Leeds ended up on top of the pile with a total of 33 points. Preston filled second spot on 28 points, with the remaining sides finishing in the following order: Halifax, Newcastle (Brough Park), Salford, Rochdale, Leicester (Stadium), Liverpool, Sheffield, Middlesbrough and Barnsley.

Despite all the problems, quite a few northern tracks were very successful and produced a galaxy of star riders, many of whom ended up moving south for better opportunities, particularly in the Metropolis. Quite a number of imaginative forenames also appeared amongst the riders in the Northern League such as 'Crazy' Hutchings of Preston, together with 'Squib' Worswick, 'Kernel' Barker and 'Ham' Burrill, whilst Halifax had 'Dusty' Haigh. The Rochdale team boasted 'Squib' Burton, 'Buster' Breaks and 'Skid' Nock, while 'Slider' Shuttleworth was a regular at Leicester. Continuing on, Sheffield were represented by 'Smoky' Stratton, Middlesbrough sported 'Broncho' Dixon, Liverpool tracked 'Skid' Plevin, and 'Skid' Skinner represented White City, Manchester. The colourful array of talent just

45

The programme from the first-ever meeting at Belle Vue's Hyde Road home on 23 March 1929.

seemed to go on and on with 'Riskit' Riley at Belle Vue and 'Cracker' Simpson at Salford, whilst 'Ginger' Lees graced Burnley.

As with the Southern League, there follows a list of the known riders who appeared in the original English Dirt-track League:

BARNSLEY:
Tommy Allott; Fred Ledger; Arthur Moore; Bert Round; Tommy Thompson; Charlie Ward.

BELLE VUE:
W. Fletcher; Arthur Franklyn; Bob Harrison; Norman Hartley; George Hazard; E. Mangnall; Jack 'Riskit' Riley; Ian Ritchings; Frank Varey.

BOLTON:
Norman Dawson; F. Greenall; W. Howard; Joe Palastrand; Jack Wood.

THE LEAGUE YEARS

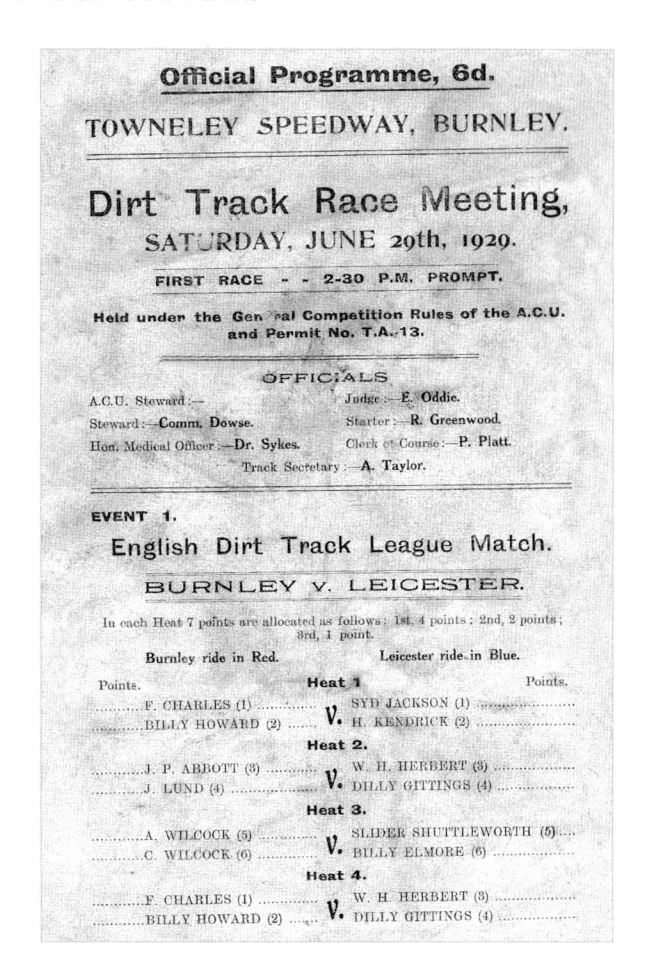

A now scarce programme from Burnley's meeting versus Leicester on 29 June 1929.

BURNLEY:
Joe Abbott; Frank Charles; Harold 'Ginger' Lees; Jack Lund; Arthur Wilcox; Cyril Wilcox.

HALIFAX:
Arthur Atkinson; Arthur Brown; Bert Clayton; George Corney; Jack Dudding; Herbert 'Dusty' Haigh; Geoff Kilburn; George 'The Fox' Reynard; Frank Smith; Geoff Taylor; George Wilson.

HANLEY:
Norman Beech; Len Blunt; George Dykes; Bob Illingworth; Walter 'Chun' Moore; Jack Rowley.

LEEDS:
Arthur Atkinson; Dennis Atkinson; Roy Barrowclough; Tommy Bullus; Billy Burrows; Tommy Gamble; George Greenwood; Alec Hill; Eric Langton; Oliver Langton; Arnold Moore; Charlie Tobin; Harry Watson.

LEICESTER:
Stan Baines; Alec Bowerman; Billy Ellmore; Jimmy Gent; Hal Herbert; Syd Jackson; 'Nobby' Kendrick; Roy Reeves; 'Slider' Shuttleworth; Alf Summersby; Harry Taft.

LIVERPOOL:
Larry Boulton; Joe Dinsmore; Charlie Hornby; Chris Hughes; Rex Kirby; George Milton; Eddie Myerscough; Syd 'Skid' Plevin; Tommy Price.

MIDDLESBROUGH:
James 'Indian' Allen; Dick Bailey; Charlie Barrett; G. Bower; Dan Buck; Col Danby; Jack 'Broncho' Dixon; Dick Evans; Norman Evans; Frank Harrison; Alec Peel; Charlie Sanderson.

NEWCASTLE:
Phil Blake; Gordon Byers; Fred Creasor; Walter Creasor; Percy Dunn; Ernie Smith; Tom Storey; Bry Vincent.

PRESTON:
Joe Abbott; Will 'Billy' Anderton; Les 'Kernel' Barker; Tony Barratt; Hamlet 'Ham' Burrill; James Carnie; Frank Charles; Frank Chiswell; Jack Chiswell; D. Chrystall; Douglas 'Crazy' Hutchings; Jack Lund; Len Myerscough; Freddy Myhill; Tommy Price; Ian Ritchings; Claude Rye; Percy Rye; Eric 'Squib' Worswick.

ROCHDALE:
Jack Atkinson; 'Buster' Breaks; Cyril 'Squib' Burton; Wally Hicklin; Ben Higginbottom; H. Leach; 'Skid' Nock; Bud Proctor; Fred Proctor; Ron Thompson.

SALFORD:
Charlie Bentley; Johnny Broughton; Sam Higgins; Tommy Mason; Sid Newiss; Tommy 'Cracker' Simpson; Cliff Wakeley; A. Ward; Cliff Watson; Arthur Wilcock; Cyril Wilcox; Freddy Williams; Stan Wynne.

SHEFFIELD:
Jack Barber; George 'Clem' Beckett; Johnny Broughton; George 'Scotty' Cumming; Fred Jenkins; William 'Gus' Platts; Spencer 'Smoky' Stratton; Arthur 'Westy' Westwood.

WARRINGTON:
G. Bell; J. Coxhead; Norman Dawson; E. Deakin; F. 'Speed' Formby; Charlie

A rare programme cover from Hanley Speedway, 1929.

Left: A Rotherham Speedway programme from 1929.

Opposite: Two more highly sought-after 1929 programmes from Glasgow (left) and Gosforth (right).

Hornby; T. Houghton; Alec McLachan; Tommy Middlehurst; George Milton; Harry Solomon; Jack Wood.

WHITE CITY:
Billy Dallison; Walter 'Wally' Hull; Arthur Jervis; Hugh Jervis; Jack Owen; 'Skid' Skinner; 'Bunny' Wilcox.

There was no cup competition in the south, but with the exception of Belle Vue, Bolton, Burnley, Hanley and Long Eaton, the teams from the north competed for the English Dirt-track Knock-Out Cup. Three open licence sides were also permitted to take part, namely the newly-opened Wombwell (South Yorkshire Sports Stadium), Leicester Super and Nottingham. The competition threw up a real war of the roses, as Preston and Halifax battled their way through to the final, but it was the Lancashire outfit who proved all-powerful to take a comfortable victory by 87 points to 39 on aggregate.

Aside from the tracks already mentioned, open licence events continued at several venues from the previous season, these being Audenshaw, Blackpool (at both the

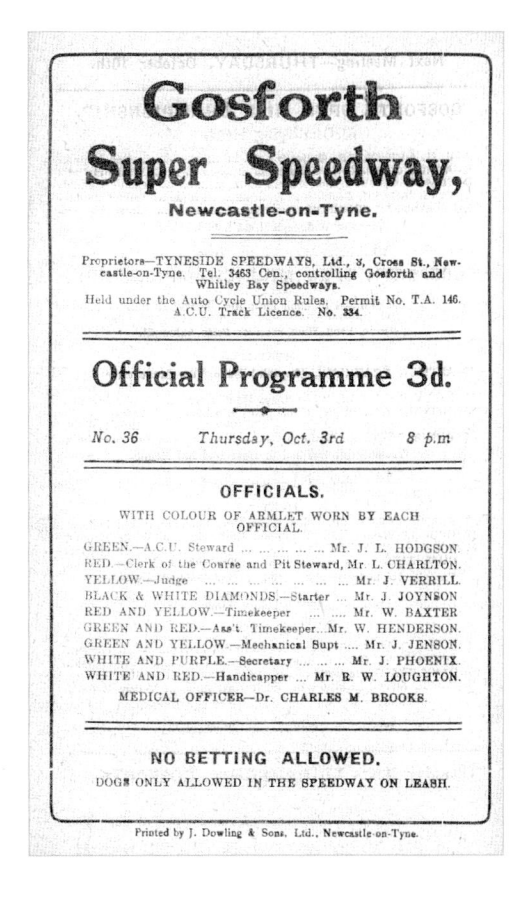

Highfield Road Sports Ground and the South Shore Greyhound Stadium), Bristol, Cardiff, Eastbourne, Edinburgh (Marine Gardens), Glasgow (White City), Greenford, High Beech, Huddersfield, Kettering, Mansfield, Swindon and Wolverhampton. The year also saw a number of other new venues, which hosted individual and open style meetings, namely Aldershot (Boxall's Lane), Crewe, Doncaster, Exeter, Newcastle (Gosforth), Northampton, Pontypridd, Portsmouth, Rotherham, Thorne, Tredegar, Whitley Bay and another at Wombwell (Ings Road Stadium). Two tracks also opened in Barnet, with the one situated at Mays Lane being used specifically for training purposes, while the other which hosted open licence events could be found on the bypass, some two miles north of Mill Hill. Meanwhile, the thrills and spills of the sport returned to Droylsden, after the venue had been dormant to the sport for a year. As in 1928, Broxburn continued to be used for trials and training, while a new practice circuit opened at Dean's Pleasure Ground in Whalley, Lancashire. At only 150 yards in length, the track was described as being circular and unbanked. Run by Whalley Dirt-Track Club, it was a facility for members only, with just two riders permitted to use the circuit at any one time due to its smallness.

SPEEDWAY – THE PRE-WAR YEARS

1929 SOUTHERN LEAGUE RESULTS

	B'ham	Coventry	C.Palace	H/Green	Harr'gay	L/Bridge	So'ton	S/Bridge	Wembley	W/Ham	W/City	Wim'don
Birmingham (P/Barr)	XX	27-35	26-16	Not Run	25-17	34-29	17-25	19-44	30-33	36-27	30-33	37-26
Coventry	48-14	XX	46-17	19-23	39-24	27-36	43-19	32-31	27-14	24-17	49-14	39-24
Crystal Palace	45-18	38-25	XX	27-14	39-23	34-29	19-23	29-34	42-21	28-35	34-29	23-19
Hall Green (Birm'ham)	Not Run	Not Run	20-12	XX	Not Run	30-12	Not Run	Not Run	Not Run	Not Run	Not Run	Not Run
Harringay	25-35	28-35	37-25	15-27	XX	27-15	37-26	27-36	24-38	30-33	29-34	42-21
Lea Bridge	36-26	29-33	31-32	Not Run	42-20	XX	26-16	14-28	30-33	44-18	44-19	30-33
Southampton	22-19	34-29	39-24	18-24	42-21	47-16	XX	33-30	43-20	44-19	48-15	45-18
Stamford Bridge	50-13	44-19	45-18	Not Run	53-10	33-9	39-24	XX	33-9	45-17	43-20	53-10
Wembley	42-21	37-26	23-40	Not Run	30-33	41-21	22-40	16-26	XX	29-12	39-24	48-15
West Ham	40-23	31-11	25-38	32-10	35-28	31-32	30-33	31-32	XX	XX	34-29	37-26
White City (London)	44-19	30-33	17-24	Not Run	28-35	37-26	29-33	33-30	25-17	22-20	XX	34-28
Wimbledon	13-28	25-38	23-19	Not Run	28-35	26-16	26-37	26-37	27-36	45-18	36-27	XX

1929 SOUTHERN LEAGUE TABLE

Team	Matches	Won	Drawn	Lost	For	Against	Points
Stamford Bridge	20	17	0	3	767	408	34
Southampton	20	16	0	4	672	500	32
Coventry	20	14	0	6	658	533	28
Crystal Palace	20	11	0	9	584	568	22
Wembley	20	11	0	9	580	570	22
West Ham	20	8	0	12	538	613	16
White City	20	8	0	12	543	651	16
Harringay	20	7	0	13	538	653	14
Birmingham	20	7	0	13	498	650	14
Lea Bridge	20	6	0	14	551	599	12
Wimbledon	20	5	0	15	495	679	10
Hall Green (Expunged)	7	5	0	2	151	141	10

Notes: (1) The match format changed from six heats to nine heats a few weeks after the competition had started, with the earlier results allowed to stand; (2) The match scores may seem odd and this is because of the scoring system used ie: 1st place = 4 points; 2nd place = 2 points; 3rd place = 1 point; (3) Hall Green resigned from the league after 7 matches, with their record expunged from the table.

1929 ENGLISH DIRT-TRACK LEAGUE RESULTS

	Barn	BV	Bolt	Burn	Hfax	Han	Leeds	Leic	Liv	Midd	Newc	Pres	Roch	Salf	Shef	Warr	WC
Barnsley	XX	36-26	NR	11-17	23-40	50-13	26-36	36-27	30-27	40-22	32-22	32-31	26-36	24-31	37-24	38-24	30-32
Belle Vue	37-25	XX	NR	NR	NR	NR	NR	NR	NR	NR	40-21	NR	43-20	NR	NR	48-15	NR
Bolton	NR	NR	XX	NR	NR	NR	NR	NR	NR	NR	36-24	NR	NR	NR	NR	NR	NR
Burnley	NR	NR	NR	XX	NR	NR	NR	NR	NR	NR	NR	41-22	NR	NR	NR	NR	NR
Halifax	35-27	27-37	NR	NR	XX	49-14	31-31	39-24	NR	46-17	43-20	39-22	29-34	42-21	39-24	49-14	30-33
Hanley	NR	NR	NR	13-49	NR	XX	NR	NR	NR	NR	NR	NR	NR	NR	NR	NR	14-48
Leeds	38-24	NR	NR	NR	42-41	NR	XX	50-13	36-27	41-21	41-22	42-41	43-20	46-16	47-16	46-16	29-33
Leicester (Stadium)	43-20	NR	NR	NR	28-34	NR	45-17	XX	44-19	38-25	25-35	34-29	41-21	33-29	41-21	31-31	34-29
Liverpool	39-23	NR	NR	28-35	44-18	NR	29-33	32-30	XX	43-18	33-23	15-48	50-12	42-21	50-11	35-26	31-32
Middlesbrough	48-15	NR	NR	NR	28-35	NR	30-33	37-24	NR	XX	20-42	37-25	33-29	44-18	43-18	38-25	NR
Newcastle (Brough Pk)	36-26	NR	NR	NR	37-23	NR	23-37	44-18	41-19	38-24	XX	24-36	40-22	41-20	44-19	NR	NR
Preston	45-18	42-21	NR	NR	35-28	NR	35-28	39-23	52-11	46-15	XX	XX	36-27	38-24	46-16	47-14	26-27
Rochdale	48-15	36-23	NR	NR	33-28	NR	31-32	29-34	43-20	33-29	XX	XX	37-26	31-31	35-28	36-27	36-27
Salford	46-17	29-34	NR	NR	38-25	NR	41-22	43-18	41-21	36-27	33-28	31-32	39-24	XX	27-36	15-44	NR
Sheffield	34-26	NR	NR	NR	26-39	NR	28-35	23-40	42-21	46-17	36-27	30-33	43-19	46-16	XX	52-11	NR
Warrington	NR	39-23	NR	NR	28-35	NR	NR	32-31	NR	46-20	NR	25-38	35-28	39-24	30-33	XX	18-44
White City (M'chester)	48-15	NR	NR	49-13	40-22	52-10	44-19	50-10	NR	47-16	48-14	45-18	42-20	51-12	50-12	XX	XX

1929 ENGLISH DIRT-TRACK LEAGUE TABLE

Team	Matches	Won	Drawn	Lost	For	Against	Points
Leeds	20	16	1	3	729	560	33
Preston	20	14	0	6	749	517	28
Halifax	19	12	1	6	654	552	25
Newcastle	20	10	0	10	620	598	20
Salford	20	10	0	10	611	629	20
Rochdale	20	9	1	10	618	631	19
Leicester	20	9	0	11	613	632	18
Liverpool	18	8	0	10	542	566	16
Sheffield	20	6	1	13	554	692	13
Middlesbrough	19	6	0	13	530	652	12
Barnsley	20	6	0	14	517	708	12
White City (Expunged)	23	21	0	2	962	460	42
Warrington (Expunged)	21	6	1	14	538	772	13
Belle Vue (Expunged)	10	6	0	4	332	290	12
Burnley (Expunged)	5	3	0	2	155	123	6
Bolton (Expunged)	1	1	0	0	36	24	2
Hanley (Expunged)	5	0	0	5	64	248	0

Notes: (1) As an experiment, the match format for the Barnsley v Burnley match was changed from nine heats to four heats, with the result allowed to stand; (2) The match scores may seem odd and this is because of the scoring system used ie: 1st place = 4 points; 2nd place = 2 points; 3rd place = 1 point; (3) Although Rochdale beat Halifax 33-28 on track, the match was subsequently awarded as a win for Halifax, due to the home side's illegal use of a rider. Despite this, the race points remained unaltered; (4) Hanley came into the league upon Bolton's withdrawal, but they themselves withdrew after just 5 matches; (5) Long Eaton also entered the league, but never raced a single match; (6) NR = Fixture not run.

1929 ENGLISH DIRT-TRACK KNOCK-OUT CUP

ROUND ONE	Agg	ROUND TWO	Agg	SEMI-FINAL	Agg	FINAL	Agg
Preston (44-19)	91						
Liverpool (16-47)	35						
		Preston (52-11)	80				
		Sheffield (35-28)	46				
Sheffield (33-30)	63						
Barnsley (32-30)	62						
				Preston (48-14)	72		
				Leicester Stadium (39-24)	53		
Leicester Stadium (34-27)	66						
Leicester Super (30-32)	57						
		Leicester Stadium (35-27)	68				
		Rochdale (30-33)	57				
Rochdale (39-25)	65						
Salford (37-26)	62						
						Preston (48-15)	87
						Halifax (24-39)	39
White City Manchester (50-13)	79						
Warrington (33-29)	46						
		White City Manchester	W/D				
		Newcastle	BYE				
Newcastle (38-24)	76						
Middlesbrough (25-38)	49						
				Newcastle (37-25)	56		
				Halifax (44-19)	69		
Wombwell (38-24)	61						
Nottingham (35-23)	59						
		Wombwell (31-31)	56				
		Halifax (35-25)	66				
Halifax (49-13)	80						
Leeds (32-31)	45						

Notes: (1) Matches were raced over nine heats, with a 3-2-1 scoring system in operation; (2) Halifax raced their 'home' leg of the final at Sheffield.

52

THE LEAGUE YEARS

1930

The Southern League swelled to fourteen participating teams in 1930, with High Beech and Nottingham joining forces with the sides that finished the previous year's campaign. There was one track that fell by the wayside during the season, however, when Birmingham (Perry Barr Greyhound Stadium) resigned after just four matches due to complications between the greyhound and dirt-track interests. The meetings were again run over the nine heats as they had predominantly been in 1929, but a change saw the scoring system amended to 3-2-1.

Having won twenty matches, and drawn another, Wembley were clear winners of the Championship on 41 points, with Southampton having to settle for the runner-up position six points behind. The victorious side boasted some terrific performers, using along the way the likes of former Leeds riders Arthur Atkinson and George Greenwood, ex-White City (London) man Colin Watson, the ex-Middlesbrough duo of Charlie Barrett and Norman Evans, plus Stan Catlett, Bert Fairweather, Buster Frogley, Jack Jackson, Wally Kilmister, Jack Ormston, Charlie Shelton, Art Warren and Harry Whitfield.

A Lea Bridge programme from 2 July 1930.

A rare programme from Nottingham, dated 16 June 1930.

THE LEAGUE YEARS

There was no national cup competition as such, although eight sides from the Metropolis contested the London Cup. Wembley and Stamford Bridge emerged to face each other in the final, when the mighty Empire Stadium team added to their league success with a convincing 105-86 aggregate victory.

Due to numerous track closures, the renamed Northern League comprised thirteen teams, with only seven remaining from the previous season. These were bolstered by Belle Vue, who returned to league competition, having resigned mid-way through the 1929 campaign. Meanwhile, also joining the set-up were former open licence venues Edinburgh (Marine Gardens), Glasgow (White City), Leicester Super, Newcastle (Gosforth) and Wombwell (South Yorkshire Sports Stadium). Meanwhile, changes to the match format saw meetings run over six heats, with a 3-2-1 points scoring system.

Sadly, the league again ended in disarray, with the fixtures incomplete. Because of poor attendance figures, Barnsley resigned after 13 matches, then Edinburgh withdrew due to the high financial demands of the top riders. They had completed 12 fixtures at the time, with White City (Manchester) following suit after 15 matches when the stadium was taken over for greyhound racing. The records of all three teams were retained in the final league table, which showed sides having ridden any number of meetings between 12 and 21.

Wimbledon 1930. Riders from left to right: Billy Lamont, Len Parker, Jim Kempster, Del Forster, Dicky Case, Ray Tauser.

55

With a total of 39 points, Belle Vue occupied top spot ahead of Liverpool, and included in their ranks Clem Cort, Percy Dunn, Arthur Franklyn, Dusty Haigh (signed from Halifax), Bob Harrison, brothers Eric and Oliver Langton (both acquired from Leeds), Bruce McCallum (signed from West Ham), Len Myerscough (signed via Preston), Frank Varey and Len Woods. Following the early closure of White City (Manchester), a further five riders were acquired by Belle Vue for their Championship charge, namely Frank Charles, Max Grosskreutz, Wally Hull, Arthur Jervis and Fred Strecker.

At the end of the season, the title-winning sides from the south and the north met over two legs to determine the British National Championship, with Wembley again proving successful with a $56\frac{1}{2}$-$43\frac{1}{2}$ victory over their counterparts from Belle Vue.

Several circuits carried on with open licence meetings from the previous year namely, Audenshaw, Barnet (Bypass), Blackpool (Highfield Road Sports Ground), Bristol, Cardiff, Crewe, Eastbourne, Exeter, Long Eaton, Northampton, Portsmouth, Rotherham, Swindon, Thorne, Tredegar and Wolverhampton. Meanwhile, new tracks opened at Barrow (Holker Street), Hull (White City), Motherwell (Paragon Speedway) and Stainforth. Two circuits also re-opened at

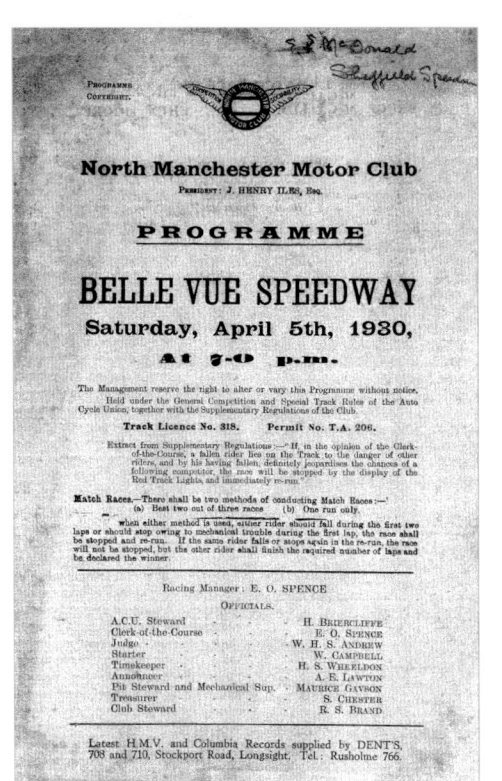

Scarce Belle Vue (left) and Hall Green (right) programmes from 1930.

An Exeter programme from 1930.

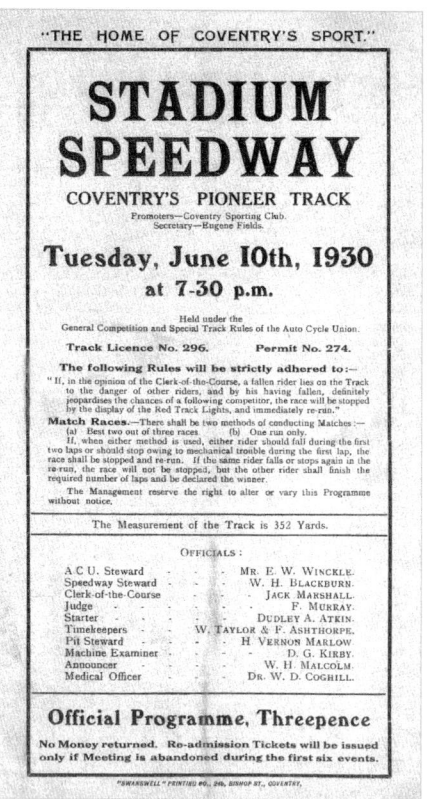

Programme illustrations from the two Coventry circuits that operated in 1930 – Brandon to the left and Foleshill to the right.

Coventry (Foleshill) and Glasgow (Carntyne), whilst former league venues Halifax, Middlesbrough and Newcastle (Brough Park) joined the long list of open licence tracks. Concluding the review of 1930, the mini-track at Whalley continued as a training facility, as did a new racing strip at Helen Street, Govan in Glasgow, while a public demonstration featured Tommy Gamble going through his paces at the newly-constructed York raceway.

THE LEAGUE YEARS

1930 SOUTHERN LEAGUE RESULTS

	B'ham	Cov	CP	HG	Harr	HB	LB	Leic	Nott	So'ton	SB	Wemb	WH	Wimb
Birmingham (P/Barr)	XX	NR	NR	18-36	NR	NR	29-25	NR	NR	NR	NR	NR	NR	NR
Coventry	NR	XX	34-20	30-23	35-19	43-11	36-18	34-19	30-22	30-22	27-26	0-36	29-25	32-22
Crystal Palace	36-18	38-16	XX	34-19	33-18	29-24	27-26	34-20	41-12	24-30	34-19	30-23	22-32	25-29
Hall Green (Birm'ham)	NR	34-19	28-26	XX	29-24	37-17	33-21	31-23	37-16	26-27	31-23	19-35	27-26	27-27
Harringay	NR	18-35	31-22	22-32	XX	30-24	33½-20½	29-24	38-16	28-25	24-29	23-31	25-28	17-37
High Beech	NR	23-29	29-22	23-29	30-23	XX	32-18	33-21	29-24	27-25	16-37	21-32	30-23	25-29
Lea Bridge	NR	31-22	30-23	29-23	27-25	35-18	XX	31-22	32-22	23-30	27-27	23-31	29-22	31-22
Leicester (Stadium)	NR	29-24	27-27	23½-30½	26-27	30-23	29-25	XX	31-23	23-27	33-20	25-29	30-22	30-20
Nottingham	NR	27-27	16-37	26-28	27-26	32-22	26-27	22-32	XX	26-28	21-31	22-31	24-30	21-33
Southampton	38-16	40-12	25-29	36-17	37-17	35-18	29-24	34-20	39-15	XX	28½-25½	26½-26½	35-18	31-22
Stamford Bridge	NR	34-20	35-19	34-19	36-18	42-12	34-19	36-17	38-14	26-28	XX	29-24	37-16	28-26
Wembley	NR	39-14	31-22	28½-24½	33-20	37-16	40-14	34-20	37-15	24-29	24-29	XX	36-18	30-22
West Ham	NR	20-33	31-23	28-24	41-13	35-19	33-21	33-20	39-11	18-36	24-29	21-33	XX	25-29
Wimbledon	NR	30-24	28-26	34-19	30-24	29-25	33-21	41-12	39-7	30-23	30-24	21-32	32-19	XX

1930 SOUTHERN LEAGUE TABLE

Team	Matches	Won	Drawn	Lost	For	Against	Points
Wembley	24	20	1	3	768	496	41
Southampton	24	17	1	6	716	560	35
Stamford Bridge	24	16	1	7	728½	551½	33
Wimbledon	24	16	1	7	695	578	33
Hall Green	24	13	1	10	647	632	27
Coventry	24	13	1	10	629	634	27
Crystal Palace	24	11	1	12	667	613	23
Lea Bridge	24	10	1	13	602½	672½	21
West Ham	24	10	0	14	627	647	20
Leicester	24	8	1	15	586½	689½	17
High Beech	24	8	0	16	555	720	16
Harringay	24	7	0	17	572½	707½	14
Nottingham	24	2	1	21	489	782	5
Birm'ham (Expunged)	4	1	0	3	81	135	2

Notes: (1) Matches were run over nine heats, with a 3-2-1 scoring system; (2) Birmingham (Perry Barr) resigned from the league in May, having completed just four meetings; (3) The match between Coventry and Wembley was awarded as a 36-0 win to Wembley after the ACU had suspended Coventry's licence due to financial difficulties; (4) League Champions Wembley subsequently raced against Northen League Champions Belle Vue for the British National Championship. The tie was decided over two legs with Wembley winning 27-20 at home and 29½-23½ at Belle Vue to secure an aggregate 56½-43½ success; (5) NR = Fixture not run

1930 LONDON CUP

ROUND ONE	Agg	SEMI-FINAL	Agg	FINAL	Agg
Wembley (71-25)	115				
High Beech (52-44)	77				
		Wembley (52-44)	108		
		Wimbledon (39-56)	83		
Wimbledon (62-33)	105				
Crystal Palace (52-43)	85				
				Wembley (59-37)	105
				Stamford Bridge (49-46)	86
Stamford Bridge (60-35)	113				
West Ham (40-53)	75				
		Stamford Bridge (58-38)	104		
		Harringay (50-46)	88		
Harringay (52-44)	99				
Lea Bridge (47-47)	91				

Note: Matches were staged over 16 heats, with a 3-2-1 scoring formula in operation.

1930 NORTHERN LEAGUE RESULTS

	Barn	BV	Edin	Glas	LS	Liv	New	Pres	Roch	Shef	Warr	W/City	Womb
Barnsley	XX	NR	NR	NR	NR	14-22	20-16	NR	NR	23-13	NR	NR	20-16
Belle Vue	27-9	XX	25-8	21-13	24-12	20-16	NR	22-13	22-14	22-14	22-14	17-19	NR
Edinburgh (M/Gardens)	22-14	13-21	XX	NR	NR	NR	26-10	NR	21-15	NR	17-19	23-12	20-4
Glasgow (White City)	NR	16-20	NR	XX	23-13	10-26	16-20	20-12	17-19	18-17	17-18	16-19	NR
Leicester Super	26-10	18-18	NR	25-11	XX	15-21	18-17	19-17	23-12	14-22	NR	11-25	26-10
Liverpool	27-9	14-20	24-12	26-10	18-17	XX	NR	20-16	NR	26-9	21-14	16-19	28-8
Newcastle (Gosforth)	15-20	12-24	8-28	24-12	11-25	XX	NR	NR	24-12	20-16	NR	NR	29-7
Preston	25-10	17½-18½	25-10	26-9	26-9	16-20	NR	XX	27-9	NR	22-14	17-18	NR
Rochdale	21-14	13-23	NR	20-13	24-11	NR	11-25	NR	XX	NR	9-27	NR	NR
Sheffield	NR	14-22	NR	26-10	22-13	21-15	30-6	NR	NR	XX	NR	12-23	NR
Warrington	26-10	10-25	22-14	23-12	NR	14-22	NR	28-8	16-15	NR	XX	11-25	NR
White City (Manch'r)	NR	15-18	NR	NR	26-9	21-15	NR	28-8	17-18	NR	25-11	XX	NR
Wombwell	24-12	16-20	NR	NR	NR	8-28	23-13	14-22	NR	NR	15-21	10-23	XX

1930 NORTHERN LEAGUE TABLE

Team	Matches	Won	Drawn	Lost	For	Against	Points
Belle Vue	21	19	1	1	451½	290½	39
Liverpool	20	15	0	5	430	284	30
White City	15	13	0	2	327	201	26
Preston	18	10	0	8	361½	275½	20
Warrington	17	8	0	9	296	307	16
Leicester Super	18	6	1	11	291	350	13
Sheffield	14	6	0	8	250	245	12
Edinburgh	12	5	0	7	198	216	10
Newcastle	15	5	0	10	233	305	10
Glasgow	17	4	0	13	259	339	8
Rochdale	12	4	0	8	172	254	8
Barnsley	13	4	0	9	185	280	8
Wombwell	12	2	0	10	155	262	4

Notes: Meetings were run over six heats, with a 3-2-1 scoring system; (2) Barnsley resigned from the league after 13 matches due to poor attendances; (3) Edinburgh withdrew from the league after 12 matches due to the high financial demands of the top riders; (4) White City (Manchester) closed after 15 matches when the stadium was taken over for greyhound racing; (5) Despite the mid-season closures of Barnsley, Edinburgh and White City, all three sides records were retained in the league table; (6) League Champions Belle Vue subsequently raced against Southern League Champions Wembley for the British National Championship. The tie was decided over two legs with Wembley winning 27-20 at home and 29½-23½ at Belle Vue to secure an aggregate 56½-43½ success; (7) NR = Fixture not run.

1931

The Southern League was contested by eleven teams in 1931, and although two of the initial starters failed to last the course, thankfully the programme of fixtures was completed due to the readiness of other tracks to come in and take over. After falling into liquidation, one of the tracks which closed prematurely after just eight fixtures was Leicester (Stadium), with Coventry (Brandon), who had initially begun the season running just open licence events, subsequently stepping in to fulfil their outstanding matches. The other track to shut its doors was Harringay after fourteen meetings, with Belle Vue Reserves taking over their fixtures under the guise of Manchester.

At the end of the campaign, having totalled 59 points, it was Wembley who repeated their Championship success of 1930, with fellow Londoners Stamford Bridge five points adrift in second position. In Stan Catlett, Norman Evans, Buster Frogley, George Greenwood, Jack Jackson, Wally Kilmister, Jack Ormston, Charlie Shelton, Col Stewart, Lionel Van Praag, Colin Watson and Harry Whitfield, the title retainers tracked a similar list of teamsters to that which had served them so well in 1930.

In the London Cup, it looked like Wembley were heading for another triumph as they brushed past Wimbledon and Stamford Bridge to reach the final, but they were to come unstuck against an inspired Crystal Palace side, who claimed a convincing 114-76 aggregate success.

The Northern League was down to just six teams, all of whom had partaken the previous year, namely Belle Vue, Glasgow (White City), Leeds, Leicester Super, Preston and Sheffield. Despite the fact that so few sides were competing, yet again the fixtures were not finished. This could be attributed to the withdrawals of Glasgow (after 12 matches) in July, and Leicester Super (after 15 matches) in August. For a second successive season, Belle Vue headed the incomplete table at the end of the term, having garnered 24 points, just three more than their nearest challengers Leeds. A quick look at the riders who carried Belle Vue to glory revealed a powerful depth of strength thus: James 'Indian' Allen, Frank Burgess, Clem Cort, Ernie Evans, Dick Fletcher, Arthur Franklyn, Max Grosskreutz, Bob Harrison, Wally Hull, Eric Langton, Oliver Langton, Walter 'Chun' Moore (signed from Sheffield), Wilf Mulliner, Frank Varey and Len Woods. Although he had later ridden for both Manchester (in the Southern League) and Leeds, the success of Belle Vue was marred by the death of Indian Allen on 12 September, three days after a crash at the Hyde Road circuit.

Along with York, which had opened with an open licence following a demonstration in 1930, non-league Wombwell lined-up alongside Belle Vue, Glasgow (White City), Leeds, Leicester Super, Preston and Sheffield to contest the Northern Cup. Having seen off Sheffield and Preston (after a replay), this was to result in another success for Belle Vue, who resisted the challenge of Leeds to win the final by 64 points to 42 on aggregate.

The National Trophy was first raced for in 1931, featuring the sides from both leagues, along with non-league outfits Exeter, Hall Green (Birmingham), Wombwell

THE LEAGUE YEARS

Nottingham 1931. Back row, left to right: Didds Haulton (Team Manager), Bert Fairweather, Nobby Kendrick, Billy Ellmore, Joe Gooding, Fred Strecker. Front row, kneeling: George Wigfield, Reg Lucas.

Wembley 1931. Back row, left to right: Wally Kilmister, Buster Frogley, Lionel Van Praag, Harry Whitfield. Front row, left to right: Norman Evans, Colin Watson, Johnnie Hoskins (Promoter), Jack Ormston, George Greenwood. Bottom, centre: Ian Hoskins (Mascot).

Very collectable High Beech programme from 6 June 1931.

and York. Interestingly, it was only the Southern League teams (plus Hall Green and Exeter) who contested the first round, with the Northern sides entering the fray in round two. After defeating West Ham, Sheffield and Wimbledon on their way to the final, Wembley then continued their monopoly on the major trophies by thumping Stamford Bridge 120-69 on aggregate.

Aside from Hall Green, Exeter, York and Wombwell, a number of other tracks continued to host open licence events, these being Audenshaw, Barnet (bypass), Crewe, Eastbourne, Middlesbrough and Motherwell (Paragon Speedway). Those venues were joined by Edinburgh (Marine Gardens) and Newcastle (Gosforth), both of which had staged league racing the season before. Two circuits also reopened with open licences after a year of inactivity, namely Aldershot (Boxall's Lane) and Greenford, while completely new venues sprung up at Barrow (Little Park), Caerphilly, Caxton, Crayford, Norwich, Plymouth and Workington (Lonsdale Park).

THE LEAGUE YEARS

Finally for 1931, and with a view to opening the following year, a track was constructed at the City Way Stadium in Rochester, with a series of trial meetings run throughout December.

1931 SOUTHERN LEAGUE RESULTS

	C.Palace	Harr/Man	H/Beech	L/Bridge	Leic/Cov	Nott'ham	South'ton	S/Bridge	Wembley	W/Ham	Wimb'don
Crystal Palace	XX	27-26 H	33-20	38-15	32-20 C	29-24	30-24	26-24	16-36	25-27	32-22
	XX	45-9 M	39-15	31-21	36-18 C	Not Run	38-15	31-23	30-23	32-22	30-22
Harringay/Manchester	30-21 H	XX	29-18 H	32-22 M	H 26-25 L	32-22 M	29-24 H	24-29 H	28-26 M	24-30 H	25-27 H
	28-26 M	XX	28-22 M	28-26 M	M 31-22 C	Not Run	29-24 M	23-31 M	16-36 M	24-28 M	20-34 M
High Beech	27-23	29-24 H	XX	32-20	35-18 C	29-21	29-23	27-26	30-24	27-26	41-12
	32-20	38-16 M	XX	34-20	31-22 C	Not Run	19-31	30-23	20-33	21-33	28-23
Lea Bridge	23-25	25-28 H	22-31	XX	33-21 L	37-16	32-22	22-31	18-36	18-32	20-34
	22-32	32-20 M	38-15	XX	35-19 C	Not Run	23-31	23-31	22-32	21-33	28-26
Leicester Stadium/Coventry	29-25 C	L 18-36 H	24-24 L	24-30 C	XX	Not Run	24-30 C	26-27 C	22-31 L	23-28 L	30-24 C
	19-35 C	C 28-24 M	26-27 C	25-29 C	XX	Not Run	32-22 C	24-28 C	29-25 C	29-25 C	28-26 C
Nottingham	29-25	28-25 M	32-22	33-21	30-23 C	XX	29-25	26-25	26-28	24½-29½	34-17
	Not Run	Not Run	Not Run	Not Run	Not Run	XX	Not Run	Not Run	Not Run	Not Run	Not Run
Southampton	36-18	36-17 H	29-24	26-27	26-18 L	38-15	XX	26-28	31-23	23-31	31½-21½
	21-31	34-19 M	37-14	32-21	32-22 C	Not Run	XX	33-20	30-24	22-31	35-16
Stamford Bridge	32-21	35-19 M	32-20	37-16	33-20 C	33-20	38-13	XX	23-30	35-15	31-22
	28-25	41-11 M	23-29	34-20	39-15 C	Not Run	31-22	XX	32-21	29-24	32-22
Wembley	41-12	37-16 M	43-11	34-20	37-17 C	37-16	31-23	31-22	XX	32-22	31-22
	34-19	30-22 M	31-23	34-18	Not Run	Not Run	32-22	34-19	XX	29½-24½	27-27
West Ham	33-19	28-25 H	31-23	35-17	34-19 L	28-23	33½-20½	23-30	24-29	XX	25-28
	23-28	30-24 M	30-21	34-19	33-21 C	Not Run	26-27	21½-32½	20-32	XX	35-17
Wimbledon	40-13	26-37 H	36-17	23-31	33-20 C	35-19	26-24	26-27	22-30	21-32	XX
	31-22	29-25 M	35-15	36-18	29-25 C	Not Run	37-17	29-23	28-25	29-25	XX

1931 SOUTHERN LEAGUE TABLE

Team	Matches	Won	Drawn	Lost	For	Against	Points
Wembley	38	29	1	8	1149½	822½	59
Stamford Bridge	38	27	0	11	1117½	890½	54
West Ham	38	23	0	15	1065	944	46
Crystal Palace	38	22	0	16	1040	964	44
Wimbledon	38	19	1	18	1014½	995½	39
High Beech	38	19	1	18	950	1036	39
Southampton	38	18	0	20	1027	990	36
Manchester/Harringay	38	14	0	24	916	1091	28
Lea Bridge	38	11	0	27	906	1115	22
Coventry/Leicester	38	8	1	29	825	1091	17
Nottingham	19	8	0	11	467½	538½	16
Harringay (Withdrew)	14	6	0	8	367	365	12
Leicester (Withdrew)	8	0	1	7	170	248	1

Notes: (1) Matches were run over nine heats, with a 3-2-1 scoring system; (2) Having completed 19 matches, Nottingham resigned in July, through being unable to raise a full team. Despite this, their record was retained in the final table; (3) Having gone into liquidation, Leicester withdrew from the league in April, with Coventry subsequently taking over their outstanding fixtures in mid-May. Results of meetings involving Leicester are identified by an 'L', while matches involving Coventry are similarly denoted by a 'C'; (4) Harringay resigned in June, with Belle Vue Reserves taking over their remaining matches under the guise of Manchester. Results of meetings involving Harringay are shown with an 'H', while those involving Manchester are identified with an 'M'; (5) The second High Beech v Southampton match was actually raced at Southampton; (6) The result of the first Leicester v High Beech match was amended from 28-23 by the ACU, due to an ineligible rider; (7) The result of the first Wimbledon v Southampton match was amended from 30-23 by the ACU, due to an ineligible rider; (8) The first Coventry v Nottingham match was awarded as a win to Coventry; (9) The second Wembley v Coventry match was rained off, but was subsequently awarded as a win for Wembley.

1931 NATIONAL TROPHY

ROUND ONE	Agg	ROUND TWO	Agg	THIRD ROUND	Agg	SEMI-FINAL	Agg	FINAL	Agg
Wembley		Bye							
		Wembley (56-37)	108						
		West Ham (44-52)	81						
West Ham (51-45)	100			Wembley (70-25)	125				
Southampton (42-49)	87			Sheffield (41-55)	66				
		Sheffield (54-40)	106						
		Leeds (39-52)	79						
Wimbledon (67-26)	116½					Wembley (48-47)	97		
Hall Green (42½-49½)	68½					Wimbledon (46-49)	93		
		Wimbledon (60-36)	108						
		Crystal Palace (48-48)	84						
Crystal Palace		Bye		Wimbledon (55-41)	101				
				Belle Vue (50-46)	91				
		Belle Vue (73-22)	137						
		Wombwell (27-64)	49						
Stamford Bridge (59-35)	113½							Wembley (71-24)	120
Leicester Stadium (39½-54½)	74½							Stamford Bridge (45-49)	69
		Stamford Bridge	W/O						
		Harringay (Withdrew)							
Harringay		Bye		Stamford Bridge (61-31)	111				
				Leicester Super (44-50)	75				
		Leicester Super (69-26)	122						
		York (42-53)	68						
High Beech (61-33)	120					Stamford Bridge (66-30)	117		
Exeter (34-59)	67					Preston (43-51)	73		
		High Beech (55-39)	93						
		Lea Bridge (52-38)	91						
Lea Bridge (59-33)	106			Preston (65-31)	107				
Nottingham (46-47)	79			High Beech (48-42)	79				
		Preston (70-26)	122						
		Glasgow (43-52)	69						

Note: (1) Matches were run over 16 heats, with a 3-2-1 scoring system; (2) The Southern League teams (plus non-league Exeter and Hall Green) took part from the first round, with the Northern League sides (plus Wombwell and York) subsequently joining the fray in round two; (3) Leicester (Stadium) staged the 'home' leg of their first round tie against Stamford Bridge at Leicester Super.

1931 LONDON CUP

ROUND ONE	Agg	SEMI-FINAL	Agg	FINAL	Agg
Crystal Palace	Bye				
		Crystal Palace (69-27)	124		
		Lea Bridge (41-55)	68		
Lea Bridge (60-35)	108				
High Beech (46-48)	81				
				Crystal Palace (59-36)	114
				Wembley (40-55)	76
Wembley (49-45)	99				
Wimbledon (46-50)	91				
		Wembley (53½-41½)	97½		
		Stamford Bridge (50-44)	91½		
Stamford Bridge (58-36)	111½				
West Ham (41½-53½)	77½				

Note: Matches were staged over 16 heats, with a 3-2-1 scoring system in operation.

1931 NORTHERN LEAGUE RESULTS

	Belle Vue	Glasgow	Leeds	Leicester Super	Preston	Sheffield
Belle Vue	XX	40-14	35-19	40-14	27-24	31-23
	XX	Not Run	34-19	Not Run	31-20	33-21
Glasgow (White City)	21-31	XX	23-31	31-23	28-25	25-28
	24-30	XX	Not Run	Not Run	Not Run	Not Run
Leeds	22-30	39-14	XX	28-26	30-23	34-18
	27-26	31-17	XX	34-18	34-17	28-26
Leicester Super	29-24	39-15	29-24	XX	34-20	31½-22½
	30-23	Not Run	Not Run	XX	34-20	28-26
Preston	27-23	35-18	26½-26½	35-19	XX	32-20
	25-29	Not Run	27-26	Not Run	XX	38-15
Sheffield	39-15	35-19	34-19	32-22	34-19	XX
	28-25	Not Run	30-22	29-25	29-24	XX

1931 NORTHERN LEAGUE TABLE

Team	Matches	Won	Drawn	Lost	For	Against	Points
Belle Vue	18	12	0	6	527	426	24
Leeds	18	10	1	7	493½	453½	21
Sheffield	17	10	0	7	474½	432½	20
Leicester Super	15	8	0	7	401½	403½	16
Preston	16	5	1	10	399½	442½	11
Glasgow	12	2	0	10	249	387	4

Notes: (1) Matches were run over nine heats, with a 3-2-1 scoring system; (2) The result of the second Preston v Sheffield match was deleted from the final table; (3) Aside from the aforementioned note, Belle Vue, Leeds, Sheffield and Preston failed to complete their fixtures, due to the withdrawals of Glasgow (in July) and Leicester Super (in August).

1931 NORTHERN CUP

ROUND ONE	Agg	SEMI-FINAL	Agg	FINAL	Agg
Belle Vue (33-20)	57				
Sheffield (29-24)	49				
		Belle Vue (27-26)	53		
		Preston (27-26)	53		
Preston (38-14)	72				
Leicester Super (20-34)	34	REPLAY			
		Belle Vue (37-17)	66	Belle Vue (37-16)	64
		Preston (25-29)	42	Leeds (26-27)	42
Leeds (35-18)	35				
Glasgow (Withdrew)	18				
		Leeds (35-15)	63		
		York (26-28)	41		
York (30-24)	55½				
Wombwell (22½-25½)	46½				

Note: Matches were run over nine heats, with a 3-2-1 scoring formula.

THE LEAGUE YEARS

1932

With the initial boom in the sport seemingly over and numerous tracks already closed down, 1932 saw the amalgamation of the Southern and Northern Leagues, the new set-up becoming known as the National League. This was initially planned to feature ten teams, made up by two former Northern Leagues sides in Belle Vue and Sheffield, along with seven ex-Southern League participants in Coventry, Crystal Palace, Southampton, Stamford Bridge, Wembley, West Ham and Wimbledon, plus league newcomers Plymouth. However, in order to pad out the fixtures, the Speedway National Association Trophy was run as a forerunner to the league competition, and this saw Southampton move their operation to Lea Bridge after completing 11 matches. Despite the move, they did manage to maintain some of their identity though, racing for the rest of the year as Clapton Saints. Run on a league basis, the competition was eventually won by Stamford Bridge, with fellow Londoners Wembley finishing in second place, 4 points behind the Pensioners' total of 32 points.

Stamford Bridge programme from 7 May 1932.

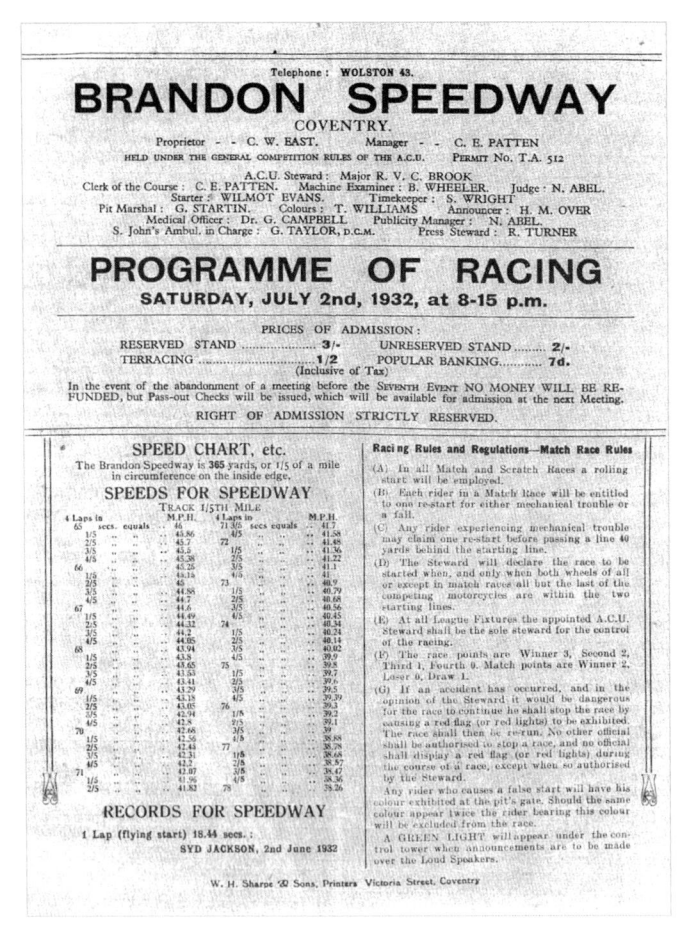

Coventry programme from 2 July 1932.

Although Sheffield had completed their fixtures in the Speedway National Association Trophy, when it came to the league, the South Yorkshire circuit unfortunately shut its doors to the sport, thus reducing the number of competing teams to just nine. For a third year in a row, the Championship went the way of Wembley, who finished 3 points ahead of their nearest rivals Crystal Palace. From the previous season the title winners tracked Stan Catlett, Norman Evans, George Greenwood, Wally Kilmister, Jack Ormston, Charlie Shelton, Lionel Van Praag, Colin Watson and Harry Whitfield, while incoming riders were Reg Bounds (from West Ham), Gordon Byers (from Leeds) and Ginger Lees (from Preston).

The same nine teams who contested the league also partook in the National Trophy, and there was little surprise when Wembley continued their winning streak by defeating Stamford Bridge and Coventry, prior to claiming an aggregate success of 103-87 over Belle Vue in the final. The year's other competition, the London Cup, also went the way of the mighty Wembley side, although they were pushed all the way in the final by Stamford Bridge, before eventually coming out on top by 99 points to 92 on aggregate.

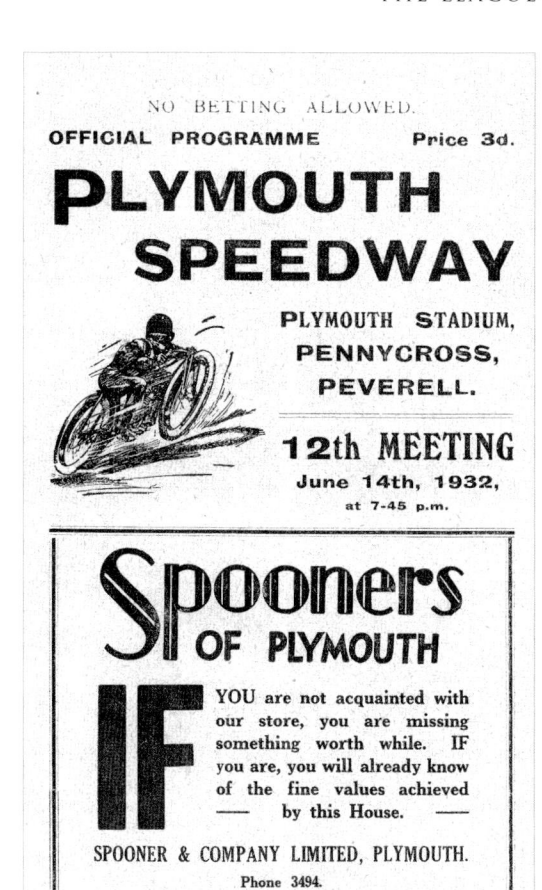

Left: A rare Plymouth programme, dated 14 June 1932.

Below: Plymouth 1932, left to right: Art Warren, Bert Jones, Bill Clibbett, H.F. Hore (Secretary & Manager), Billy Ellmore, Frank Pearce, Jack Barber, Jimmy Ewing, Stan Lupton.

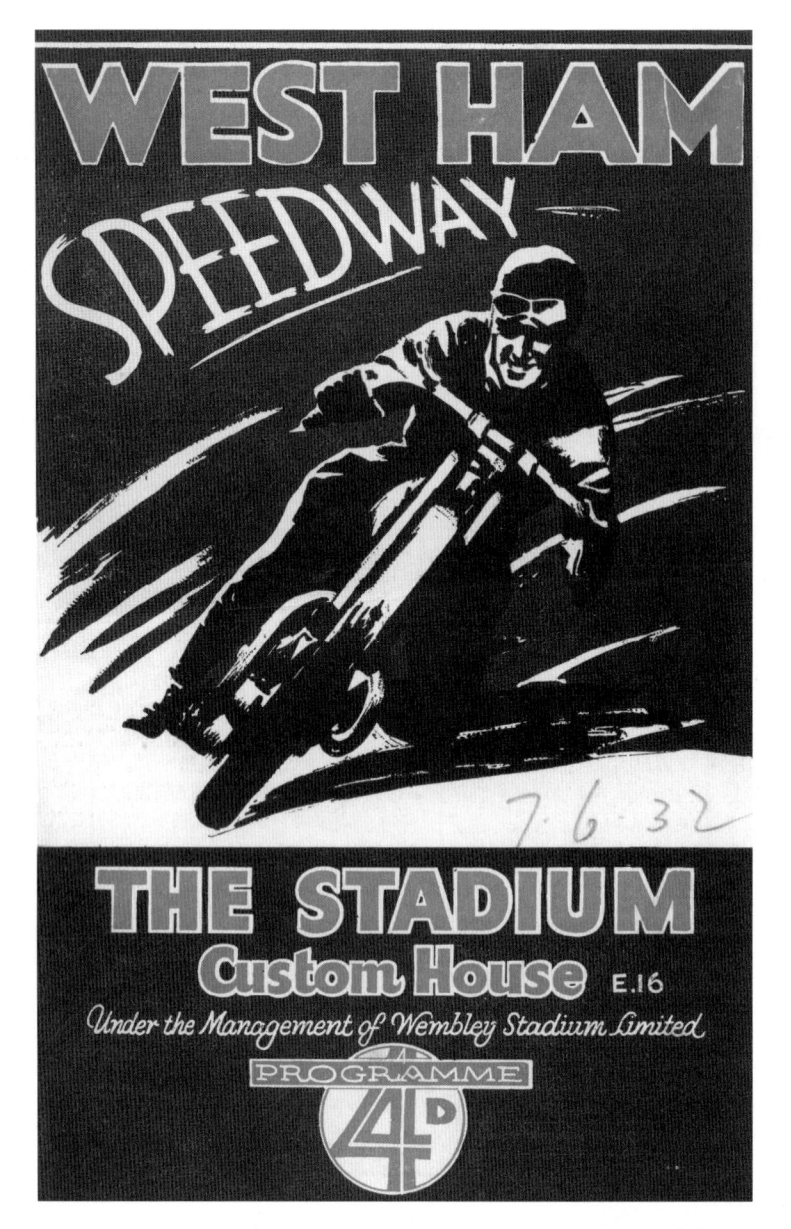

The West Ham programme from their league encounter with Wembley on 7 June 1932.

Completing the picture for 1932, other tracks running open licence meetings were former league outfits High Beech, Leeds, Leicester (Stadium) and Preston, as well as Barnet (Bypass), Caxton, Caerphilly, Crewe, Eastbourne, Motherwell (Paragon Speedway), Norwich and Workington (Lonsdale Park). In addition, there were new circuits at Catford, Dagenham and Tamworth (Mile Oak Speedway), while Rochester also opened following their successful trials at the end of 1931.

THE LEAGUE YEARS

1932 SPEEDWAY NATIONAL ASSOCIATION TROPHY RESULTS

	Belle Vue	Coventry	C.Palace	Plymouth	Sheffield	South'pton	S.Bridge	Wembley	West Ham	Wimbledon
Belle Vue	XX	43-10	24-29	36-18	32-22	42-12 S	24-28	29-25	39-15	35-18
Coventry	21-32	XX	26-23	28-23	34-18	23-31 C	24-29	20-34	23-31	21-32
Crystal Palace	34-18	35-18	XX	35-19	36-17	31-23 S	18-36	27-26	33-21	37-17
Plymouth	25-28	34-20	16-37	XX	39-14	16-34 S	26-27	15-36	20-33	24-28
Sheffield	15-37	14-35	38-16	37-17	XX	34-19 S	22-32	20-34	17-35	23-26
Southampton/Clapton	20-33 S	25-29 C	22-32 C	37-16 C	29-22 S	XX	22-31 C	24-29 S	27-26 S	23-28 S
Stamford Bridge	29-25	36-18	30-24	39-12	43-11	37-17 S	XX	37-17	37-17	41-12
Wembley	28-25	33-20	32-22	36-16	41-11	37-16 S	31-21	XX	31-23	28-24
West Ham	34-20	36½-16½	28-24	34-15	35-18	34-17 C	30-24	25-29	XX	27-25
Wimbledon	28-26	38-15	25-29	34-13	34-18	33-19 C	24-30	28-26	31-21	XX

1932 SPEEDWAY NATIONAL ASSOCIATION TROPHY TABLE

Team	Matches	Won	Drawn	Lost	For	Against	Points
Stamford Bridge	18	16	0	2	587	374	32
Wembley	18	14	0	4	553	403	28
Crystal Palace	18	12	0	6	522	436	24
Belle Vue	18	11	0	7	548	411	22
West Ham	18	11	0	7	505½	446½	22
Wimbledon	18	11	0	7	485	456	22
Clapton/Southampton	18	5	0	13	417	533	10
Coventry	18	5	0	13	401½	547½	10
Sheffield	18	3	0	15	371	574	6
Plymouth	18	2	0	16	364	573	4
South'pton (Withdrew)	11	3	0	8	244	335	6

Notes: (1) Matches were run over nine heats, with a 3-2-1 scoring system; (2) The Speedway National Association Trophy was run in the first half of the season, while the National League Championship followed in the second half of the year; (3) Having completed 11 matches, Southampton moved their operation to Lea Bridge, where they rode as Clapton Saints for the remainder of the competition. Results of meetings involving Southampton are marked with an 'S', while those involving Clapton are identified with a 'C'; (4) Although Sheffield did participate in this competition, they did not compete in the National League Championship which followed.

1932 NATIONAL LEAGUE CHAMPIONSHIP RESULTS

	Belle Vue	Clapton	Coventry	C.Palace	Plymouth	S.Bridge	Wembley	West Ham	Wimbledon
Belle Vue	XX	38-16	38-15	32-22	35-15	31-23	29-25	35-18	26-26
Clapton	21-32	XX	24-27	28-25	36-18	31-23	20-34	21-31	35-19
Coventry	32½-21½	28-25	XX	22-31	34-18	29-25	22-29	20-34	24-29
Crystal Palace	30-24	35-19	31-22	XX	31-20	27-27	30-24	25-27	34-20
Plymouth	23-25	33-20	31-22	19-35	XX	30-22	16-35	32-18	22-29
Stamford Bridge	30-22	39-15	37-16	25-29	39-15	XX	29-25	31-22	34-19
Wembley	41-13	33-20	30-24	29-25	27-24	30-24	XX	33-20	29-25
West Ham	29-25	35-18	25-26	34-20	20-33	14-40	XX	28-25
Wimbledon	27-26	35-17	35-19	23-31	33½-20½	28-26	23-31	31-23	XX

1932 NATIONAL LEAGUE CHAMPIONSHIP TABLE

Team	Matches	Won	Drawn	Lost	For	Against	Points
Wembley	16	13	0	3	495	358	26
Crystal Palace	16	11	1	4	467	386	23
Belle Vue	16	9	1	6	452½	393½	19
Stamford Bridge	16	8	1	7	467	389	17
Wimbledon	16	8	1	7	427½	425½	17
West Ham	16	7	0	9	397	447	14
Coventry	16	6	0	10	384½	463½	12
Clapton	16	4	0	12	370	479	8
Plymouth	16	4	0	12	356½	475½	8

Notes: (1) Matches were run over nine heats, with a 3-2-1 scoring system; (2) The National League Championship was run in the second half of the season; (3) Having taken part in the Speedway National Association Trophy which preceded it, Sheffield did not enter the National League Championship.

1932 NATIONAL TROPHY

ROUND ONE	Agg	ROUND TWO	Agg	SEMI-FINAL	Agg	FINAL	Agg
		Wembley (54-42)	99				
		Stamford Bridge (46-45)	88				
				Wembley (63-33)	119		
				Coventry (38-56)	71		
Clapton (57-35)	107	Coventry (55-41)	99				
Plymouth (44-50)	79	Clapton (50-44)	91				
						Wembley (66-29)	103
						Belle Vue (58-37)	87
		Belle Vue (64-32)	106				
		West Ham (51-42)	83				
				Belle Vue (56-37)	102		
				Wimbledon (50-46)	87		
		Wimbledon (54-42)	97				
		Crystal Palace (51-43)	93				

Note: Matches were run over 16 heats, with a 3-2-1 scoring system in operation.

1932 LONDON CUP

ROUND ONE	Agg	SEMI-FINAL	Agg	FINAL	Agg
Wembley	Bye				
		Wembley (65-30)	102		
		Crystal Palace (56-37)	86		
Crystal Palace (54-42)	102				
Clapton (42-48)	84				
				Wembley (52-44)	99
				Stamford Bridge (48-47)	92
Stamford Bridge (57-37)	95				
Wimbledon (53-38)	90				
		Stamford Bridge (46½-41½)	95½		
		West Ham (47-49)	88½		
West Ham	Bye				

Note: Matches were run over 16 heats, with a 3-2-1 scoring system in operation.

69

1933

The National League consisted of ten teams in 1933, with only Belle Vue, Clapton, Coventry, Crystal Palace, Plymouth, plus the big three W's of Wembley, West Ham and Wimbledon remaining in place from the previous year. These were bolstered by the inclusion of Nottingham and Sheffield, both of whom re-opened to the sport. To form a more meaningful fixture list, the league programme was extended and saw all the sides face each other four times over the course of the season – twice at home and twice away. In a change to the format, the nine-heat meetings were run with a 4-2-1 scoring system, but that only seemed to inspire Belle Vue as they stormed to their third League Championship in four years, finishing a massive 16 points ahead of second-placed Wimbledon, while the usually formidable Wembley could only claim sixth position in the final analysis. The Aces used ten riders on their glory march, with the names recorded for posterity thus: Joe Abbott, Frank Charles, Broncho Dixon, Eric Gregory, Max Grosskreutz, Bob Harrison, Bill Kitchen, Eric Langton and Frank Varey.

The London Cup was contested by five teams, with Wembley overcoming West Ham to reach the final, having had a first round bye. Meanwhile, the other half of the draw saw Wimbledon brush past Crystal Palace and Clapton for the right to face

Belle Vue 1933. Left to right: Eric Langton, Max Grosskreutz, Broncho Dixon, Bob Harrison, Frank Varey (on bike), Eric Gregory, Bill Kitchen, Joe Abbott.

THE LEAGUE YEARS

Crystal Palace 1933. Left to right: Triss Sharp, Joe Francis, Nobby Key, Fred Mockford (Promoter), Ron Johnson, Tom Farndon, Harry Shepherd, George Newton.

Sheffield 1933. Back row, left to right: Henry Walker, Eric Blain, Squib Burton, John Deeley. Front row, left to right: Chun Moore, Dusty Haigh, Tommy Gamble.

the Lions. However, when it came to the final, the Dons were no match for their illustrious opponents, suffering defeat in both legs as Wembley cantered to an aggregate success of 140-109.

In the National Trophy, the same ten league teams took part, and in a repeat of the previous year's final, it was Wembley and Belle Vue who met for the coveted trophy. However, it was the Aces who gained revenge for their 1932 defeat by scorching to a huge 164-87 success on aggregate. Wembley staged the first leg on 28 September, and after slipping to a 54-72 reverse, the overall outcome was a foregone conclusion, although nobody could possibly have predicted that Belle Vue would blast their way to a massive 92-33 victory two days later in the second leg at Hyde Road.

Aside from the ten league circuits, open licence racing could also be seen at Barnet (Bypass), Dagenham, Eastbourne, Norwich and Tamworth (Mile Oak Speedway), along with three new venues at California (Longmoor Speedway), New Brighton (The Tower Ground) and Rayleigh (Laindon). Sadly, that meant a total of only 18 British tracks were staging speedway of one form or another, compared to a high of some 67 circuits in 1929.

More rare programme covers from the 1933 season – Nottingham (left) and Plymouth (right).

THE LEAGUE YEARS

1933 NATIONAL LEAGUE RESULTS

	Belle Vue	Clapton	Coventry	C.Palace	Nott'gham	Plymouth	Sheffield	Wembley	West Ham	Wimbledon
Belle Vue	XX	27-36	46-17	45-14	46-16	44-19	45-18	32-30	41-21	34-29
	XX	33-30	50-13	33-30	49-14	52-11	45-17	32-31	37½-24½	43-20
Clapton	28-35	XX	45-17	37-21	48-13	40-23	53-10	44-18	31-31	27-35
	35-27	XX	39-24	33-30	31-32	45-18	41-22	34-28	22-41	32-30
Coventry	25-38	25-38	XX	33-29	41-21	18-45	38-25	27-34	24-39	20-42
	28-35	31½-31½	XX	26-34	45-17	51-12	43-18	42-21	34-28	26½-36½
Crystal Palace	37-26	40-20	44-18	XX	41-22	45-17	49-11	39-23	41-21	42-21
	30-33	32-29	32-30	XX	37-25	41-22	32-31	42-21	29-31	46-17
Nottingham	18-41	41-22	41-21	24-38	XX	45-17	33-30	24-35	0-36	22-41
	29-34	40-18	30-33	32-31	XX	40-21	39-23	25-37	30-30	27-35
Plymouth	34-29	20-42	38-21	33-30	46-16	XX	32-31	34-29	32-31	31-32
	21-42	24-38	18-45	30-32	36-23	XX	31-30	35-27	21-42	30-33
Sheffield	25-38	18-45	44-18	23-40	35-23	32-31	XX	25-38	36-26	32-29
	25-38	30-33	39-23	41-22	37-26	38-25	XX	33-30	29-34	36-26
Wembley	38-23	49½-13½	37-21	34-29	45-16	46-17	37-26	XX	38-24	25-37
	21-42	24-38	35-27	35-27	46-17	48-15	51-12	XX	28-35	24-38
West Ham	23-39	34-29	44-15	36-24	44-18	40-22	46-16	46½-16½	XX	36-23
	26-36	32-30	31-31	26-37	43-16	40-23	37-26	36-27	XX	37-25
Wimbledon	28-35	36-27	43-19	33-29	38-24	38-23	46-14	25-38	46-16	XX
	28-33	37-26	37-26	34-29	44-19	47-15	39-23	30-32	34½-28½	XX

1933 NATIONAL LEAGUE TABLE

Team	Matches	Won	Drawn	Lost	For	Against	Points
Belle Vue	36	31	0	5	1358½	889½	62
Wimbledon	36	23	0	13	1213	1027	46
West Ham	36	21	3	12	1196½	1007½	45
Crystal Palace	36	21	0	15	1225	1006	42
Clapton	36	19	3	14	1204	1036	41
Wembley	36	19	1	16	1184	1057	39
Coventry	36	10	2	24	998	1237	22
Sheffield	36	11	0	25	961	1282	22
Plymouth	36	11	0	25	922	1323	22
Nottingham	36	9	1	26	898	1295	19

Notes: (1) Matches were run over 9 heats, with a 4-2-1 scoring system; (2) The first match between Nottingham and West Ham was awarded as a 36-0 victory to the visitors as Nottingham had temporarily closed down; (3) The second match between Coventry and Crystal Palace originally ended 26-36, but was amended due to an oversized tyre used by visiting rider George Newton; (4) The second match between Crystal Palace and West Ham originally ended in a 32-30 win for the visitors; however, the match was declared void by the ACU. As shown, the rematch subsequently also ended in an away success for West Ham.

1933 NATIONAL TROPHY

PRELIMINARY ROUND	Agg	ROUND ONE	Agg	SEMI-FINAL	Agg	FINAL	Agg
		Belle Vue (74-51)	134				
		Wimbledon (64-60)	115				
Clapton (69-56)	130			Belle Vue (98-28)	168		
Coventry (63-61)	119			Clapton (54-70)	82		
		Clapton (80-43)	135				
		Sheffield (71-55)	114				
						Belle Vue (92-33)	164
						Wembley (54-72)	87
		Wembley (103-22)	182				
		Nottingham (44-79)	66				
Nottingham (81-42)	143			Wembley (77-48)	140		
Plymouth (64-62)	106			Crystal Palace (62-63)	110		
		Crystal Palace (63-63)	132				
		West Ham (55-69)	118				

Note: Matches were run over 18 heats, with a 4-2-1 scoring system in operation.

1933 LONDON CUP

ROUND ONE	Agg	SEMI-FINAL	Agg	FINAL	Agg
Wembley	Bye				
		Wembley (77-46)	143		
		West Ham (60-66)	106		
West Ham	Bye				
				Wembley (69-56)	140
				Wimbledon (53-71)	109
Wimbledon (60-65)	137				
Crystal Palace (49-77)	114				
		Wimbledon (71-54)	139		
		Clapton (57-68)	111		
Clapton	Bye				

Note: Matches were run over 18 heats, with a 4-2-1 scoring system in operation.

SPEEDWAY - THE PRE-WAR YEARS

1934

From the previous season, just six tracks continued in the National League, five of which were Belle Vue, Plymouth, Wembley, West Ham and Wimbledon. The sixth circuit continuing with league racing was Lea Bridge, which had reverted to its original name, having run as Clapton since taking over Southampton's fixtures in June 1932. Those teams were augmented by a new circuit in the Metropolis at New Cross, with promoter Fred Mockford transferring his entire operation from Crystal Palace to the Old Kent Road venue. Aside from that, a further two tracks re-opened to take the total of competing sides to nine, these being Hall Green (Birmingham) and Harringay.

Matches were again run over nine heats, but following the experimental scoring system of 1933, the trusted 3-2-1 formula was restored. Unfortunately, one side failed to last the course, with Lea Bridge closed down by the Control Board on 27 July, due to what were described as 'continuing irregularities'. Thankfully though, their results and remaining fixtures were taken over by Walthamstow, which was opened in August under the promotion of Fred Mockford and Dicky Maybrook.

The battle for the Championship brought together the two teams that had virtually dominated the sport domestically since 1930, with just two points separating table-toppers Belle Vue from gallant runners-up Wembley at the end of the head-to-head battle. Interestingly, Wembley took victory in the first of their two matches at Belle Vue, though crucially as it turned out, the Aces won both fixtures at the Lions' den. As with the other years covered in this section, it is worth recalling the names associated with the title winners, with the men bearing the famous Aces race-jacket in 1934 being Joe Abbott, Frank Charles, Eric Gregory (for part of the year before linking with Wembley), Max Grosskreutz, Jack Hargreaves, Bob Harrison, Bill Kitchen, Eric Langton, Bill O'Neil, Ron Thompson and Frank Varey.

Running alongside the senior competition was a Reserve League featuring Belle Vue (who interestingly raced with a 'Goats' nickname), Hall Green, Harringay, New Cross, Wembley, West Ham and Wimbledon. Matches were run over six heats, with each team comprising four riders and a reserve. Unlike the National League, the sides only faced each other on two occasions (once at home and once away), and it was West Ham who went through the 12-match programme unbeaten to take the Championship, having won 11 fixtures and drawn the other at home to Wembley.

For a third successive season, it was Belle Vue and Wembley who graced the National Trophy final, the Manchester club seeing off Hall Green and Wimbledon, while Wembley defeated Harringay and New Cross on their way through. As in 1933, the Aces were to prove far too powerful for the Londoners, storming to victory in both legs for an 145-70 aggregate success.

The London Cup featured six sides, with New Cross grabbing a place in the final after seeing off the challenges of Harringay and then Walthamstow. Meanwhile, it was West Ham who made it through to the first of two finals by virtue of a round one bye, before beating Wembley in a closely fought semi-final encounter. New Cross took a firm grip on the final by gaining a 62-44 victory in the first leg on

74

Rare Lea Bridge programme from 11 April 1934.

Harringay 1934. Back row, left to right: Cliff Parkinson, Phil Bishop, Charlie Blacklock, Norman Evans. Front row, left to right: Norman Parker, Tom Bradbury-Pratt (Co-promoter), Jack Parker, Charlie Knott (Co-promoter), Frank Arthur.

19 September, with the Hammers unable to achieve anything more than a narrow 53-52 win six days later in the return leg at their Custom House home. That gave the intriguingly nicknamed 'Lambs' an aggregate 114-97 triumph, and everyone connected with the club was overjoyed at the marking of their opening season with a trophy.

A new competition called the ACU Cup was inaugurated in 1934, with the ties run over just one match as drawn from the hat. Due to the uneven number of competing teams, just one first round match saw Wembley overcome Hall Green, only to be rewarded with a trip to Belle Vue. That subsequently resulted in a big 79-29 win for the Aces, who then dismissed Harringay to face West Ham in the final. The Hammers had previously seen off Walthamstow and New Cross in all-London ties, prior to producing a determined performance in the grand showdown, held at the Plough Lane home of Wimbledon. However, despite their heroics, it wasn't quite enough to prevent the Belle Vue boys from claiming a narrow victory by 56 points to 51.

Meanwhile, the number of other tracks running on an open licence showed an increase in 1934, with Barnet (Bypass), California (Longmoor Speedway), Dagenham, Eastbourne, New Brighton (The Tower Ground), Norwich and Tamworth (Mile Oak Speedway) remaining operational from the previous year. As well as those seven venues, new circuits were opened at Catford (Greyhound Stadium), Liverpool (Seaforth Greyhound Stadium), Luton (Greyhound Stadium)

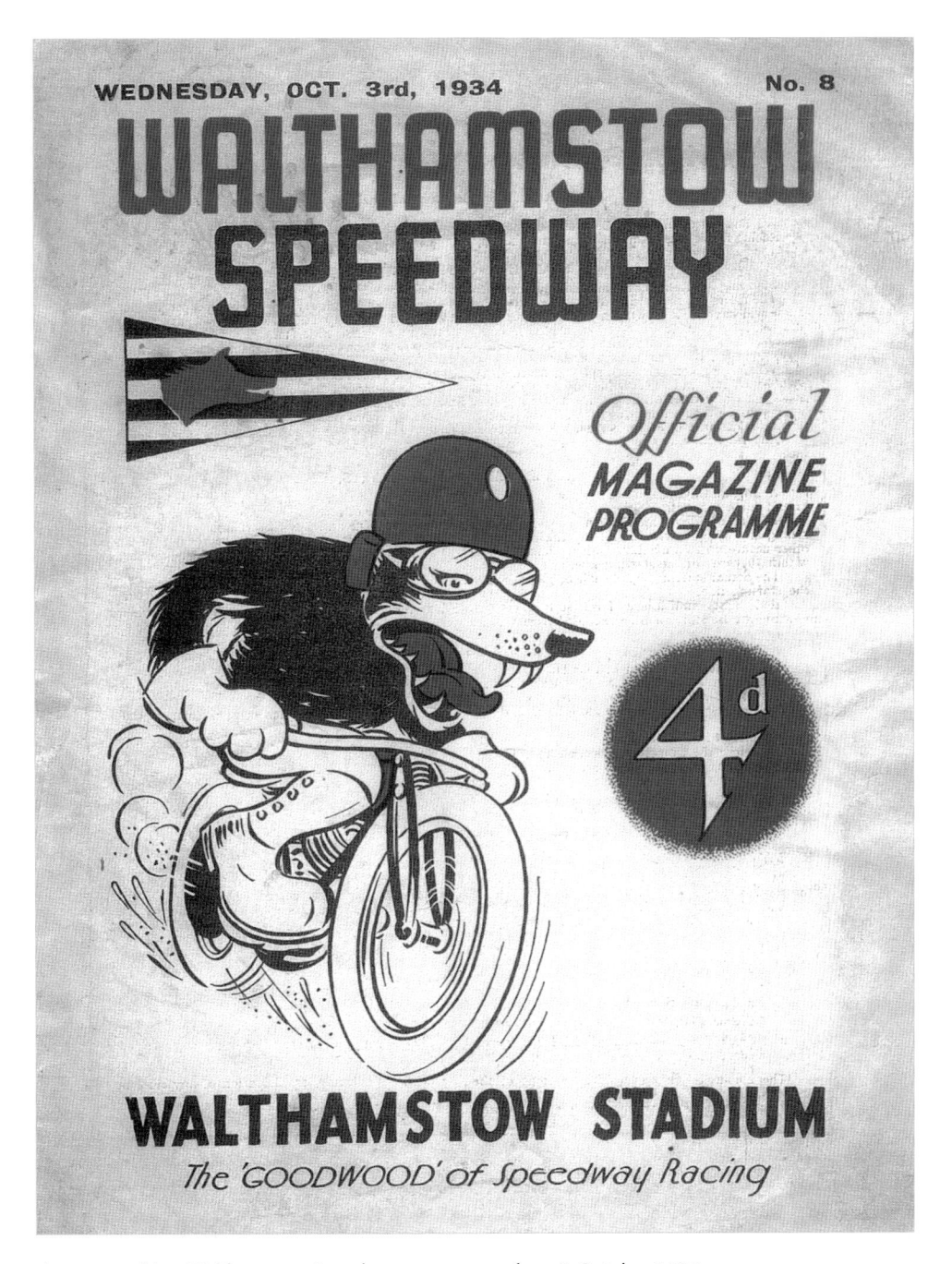

An eye-catching Walthamstow Speedway programme from 3 October 1934.

SPEEDWAY – THE PRE-WAR YEARS

Above: New Cross 1934. Back row, left to right: Harry Shepherd, Roy Dook, Stan Greatrex, George Newton. Front row, left to right: Joe Francis, Tom Farndon, Fred Mockford (Promoter) Ron Johnson, Nobby Key.

Left: An ultra-rare programme from New Brighton, dated 8 September 1934.

THE LEAGUE YEARS

and Rye House (Hoddesdon Stadium), with Cardiff re-opening its doors having not staged the sport since 1930. Another returnee was Exeter, which hadn't run since 1931, while both Coventry (Brandon) and Nottingham resumed on open licences, having been league participants in 1933. Earlier in the year, a track of sorts was also laid in the car park at Wembley, purely for the purpose of practising, as the main Empire Stadium circuit wasn't available prior to the season.

1934 NATIONAL LEAGUE RESULTS

	Belle Vue	Hall Green	Harringay	LB/Wal'stw	New Cross	Plymouth	Wembley	West Ham	Wimbledon
Belle Vue	XX	38-16	33-21	33-21 L	26-25	36-0	26-28	32-19	34-19
	XX	42-11	36-18	40-14	28-26	41-12	35-19	30-24	38-16
Hall Green (Birmingham)	21-33	XX	22-32	31-23 L	28-25	31-23	20-34	32-22	26-27
	12-40	XX	21-33	28-26 L	30-23	39-14	22-32	31-23	32-22
Harringay	21-33	28-24	XX	35-18 L	20-33	35-15	26-28	32-21	26-28
	21-33	32-20	XX	34-20 L	26½-27½	40-14	22-32	33-20	23-29
Lea Bridge/Walthamstow	18-32 L	31-22 L	19-33 L	XX	18-33 L	28-25 L	23-31 L	23-29 L	23-31 L
	17-36	29-25 L	25-29	XX	23-30	22-31 L	22-32	21-32	29-25
New Cross	31-21	26-24	29-25	38-16 L	XX	31-22	24-29	32-21	30-24
	20-34	33-21	39-14	36-17	XX	42-9	28-26	29-25	38-16
Plymouth	18-36	32-20	26-26	29-22 L	23-31	XX	23-30	27-27	27-22
	31-22	30-23	28-26	25-28 L	21-32	XX	22-32	22-32	28-25
Wembley	23-31	35-19	23-31	35-17 L	33-20	40-14	XX	35-17	31-23
	23-31	36-17	22-30	32-21 L	28-25	41-12	XX	36-18	29-24
West Ham	22-32	27-26	30-23	33-21 L	27-26	40-11	24-30	XX	20-33
	35-19	33-21	31-23	36-17	33-21	40-14	23-31	XX	34-19
Wimbledon	21-33	36-17	31-23	31-23 L	29-24	33-20	21-32	37-15	XX
	27-26	29-25	27-26	34-19	25-28	34-20	20-32	22-32	XX

1934 NATIONAL LEAGUE TABLE

Team	Matches	Won	Drawn	Lost	For	Against	Points
Belle Vue	32	27	0	5	1040	650	54
Wembley	32	26	0	6	980	731	52
New Cross	32	21	0	11	935½	762½	42
West Ham	32	16	1	15	865	841	33
Wimbledon	32	16	0	16	840	863	32
Harringay	32	14	1	17	867½	837½	29
Hall Green	32	9	0	23	757	949	18
Plymouth	32	8	2	22	668	1007	18
Walthamstow/L.Bridge	32	5	0	27	694	1006	10
Lea Bridge (Withdrew)	22	4	0	18	490	676	8

Notes: (1) Matches were run over nine heats, with a 3-2-1 scoring system; (2) Lea Bridge were closed down by the Control Board on 27 July due to 'continuing irregularities'. The results and remaining fixtures of the side were taken over by Walthamstow. Results of matches ridden by Lea Bridge are indicated by an 'L'; (3) The match between Belle Vue and Plymouth was not raced, but was subsequently awarded as a 36-0 victory to the home team.

1934 NATIONAL TROPHY

ROUND ONE	Agg	ROUND TWO	Agg	SEMI-FINAL	Agg	FINAL	Agg
		Belle Vue (81-27)	150				
		Hall Green (36-69)	63				
				Belle Vue (80-27)	155		
				Wimbledon (32-75)	59		
Lea Bridge (Walkover)	57	Wimbledon (67-38)	114				
Plymouth (49-57)	49	Lea Bridge (60-47)	98				
						Belle Vue (71-36)	145
						Wembley (34-74)	70
		Wembley (59-49)	133				
		Harringay (33-74)	82				
				Wembley (67½-40½)	129½		
				New Cross (42-62)	82½		
		New Cross (69-36)	128½				
		West Ham (48½-59½)	84½				

Note: Matches were run over 18 heats, with a 3-2-1 scoring system in operation.

1934 ACU CUP

ROUND ONE	Agg	ROUND TWO	Agg	SEMI-FINAL	Agg	FINAL	Agg
		Plymouth	44				
		Harringay	62				
				Harringay	45		
				Belle Vue	62		
Hall Green	49	Belle Vue	79				
Wembley	59	Wembley	29				
						Belle Vue	56
						West Ham	51
		West Ham	66			(Raced at Wimbledon)	
		Walthamstow	37				
				West Ham	58		
				New Cross	49		
		New Cross	62				
		Wimbledon	44				

Notes: (1) Matches were run over 18 heats, with a 3-2-1 scoring system; (2) The second round match between New Cross and Wimbledon originally ended 63-43, but was subsequently amended by the ACU.

1934 LONDON CUP

ROUND ONE	Agg	SEMI-FINAL	Agg	FINAL	Agg
New Cross (66-41)	129				
Harringay (44-63)	85				
		New Cross (69-38)	134		
		Walthamstow (41-65)	79		
Walthamstow	Bye				
				New Cross (62-44)	114
				West Ham (53-52)	97
West Ham	Bye				
		West Ham (62-46)	113		
		Wembley (57-51)	103		
Wembley (60-47)	117				
Wimbledon (48-57)	95				

Note: Matches were run over 18 heats, with a 3-2-1 scoring system in operation.

1934 RESERVE LEAGUE RESULTS

	Belle Vue	Hall Green	Harringay	New Cross	Wembley	West Ham	Wimbledon
Belle Vue	XX	23-12	22-13	15-18	7-26	13-23	16-19
Hall Green	23-13	XX	22-13	22-13	21-13	16-18	17-19
Harringay	23-13	25-11	XX	20-13	15-18	9-24	26-9
New Cross	14-21	17-13	11-25	XX	7-28	15-21	12-22
Wembley	23-11	22-13	18-18	19-17	XX	8-28	22-12
West Ham	20-13	25-11	22-12	25-11	18-18	XX	22-13
Wimbledon	27-7	20-15	17-19	18-18	22-13	10-25	XX

1934 RESERVE LEAGUE TABLE

Team	Matches	Won	Drawn	Lost	For	Against	Points
West Ham	12	11	1	0	271	149	23
Wembley	12	7	2	3	228	189	16
Harringay	12	6	1	5	218	200	13
Wimbledon	12	6	1	5	208	212	13
Hall Green	12	4	0	8	196	221	8
Belle Vue	12	3	0	9	174	241	6
New Cross	12	2	1	9	166	249	5

Notes: (1) Matches were run over six heats, with a 3-2-1 scoring system; (2) Each team comprised four riders and a reserve.

THE LEAGUE YEARS

1935

The National League was contested by only seven teams, and all were based in London, with the one exception being Belle Vue. The capital outfits were Harringay, New Cross, Wembley, West Ham and Wimbledon, with the addition of a new circuit at Hackney Wick, which opened under the promotion of Fred Whitehead.

Belle Vue's amazing glory run continued as they lifted the league title not only for the third year in a row, but for the fifth time in six incredible years! The Aces didn't just win the Championship, they literally blitzed to it, losing just four matches as they finished twelve points ahead of their nearest challengers, Harringay. While mentioning Harringay, it is interesting to note that due to reaching no less than three cup finals during the year, the Tigers actually had to run two 'home' matches at the non-league venues of Portsmouth and Southampton. Going back to Belle Vue, the backbone of their regular line-up showed little change to 1934, with them again being well served by Joe Abbott, Max Grosskreutz, Bob Harrison, Bill Kitchen, Eric Langton, Oliver Langton and Frank Varey. Meanwhile, with Frank Charles departing for Wembley, the Aces were bolstered by a couple of new acquisitions in Tommy Allott, signed from West Ham, and Eric Blain, who arrived via Lea Bridge/Walthamstow. It was a welcome return too for Wally Hull, who had represented Wimbledon (1932), Sheffield (1933) and Lea Bridge/Walthamstow (1934) since last appearing for the Aces in 1931,

Illustration of a Wembley programme from 16 May 1935. Note the reference to the 'Ascot' of the Speedways.

while having represented the Goats in the Reserve League of the previous season, Stanley 'Acorn' Dobson also got in on the act and took some rides for the Aces.

A change to the running of the ACU Cup saw the seven National League teams split into two pools, one of three sides (Belle Vue, Wembley and Wimbledon), and the other of four (Hackney Wick, Harringay, New Cross and West Ham). The participants faced each other home and away, with the winner of each section decided purely on the basis of the highest aggregate total of race points accumulated. With 255 points from four matches in pool one, Belle Vue dashed into the final to face pool two victors Harringay, who amassed 366 points from their six fixtures. The final was duly run over two legs, but was effectively over after the Aces had stormed to a 73-34 victory in the first leg around their own patch on 31 August. Valiantly, Harringay then managed to force a 54-54 draw at their Green Lanes home on 21 September, as Belle Vue wrapped up another trophy by 127 points to 88 on aggregate.

The Belle Vue bandwagon just rolled on in the National Trophy, but they were made to work extremely hard as they squeezed past New Cross by only 3 points on aggregate in the opening round. Life was a little easier for the Aces in the semi-final, with a 20-point success over West Ham, while fellow finalists Harringay disposed of Hackney Wick and Wimbledon along their route. Unfortunately for the Londoners, the mighty Manchester side were again in a class of their own in the final, winning both legs comfortably for an aggregate 126-88 success.

Having had to settle for second place in three competitions, the London Cup gave Harringay the opportunity to gain some deserved silverware, safe in the knowledge they wouldn't have to take on Belle Vue! After turning over Wimbledon in the first round, the Tigers rode very well to take a 30-point aggregate victory over Wembley in the semi-final, thereby setting up a showdown with West Ham, who had beaten Hackney Wick and New Cross. Showing they weren't prepared to be the 'nearly team' again, a very determined Harringay outfit fairly ripped to a 68-37 win in their home leg on 28 September. It was to prove too great a deficit for the Hammers, who could only manage to eke out a 55-52 victory in the second leg at their Custom House Stadium on 1 October. Having ridden so well as a team all season long, Harringay's aggregate success of 120-92 must surely have been welcomed by most in British speedway – with the exception of the diehard West Ham supporters of course.

Briefly looking at the other racing strips of the year, open licence meetings were again hosted by Barnet (Bypass), California (Longmoor Speedway), Cardiff, Dagenham, Eastbourne, Liverpool (Seaforth Greyhound Stadium), Luton, New Brighton (The Tower Ground), Norwich and Rye House (Hoddesdon Stadium). Meanwhile, having dropped out of league competition at the end of 1934, Plymouth ran several challenge meetings during the summer, including a junior international between England and Australia on 30 July. Track action was also seen at Crayford, which re-opened having last staged the sport in 1931, while two other circuits reappeared as training venues, namely High Beech and Lea Bridge. It is also known that a demonstration of just a few laps took place at Stenhouse Greyhound Stadium in Edinburgh during the year. As mentioned in the summary of the National League competition, the sport made a return to Southampton, with some late season

THE LEAGUE YEARS

meetings, including one of Harringay's league fixtures. Finally, a new track opened at Portsmouth Greyhound and Sports Stadium in Tipnor, but aside from staging another of Harringay's league matches on 2 October, the track sadly saw no further activity.

1935 NATIONAL LEAGUE RESULTS

	Belle Vue	Hackney Wick	Harringay	New Cross	Wembley	West Ham	Wimbledon
Belle Vue	XX	45-27	45-26	41-30	46-25	35-35	41-31
	XX	30-41	44-25	47-25	49-23	46-26	43-26
Hackney Wick	35-37	XX	40-30	29-43	43-28	38-33	29-43
	35-35	XX	34½-37½	31-41	40-32	39-31	47-25
Harringay	31-41	43-29	XX	44-27	41-30	40-31	30-39
	46-25	32-35	XX	42-29	43-28	43-27	43-29
New Cross	31-40	43-24	38-33	XX	34-38	43-29	38-33
	25-47	35-37	30-41	XX	40-31	35-37	43-28
Wembley	37-34	42-28	41-31	38-34	XX	28-42	35-36
	30-42	45-26	32-39	50-22	XX	45-25	48-22
West Ham	34-38	38-34	37-35	35-36	40-31	XX	45-26
	39-33	42-28	39-33	44-28	41-31	XX	45-27
Wimbledon	34-37	43-29	38-30	29-42	29-41	37-34	XX
	35-36	26-46	35-36	41-30	25-46	43-27	XX

1935 NATIONAL LEAGUE TABLE

Team	Matches	Won	Drawn	Lost	For	Against	Points
Belle Vue	24	18	2	4	957	752	38
Harringay	24	13	0	11	874½	823½	26
West Ham	24	12	1	11	856	852	25
Wembley	24	11	0	13	855	852	22
Hackney Wick	24	10	1	13	824½	879½	21
New Cross	24	10	0	14	822	889	20
Wimbledon	24	8	0	16	780	921	16

Notes: (1) Matches were run over 12 heats, with a 3-2-1 scoring system; (2) The second Harringay versus Hackney Wick match was raced at Portsmouth; (3) The second Harringay versus West Ham match was staged at Southampton.

1935 NATIONAL TROPHY

ROUND ONE	Agg	SEMI-FINAL	Agg	FINAL	Agg
Belle Vue (55-52)	109				
New Cross (54-54)	106				
		Belle Vue (64-43)	117		
		West Ham (54-53)	97		
West Ham (67-41)	119				
Wembley (55-52)	96				
				Belle Vue (63-43)	126
				Harringay (45-63)	88
Harringay (70-35)	137				
Hackney Wick (41-67)	76				
		Harringay (69-39)	133		
		Wimbledon (41-64)	80		
Wimbledon	Bye				

Note: Matches were run over 18 heats, with a 3-2-1 scoring system in operation.

1935 ACU CUP

POOL ONE	Belle Vue	Wembley	Wimbledon		RACE POINTS	FINAL	Agg
Belle Vue	XX	74-34	67-40		255		
Wembley	43-64	XX	72-35		211		
Wimbledon	57-50	43-62	XX		175		
						Belle Vue (73-34)	127
						Harringay (54-54)	88
POOL TWO	Hackney Wick	Harringay	New Cross	West Ham			
Hackney Wick	XX	46-61	42-62	54-53	273		
Harringay	64-44	XX	62-45	64-43	366		
New Cross	63-44	41-67	XX	66-42	329		
West Ham	65-43	60-48	53-52	XX	316		

Notes: (1) Matches were run over 18 heats, with a 3-2-1 scoring system; (2) The finalists were decided purely on the basis of the highest aggregate race points scored in each group.

1935 LONDON CUP

ROUND ONE	Agg	SEMI-FINAL	Agg	FINAL	Agg
Harringay (75-32)	139				
Wimbledon (39-64)	71				
		Harringay (66-41)	121		
		Wembley (50-55)	91		
Wembley	Bye				
				Harringay (68-37)	120
				West Ham (55-52)	92
New Cross	Bye				
		West Ham (63½-41½)	110½		
		New Cross (58-47)	99½		
West Ham (69-39)	126				
Hackney Wick (48-57)	87				

Notes: Matches were run over 18 heats, with a 3-2-1 scoring system in operation.

83

1936

The National League was contested by the same seven sides as in the previous year, with Belle Vue losing just five matches on their way to a fourth successive Championship, ahead of runners-up Wembley. Again representing the mighty Aces during the season were long-term regulars Joe Abbott, Max Grosskreutz, Bob Harrison, Bill Kitchen, brothers Eric and Oliver Langton, plus Frank Varey. Meanwhile several others also got rides and made a contribution along the way, namely Tommy Allott, Acorn Dobson, Wally Hull, Walter 'Chun' Moore, Lancashire-born Tommy Price (not to be confused with his namesake at Wembley) and Jack Tye.

As in 1935, the ACU Cup was spread over two groups, with the finalists determined by the highest aggregate race points attained in each. With a tally of 221 points, Wembley were the clear winners of pool one, and rather unsurprisingly it was Belle Vue who topped pool two on 326 points. Run over two legs, Wembley fought bravely to contain the Aces, actually winning their home leg 48-47 on 16 July. However, it was the Aces who claimed aggregate victory by 98 points to 92, after gaining a hard-fought 51-44 success in the return encounter at Hyde Road two days later.

New Cross 1936. Back row, left to right: Stan Greatrex, Nobby Key, Jack Milne, Henry Collins, Ernie Evans, Harry Shepherd. Front row, left to right: Ron Johnson, Mike Erskine, Fred Mockford (Promoter), Norman Evans, George Newton.

A Liverpool programme from their Provincial League clash versus Bristol on 10 August 1936.

Belle Vue continued to sweep all before them in the National Trophy, defeating West Ham and Wembley as they strode into the final, before lifting yet another piece of silverware with a decisive 121-90 aggregate result over Hackney Wick.

The London Cup at least gave the six other teams an opportunity of winning something, and following a first round bye, it was Hackney Wick who marched through to the final by defeating New Cross. The Waterden Road outfit were duly joined by Harringay, who waltzed past Wimbledon, prior to narrowly seeing off Wembley in a tight semi-final tie. Despite staging the first leg of the final, Harringay were unable to prevent Hackney Wick from racing to a 58-49 win, with the Wolves (as Hackney Wick were then nicknamed) completing a fine overall 127-88 success when thundering to a 69-39 victory in the second match.

A six-team Provincial League started in 1936, with the participating sides being Bristol, Cardiff, Liverpool, Nottingham, Plymouth and Southampton. Unfortunately, this number was reduced to five when Cardiff dropped out, having completed nine fixtures. This was a shame as the Welsh outfit had reported a handsome profit from running a series of open licence meetings in 1935, but the gamble to operate league racing had simply not brought the hoped-for response from the public. Of the other teams, both Plymouth and Southampton had also operated on an open licence the year before, whereas Bristol, Liverpool (Stanley Stadium) and Nottingham had re-opened their doors to the sport. Although speedway had been staged in Liverpool at Seaforth Greyhound Stadium in 1934 and 1935, the Stanley Stadium venue had not seen any of the motorized action since way back in 1930. Bristol's Knowle Stadium had also remained dormant to speedway since 1930, while Nottingham's White City Stadium had last hosted racing in 1934.

With two different leagues running, many riders often 'doubled-up', examples of which saw three of the Belle Vue teamsters appear in the Provincial League thus: Tommy Allott also had spells at both Bristol and Nottingham, Tommy Price also represented Liverpool, and Chun Moore also rode for Nottingham.

The race for the title was a close-run thing between Southampton and Bristol, both of whom finished level on 20 points after the Saints had gained a thrilling $41\frac{1}{2}$-$29\frac{1}{2}$ victory over the Bulldogs at their Banister Court home on 24 September. The win, however, clinched the Championship for Southampton by virtue of a superior race points difference, with their representatives over the season being Cyril Anderson, Vic Collins, Billy Dallison, Arthur 'Artie' Fenn, Frank Goulden, Sid

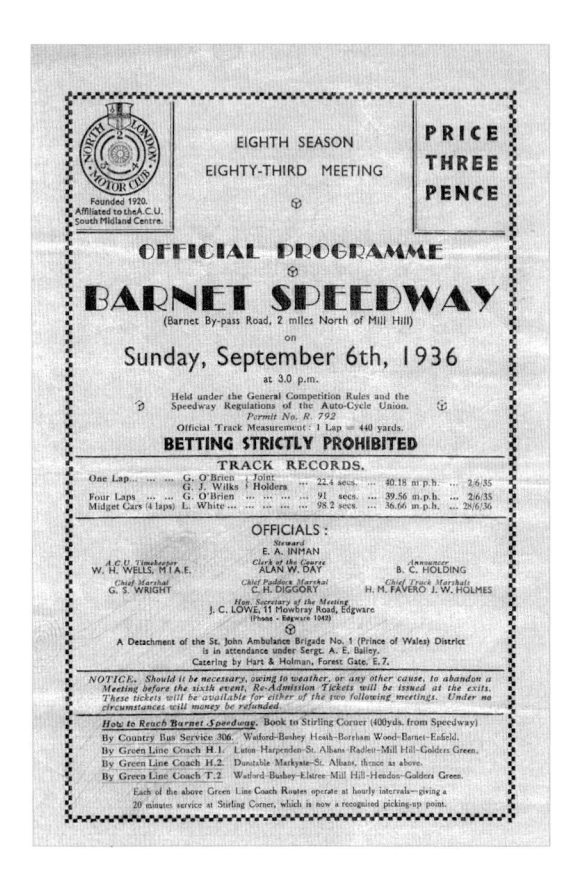

Scarce Barnet Speedway programme from 6 September 1936.

Griffiths, Bert Jones, Harry 'Tiger' Lewis (who linked with Nottingham in mid-season), Bob Lovell (who also had a spell with Nottingham), Dicky Smythe, Alec Statham, Fred Strecker and S. Webb. A number of the Southampton boys also made appearances in the National League, with Billy Dallison, Artie Fenn, Frank Goulden, Bert Jones, Bob Lovell and Fred Strecker all identified with Harringay.

Meanwhile, seven teams initially entered the Provincial Trophy, these being the six league contestants, plus a second West Ham side (complete with a 'Hawks' nickname), who raced their 'home' matches at Southampton. This number was reduced by the June closure of Cardiff, who had ridden just one match in the competition at the time. As with the league, it boiled down to a straight contest between Southampton and Bristol, with the Saints again coming out on top, having accumulated 2 points more than the Bulldogs' total of 14.

Racing could also be seen at Barnet (Bypass), California (Longmoor Speedway), Crayford, Dagenham, Eastbourne, Luton, Middlesbrough, Norwich and Rye House (Hoddesdon Stadium), all of which continued to run with open licences. In addition, Coventry (Brandon), Crystal Palace and Rayleigh (Laindon) could be added to the list after re-opening, whilst new venues started at Holbeach and Smallford (St Albans). Concluding the venues of 1936, High Beech was again used for training purposes (under the guidance of Roger Frogley), as was a new circuit at Melton Mowbray, while as had occurred in 1934, a practice strip was laid in the car park at Wembley.

1936 NATIONAL LEAGUE RESULTS

	Belle Vue	Hackney Wick	Harringay	New Cross	Wembley	West Ham	Wimbledon
Belle Vue	XX	47-25	47-24	45-27	41-30	53-19	43-29
	XX	47-25	50-22	36-32	45-27	36-36	55-17
Hackney Wick	44-21	XX	42-29	26-44	30-42	43-28	51-19
	32-39	XX	41-31	32-40	30-42	48-24	46-26
Harringay	32-40	51-21	XX	40-32	39-33	50-22	39-33
	42-30	34-38	XX	38-33	45-26	31-38	51-21
New Cross	35-37	39-30	34-38	XX	28-43	43-29	35-36
	43-27	43-29	44-26	XX	42-30	43-28	35-37
Wembley	32-40	43-29	44-28	47-25	XX	43-28	33-38
	37-34	28-44	43-29	36-35	XX	43-28	34-38
West Ham	37-34	27-44	33-37	49-22	27-45	XX	32-40
	27-44	33-38	49-23	44-28	34-37	XX	52-20
Wimbledon	30-38	37-33	32-40	40-31	34-37	44-27	XX
	27-44	37-34	42-29	40-31	35-36	33-37	XX

1936 NATIONAL LEAGUE TABLE

Team	Matches	Won	Drawn	Lost	For	Against	Points
Belle Vue	24	18	1	5	973	731	37
Wembley	24	15	0	9	891	826	30
Harringay	24	12	0	12	848	868	24
Hackney Wick	24	11	0	13	855	851	22
Wimbledon	24	11	0	13	785	923	22
New Cross	24	9	0	15	844	863	18
West Ham	24	7	1	16	788	922	15

Note: Matches were run over 12 heats, with a 3-2-1 scoring system.

1936 NATIONAL TROPHY

PROVINCIAL LEAGUE ROUND 1	Agg	PROVINCIAL LEAGUE ROUND 2	Agg	QUARTER-FINAL	Agg	SEMI-FINAL	Agg	FINAL	Agg
				Belle Vue (68-40)	133				
				West Ham (43-65)	83				
						Belle Vue (78-30)	131		
						Wembley (54-53)	84		
				Wembley (61-47)	126				
				Wimbledon (42-65)	89				
								Belle Vue (72-31)	121
								Hackney Wick (59-49)	90
Southampton (38-33)	76			Hackney Wick (65-42)	116				
Cardiff (33-38)	66			New Cross (55-51)	97				
		Southampton (42-28)	73			Hackney Wick (58-50)	110		
		Liverpool (39-31)	67			Harringay (55-52)	105		
Liverpool (35-34)	73			Southampton (30-41)	30				
Nottingham (34-38)	68			Harringay (Walkover)	41				

Note: Matches were run over 18 heats, with a 3-2-1 scoring system in operation.

1936 ACU CUP

POOL ONE	New Cross	Wembley	Wimbledon		RACE POINTS	FINAL	Agg
New Cross	XX	37-59	51-45		178		
Wembley	54-42	XX	59-37		221		
Wimbledon	47-48	45-49	XX		174		
						Wembley (48-47)	92
POOL TWO	Belle Vue	Hackney	Harringay	West Ham		Belle Vue (51-44)	98
Belle Vue	XX	65-30	53-41	60-35	326		
Hackney Wick	38-57	XX	45-51	57-39	246		
Harringay	45-51	51-44	XX	61-35	306		
West Ham	56-40	63-32	38-57	XX	266		

Notes: (1) Matches were run over 16 heats, with a 3-2-1 scoring system; (2) The finalists were decided purely on the basis of the highest aggregate race points scored in each group.

1936 LONDON CUP

ROUND ONE	Agg	SEMI-FINAL	Agg	FINAL	Agg
Hackney Wick	Bye				
		Hackney Wick (63-43)	115		
		New Cross (54-52)	97		
New Cross (67-41)	117				
West Ham (58-50)	99				
				Hackney Wick (69-39)	127
				Harringay (49-58)	88
Wembley	Bye				
		Harringay (63-44)	110		
		Wembley (60-47)	104		
Harringay (65-43)	136				
Wimbledon (37-71)	80				

Note: Matches were run over 18 heats, with a 3-2-1 scoring system in operation.

1936 PROVINCIAL LEAGUE RESULTS

	Bristol	Cardiff	Liverpool	Nottingham	Plymouth	Southampton
Bristol	XX	38-33	41-30	43-29	40-32	38-32
	XX	Not Run	52-19	43-29	49-23	35-37
Cardiff	39-33	XX	42-28	35-36	37-34	33-37
	Not Run	XX	Not Run	Not Run	Not Run	Not Run
Liverpool	36-35	Not Run	XX	29-40	43-24	40-31
	39-33	Not Run	XX	34-37	44-26	40-30
Nottingham	33-34	38-34	30-41	XX	39½-32½	30-41
	53-19	Not Run	55-17	XX	48-23	47-24
Plymouth	35-37	57-15	25-47	35-37	XX	47-25
	35-36	Not Run	40-32	27-44	XX	29-43
Southampton	43-29	50-22	35-37	53½-17½	49-20	XX
	41½-29½	Not Run	43-27	42-30	49-23	XX

1936 PROVINCIAL LEAGUE TABLE

Team	Matches	Won	Drawn	Lost	For	Against	Points
Southampton	16	10	0	6	619	519	20
Bristol	16	10	0	6	593½	546½	20
Nottingham	16	9	0	7	599	538	18
Liverpool	16	9	0	7	555	577	18
Plymouth	16	2	0	14	476½	662½	4
Cardiff (Expunged)	9	3	0	6	290	351	6

Notes: (1) Matches were raced over twelve heats, with a 3-2-1 scoring system; (2) Cardiff closed down in June due to poor crowds, with their record expunged from the table.

1936 PROVINCIAL TROPHY RESULTS

	Bristol	Cardiff	Liverpool	Nottingham	Plymouth	Southampton	West Ham II
Bristol	XX	Not Run	32-40	45-24	50-22	32-38	43-29
Cardiff	Not Run	XX	Not Run	Not Run	Not Run	Not Run	43-28
Liverpool	30-42	Not Run	XX	47-23	46-23	33-39	44-28
Nottingham	27-43	Not Run	30-41	XX	38-33	31-39	47-24
Plymouth	46-25	Not Run	38-34	Not Run	XX	42-30	53-18
Southampton	29-40	Not Run	43-27	42-28	44-27	XX	52-20
West Ham II	33-39	Not Run	37-34	29-42	34-34	28-44	XX

1936 PROVINCIAL TROPHY TABLE

Team	Matches	Won	Drawn	Lost	For	Against	Points
Southampton	10	8	0	2	400	308	16
Bristol	10	7	0	3	391	318	14
Liverpool	10	5	0	5	376	335	10
Plymouth	10	4	1	5	318	319	9
Nottingham	10	4	0	6	290	343	8
West Ham II	10	1	1	8	280	432	3
Cardiff (Expunged)	1	1	0	0	43	28	2

Notes: Matches were raced over twelve heats, with a 3-2-1 scoring system; (2) Cardiff closed down in June due to poor crowds, with their record expunged from the table; (3) Although Plymouth v Nottingham was not raced, the match points were awarded to the away side; (4) Aside from the main West Ham side, which operated in the National League, a second team (known as West Ham Hawks) competed in the Provincial Trophy, with their 'home' matches being staged at Southampton.

THE LEAGUE YEARS

1937

Despite there not being many tracks staging regular domestic fare, at least the National League remained constant with the same seven sides that had partaken in the previous two seasons. However, in a change from what had become the norm, Belle Vue failed to retain the Championship, and in fact could only manage to finish in fourth position. This could be attributed to the non-return of Max Grosskreutz (who opted to take over as speedway manager at Norwich), and a broken leg suffered by Bob Harrison, which caused him to miss more than two months of action at the end of the campaign. With a total of 36 points, the title instead went to a powerful West Ham outfit, who were represented over the year by an embarrassment of riches in Arthur Atkinson, Phil Bishop, Ken Brett, Eric Chitty, Tommy Croombs, Broncho Dixon, Lloyd 'Cowboy' Goffe (who also rode in the Provincial League for Leicester), Charlie Spinks, Tiger Stevenson, Jack Tidbury (who also raced for both Leicester and Birmingham in the Provincial League) and Bluey Wilkinson.

A Wembley programme from their ACU Cup match against Harringay on 22 July 1937.

West Ham 1937. Back row, left to right: Eric Chitty, Tommy Croombs, Arthur Atkinson, Phil Bishop, Johnnie Hoskins (Promoter), Alec Moseley (Mechanic), Broncho Dixon, Charlie Spinks. Front, on bike: Tiger Stevenson.

In contrast to their league form, Belle Vue remained a dominant force in the National Trophy, sweeping past Wimbledon and Hackney Wick to incredibly reach their sixth final in a row. The other half of the draw saw New Cross thump Harringay, prior to reaching the final with a 19-point aggregate success over Wembley. The final itself might have appeared a foregone conclusion after Belle Vue had dashed to a 70-38 win in the first leg at Hyde Road on 21 August, but four days later, the Rangers (as they had become known at the start of the season) fought tooth and nail in the second leg on their mini 262-yard circuit. Although they ultimately failed to claw back the large deficit, they were gallant victors on the night by 62 points to 45, as the Aces claimed the National Trophy for a fifth successive year by an aggregate score of 115-100.

The ACU Cup was run on the same lines as previously, with the two group winners on aggregate race points being Belle Vue and Wembley. The first leg of the final took place at Wembley on 7 October, when the Lions managed to eke out a narrow 49-45 win. That meant it was always going to be an uphill task for the Londoners in the second leg two days later, and so it proved as the Aces blasted to a 61-35 victory, giving them an aggregate success of 106-84.

In the London Cup, it was New Cross and West Ham who met in the final, the Rangers getting there via Wimbledon and Wembley, while the Hammers' passage was a little less strenuous as they had a first round bye, before thrashing Hackney Wick in the semi-final. West Ham hosted the first leg of the final on 28 September, but it was New Cross who gained the initiative with a 55-52 victory, thereby setting themselves up nicely for the return match the following evening. Wanting to at least gain some consolation for their defeat in the National Trophy final, the Rangers were in no mood for complacency as they sped to a 62-45 success to achieve an overall win by 117 points to 97.

In Bristol, Liverpool, Nottingham and Southampton, the Provincial League only had four starters from the previous season; however, these were augmented by the revival of both Birmingham (Hall Green) and Leicester (Stadium). Having previously operated under the name of Hall Green, the West Midlands outfit took to the track as Birmingham, but with a new Bulldogs moniker. Meanwhile, having run without an ACU licence since opening in 1931, Norwich obtained the necessary documentation to take the number of competing sides to seven, installing former Belle Vue star Max Grosskreutz as their speedway manager as previously mentioned.

Unfortunately, the league was quickly reduced to six participants when Leicester resigned, having completed just half a dozen fixtures. Meanwhile, after fulfilling 11 matches, Liverpool promoter E.O. Spence transferred their operation to his other track at Belle Vue, with the result that the famous Manchester circuit again housed two teams as they had done previously in both 1931 and 1934.

The High Beech programme from 15 August 1937.

In a repeat of what happened in 1936, the race for the Championship again featured Bristol and Southampton, but in the final analysis it was the Bulldogs who scooped top spot, their 30-point tally being four more than the Saints. With Bristol being promoted by Ronnie Greene and Fred Mockford, who both also ran National League venues Wimbledon and New Cross respectively, it was only natural that the Bulldogs would employ a number of riders to 'double up' during their charge to glory. Examples of this were Roy Dook, Fred Leavis, Bill Maddern, Bill Rogers, Harry Shepherd, Rol Stobart and Reg Vigor, all of whom also rode for the Dons.

Aside from those seven representatives, Jack Dalton and Bill Longley also made appearances for New Cross. Meanwhile, the remaining men who sported the Bulldogs race-jacket during the campaign were Harold Bain, Harry Bowler (who joined following the premature closure of Leicester), Reg Gore, Reg Hay (who moved to Norwich late in the season), Reg Lambourne, Fred Lewis, Johnnie Millett (who also rode for Birmingham) and George Saunders. Bristol's title glory was tinged with sadness though, when Reg Vigor lost his life three days after being involved in a track accident while riding for Wimbledon against visiting Harringay in a National League match on 27 September.

Following the early closure of Leicester, the Provincial Trophy was contested by six teams, with Liverpool completing six of their ten match programme prior to the previously mentioned move to Belle Vue. The competition developed into a battle between Nottingham and Bristol, with the White City Stadium-based side eventually emerging victorious after pipping the Bulldogs by a single point.

One further event saw the Coronation Cup raced for on a two-legged knock-out basis, with Nottingham reaching the final after a first round bye, and subsequent semi-final success over Bristol. Meanwhile, their opponents in the final turned out to be Southampton, who dispatched Liverpool and Birmingham en route. Nottingham duly staged the first leg of the final on 10 August, and coasted to a 61-23 win, making the following evening's return match somewhat academic. However, the Saints at least managed to register a home victory by 46 points to 37, as Nottingham completed an overall 98-69 success.

Rounding off the story of the season, open licence meetings continued at California (Longmoor Speedway), Crayford, Crystal Palace, Dagenham, Eastbourne, Holbeach, Middlesbrough, Rye House (Hoddesdon Stadium) and Smallford (St Albans). Added to those ten venues, both Portsmouth (Greyhound and Sports Stadium) and Workington (Lonsdale Park) re-opened, having last operated in 1935 and 1932 respectively. Meanwhile, Cardiff and Plymouth resumed on open licences, having been league outfits the year before, although the Welsh side had failed to last the distance of course. Three new tracks started up at Carlisle (Moorville Park), Ringwood and Stockport, while High Beech reverted to open meetings after running purely as a training venue throughout 1935 and 1936. Finally, the spacious car park at Wembley was again used for practice purposes, with the management even erecting the original starting gate to allow the riders to hone their gating techniques.

THE LEAGUE YEARS

1937 NATIONAL LEAGUE RESULTS

	Belle Vue	Hackney Wick	Harringay	New Cross	Wembley	West Ham	Wimbledon
Belle Vue	XX	47-37	52-31	54-29	48-36	39-45	62-22
	XX	60-24	62-22	53-31	52-31	38-45	61-23
Hackney Wick	45-39	XX	46-37	40-42	38-46	42-41	53-31
	44-39	XX	43½-38½	43-40	34-49	49-32	54-29
Harringay	41-43	54-30	XX	49-35	46-36	35-48	47-32
	49-35	46-37	XX	30-54	43-41	40-43	42-41
New Cross	51-33	44-39	49½-34½	XX	49-35	56-28	48-35
	46-37	58-26	47-37	XX	42-41	47-37	55-28
Wembley	43-40	44-40	48-36	52-31	XX	52-30	56-28
	50-34	45-39	53-28	47-36	XX	44-40	55-28
West Ham	53-31	57-25	54-28	53-30	68-16	XX	47-37
	43-38	52-31	59-24	55-28	49-34	XX	65-19
Wimbledon	30-53	40-44	45-38	40-42	31-49	38-43	XX
	38-44	52-32	30-53	31-52	33-51	38-42	XX

1937 NATIONAL LEAGUE TABLE

Team	Matches	Won	Drawn	Lost	For	Against	Points
West Ham	24	18	0	6	1129	859	36
Wembley	24	16	0	8	1054	943	32
New Cross	24	16	0	8	1042½	957½	32
Belle Vue	24	13	0	11	1094	909	26
Hackney Wick	24	10	0	14	935½	1062½	20
Harringay	24	9	0	15	929	1064	18
Wimbledon	24	2	0	22	799	1188	4

Note: Matches were run over 14 heats, with a 3-2-1 scoring system.

1937 NATIONAL TROPHY

PROVINCIAL LEAGUE ROUND 1	Agg	PROVINCIAL LEAGUE ROUND 2	Agg	QUARTER-FINAL	Agg	SEMI-FINAL	Agg	FINAL	Agg
				Belle Vue (80-28)	148				
				Wimbledon (39-68)	67				
						Belle Vue (69-39)	121		
						Hackney Wick (56-52)	95		
				Hackney Wick (65-43)	118				
Southampton (55-28)	100			West Ham (55-53)	98				
Liverpool (39-45)	67							Belle Vue (70-38)	115
		Southampton (51-32)	93					New Cross (62-45)	100
		Bristol (41-42)	73						
Bristol (48-36)	85			Southampton (40-44)	40				
Nottingham (46-37)	82			Wembley (Walkover)	44				
						New Cross (59-48)	117		
						Wembley (50-58)	98		
				New Cross (76-31)	141				
				Harringay (41-65)	72				

Notes: (1) Matches were run over 18 heats, with a 3-2-1 scoring system; (2) The quarter-final tie between Hackney Wick and West Ham originally ended in a 106-106 draw, Hackney winning their leg 60-48, while West Ham won their home match 58-46. The results shown in the above grid relate only to the replay.

1937 ACU CUP

POOL ONE	Belle Vue	Hackney Wick	West Ham		RACE POINTS	FINAL	Agg
Belle Vue	XX	69-27	47-48		202		
Hackney Wick	52-44	XX	62-34		181		
West Ham	52-42	56-40	XX		190		

POOL TWO	Harringay	New Cross	Wembley	Wimbledon			
						Belle Vue (61-35)	106
						Wembley (49-45)	84
Harringay	XX	52-41	44-52	47-46	269		
New Cross	62-34	XX	47-48	60-34	311½		
Wembley	53-42	54½-41½	XX	58-38	319½		
Wimbledon	46-50	34-60	42-54	XX	240		

Notes: (1) Matches were run over 16 heats, with a 3-2-1 scoring system; (2) The finalists were determined purely on the basis of the highest aggregate race points scored in each group.

1937 LONDON CUP

ROUND ONE	Agg	SEMI-FINAL	Agg	FINAL	Agg
New Cross (65-43)	130				
Wimbledon (42-65)	85				
		New Cross (62-46)	118		
		Wembley (50-56)	96		
Wembley (58-49)	119				
Harringay (46-61)	95				
				New Cross (62-45)	117
				West Ham (52-55)	97
West Ham	Bye				
		West Ham (87-21)	146		
		Hackney Wick (49-59)	70		
Hackney Wick	Bye				

Note: Matches were raced over 18 heats, with a 3-2-1 scoring system in operation.

93

1937 PROVINCIAL LEAGUE RESULTS

	Birmingham	Bristol	Leicester	Liverpool/BV II	Norwich	Nottingham	Southampton
Birmingham (Hall Green)	XX	39-44	39-45	41-40	39-44	26-57	30-53
	XX	38-45	Not Run	53-31 B	55-28	44-39	60-24
Bristol	48-34	XX	68-15	58-25	64-18	49-31	45-36
	50½-33½	XX	Not Run	59-24	60-23	48-35	55-28
Leicester	47-33	23-57	XX	Not Run	Not Run	Not Run	Not Run
	Not Run	Not Run	XX	Not Run	Not Run	Not Run	Not Run
Liverpool / Belle Vue II	58-26	29-55	Not Run	XX	30-54 B	42-40	37-46
	54-27	31-52 B	Not Run	XX	44-35 B	46-37 B	49-35 B
Norwich	48-35	27-54	57-27	32-50	XX	28-49	37-47
	50-34	44-39	Not Run	48-34 B	XX	46-37	46-37
Nottingham	51-31	42-40	65-19	31-53	60-24	XX	54-30
	50-33	45-35	Not Run	58-26 B	53-31	XX	45-38
Southampton	57-26	46-38	Not Run	43-41	59-22	44-40	XX
	59-25	52-31	Not Run	53-30 B	61-22	44-38	XX

1937 PROVINCIAL LEAGUE TABLE

Team	Matches	Won	Drawn	Lost	For	Against	Points
Bristol	20	15	0	5	969½	680½	30
Southampton	20	13	0	7	892	771	26
Nottingham	20	11	0	9	892	758	22
Belle Vue II / Liverpool	20	8	0	12	774	883	16
Norwich	20	8	0	12	707	941	16
Birmingham	20	5	0	15	729½	930½	10
Liverpool (Withdrew)	11	5	0	6	453	458	10
Leicester (Expunged)	6	2	0	4	176	319	4

Notes: (1) Matches were run over 14 heats, with a 3-2-1 scoring system; (2) Leicester resigned from the league after just six matches, with their record expunged from the table; (3) The first match between Southampton and Leicester did start, but was abandoned with the home side leading 33-7; (4) Liverpool transferred to Belle Vue in mid-season. A second Belle Vue side, riding with a 'Merseysiders' moniker, subsequently completed their remaining fixtures and these are indicated by a 'B' next to the relevant result.

1937 PROVINCIAL TROPHY RESULTS

	Birmingham	Bristol	Liverpool/BV II	Norwich	Nottingham	Southampton
Birmingham	XX	54-54	67-41	72-34	60-47	54-50
Bristol	50-58	XX	59-49 B	62-44	46-61	41-64
Liverpool / Belle Vue II	72-36 B	43-62	XX	59-46 B	56-50	59-47 B
Norwich	68-38	45-62	61-47	XX	36-72	68-37
Nottingham	75-32	68-40	73-32	69-39	XX	59-48
Southampton	75-33	59-48	68-40	73-33	69-38	XX

1937 PROVINCIAL TROPHY TABLE

Team	Matches	Won	Drawn	Lost	For	Against	Points
Nottingham	10	7	0	3	612	458	14
Bristol	10	6	1	3	569	499	13
Southampton	10	6	0	4	590	473	12
Belle Vue II / Liverpool	10	4	0	6	498	569	8
Birmingham	10	3	1	6	459	612	7
Norwich	10	3	0	7	474	591	6
Liverpool (Withdrew)	6	1	0	5	259	381	2

Notes: Matches were raced over 18 heats, with a 3-2-1 scoring system; (2) Liverpool transferred to Belle Vue in mid-season. A second Belle Vue side, riding with a 'Merseysiders' moniker, subsequently completed their remaining fixtures and these are indicated by a 'B' next to the relevant result; (3) Norwich v Birmingham originally ended 61-45, but the result was subsequently cancelled by the ACU and the match restaged.

1937 CORONATION CUP

ROUND ONE	Agg	SEMI-FINAL	Agg	FINAL	Agg
Nottingham (Walkover)	W/O				
Leicester (Withdrew)					
		Nottingham (55-29)	92		
		Bristol (47-37)	76		
Bristol (53-29)	100				
Norwich (35-47)	64				
				Nottingham (61-23)	98
				Southampton (46-37)	69
Southampton (41-42)	89				
Liverpool (35-48)	77				
		Southampton (80-28)	120		
		Birmingham (41-40)	69		
Birmingham	Bye				

Note: Matches were run over 14 heats, with a 3-2-1 scoring system. There was one exception, however, as the semi-final match between Southampton and Birmingham was staged over 18 heats.

1938

An alteration to the domestic set-up in 1938 saw all the regularly active tracks competing in the National League, which was split into Divisions One and Two. The top flight comprised six of the seven teams that had contested the National League in 1937, namely Belle Vue, Harringay, New Cross, Wembley, West Ham and Wimbledon. The seventh member was Bristol, who exchanged licences with Hackney Wick – the London side having opted for the cheaper running costs of the Second Division.

With 15 wins and a draw, New Cross proved to be the most consistent side in Division One, taking the Championship with a 4-point cushion from their nearest challengers West Ham, who themselves filled the runner-up spot on race points difference from Wembley and Wimbledon. It really was a glorious campaign for the Rangers, who were represented by the likes of Harry Bowler, Ray Duggan, Ernie Evans, Joe Francis, Stan Greatrex, Ron Johnson, Bill Longley, Jack Milne, Clem Mitchell, George Newton and Godwin 'Goldy' Restall.

For a fourth successive year, the ACU Cup was spread over two groups, with the finalists again decided purely on the highest aggregate of race points scored. Just for a change, neither Belle Vue or Wembley qualified for the final, instead it was West Ham and Wimbledon who contested the prestigious two-legged event. The Dons, for whom former teamster Wal Phillips was non-riding captain, played host for the

Wembley 1938. Back row, left to right: Alec Jackson (Manager), Tommy Price, Eric Gregory, Cliff Parkinson, Malcolm Craven. Front row, on bikes: Wally Kilmister, Lionel Van Praag, George Wilks, Frank Charles.

first leg on 5 September, but they were unable to prevent West Ham from taking the initiative courtesy of a 58-50 win. The Hammers duly pressed home their advantage in the second leg one night later, racking up a 64-43 victory to achieve an overall 122-93 success.

In the National Trophy, Wimbledon reached their second final of the year, having firstly disposed of New Cross and then turning West Ham over in the semi-final. Their opponents for the showpiece event were Wembley, who narrowly squeezed past Belle Vue, prior to comfortably defeating Second Division Norwich in the semi-final. Any disappointment the Dons might have felt over their ACU Cup final defeat was soon forgotten when they amazingly came away from Wembley with a 65-43 win under their belts from the first leg on 15 September. Completing a job well done, Wimbledon eased their way to a 58-49 victory in the return match four days later, giving them an aggregate success by 123 points to 92.

The London Cup culminated in October, with Wimbledon making it a hat-trick of final appearances for the year after nullifying Wembley's semi-final challenge. Having beaten West Ham in the other last-four tie, New Cross provided the opposition for the Dons, hosting the initial leg on 5 October, when they got the

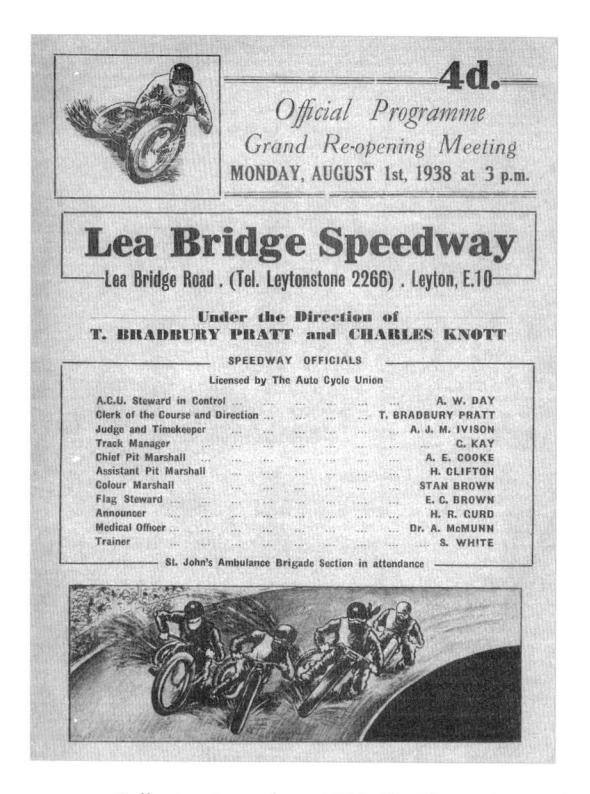

Collectors items from 1938. The illustration on the left shows the programme used at Lea Bridge's re-opening meeting on 1 August. To the right is the Norwich versus Lea Bridge programme from 27 August.

better of a closely-fought encounter by 55 points to 52. That left things finely balanced for the second leg on 10 October, but it was the Dons who eventually claimed their second trophy of the season by virtue of a 57-49 win, which left an aggregate score-line of 109-104.

The new Second Division comprised nine teams, of which just three had competed in the previous year's Provincial League, namely Birmingham (Hall Green), Norwich and Southampton. One of the other competing sides was Hackney Wick, who, as mentioned before, decided to drop down a rung. Added to these were three tracks which re-opened to the sport, these being Lea Bridge, Newcastle (Brough Park) and Sheffield, while as they had done in 1936, West Ham again operated a second side with a 'Hawks' nickname. Finally, Nottingham, who had run in the Provincial League of 1937, were named as one of the starters in the Second Division, however, after competing in the English Speedway Trophy, they closed down before racing a single league match. Their demise was offset by Leeds, who had initially re-opened at Fullerton Park on an open licence, but were happy to take over the fixtures of the defunct club.

The race for the Championship developed into a scrap between Hackney Wick and Norwich, with neither side giving an inch in a neck-and-neck battle. Both sides tasted victory in 12 of their 16 matches to finish level on 24 points; however, it was the East London outfit who took the title thanks to a superior race points difference. The move down a division had certainly proved beneficial for the Wolves, with the men who played an active part along the way being Charlie Appleby, Tommy Bateman, Jim Baylais, Ken Brett, Stan Dell, Frank Hodgson, Charlie Page, George Saunders, Nobby Stock, Jack Tidbury, Doug Wells and Archie Windmill.

With a place at stake amongst the elite in the First Division version of the National Trophy, the Division Two sides began their quest early, and Norwich clearly looked like they meant business, scorching to a big win over Newcastle in the first round. However, the Stars were then held to a thrilling draw by Southampton in the semi-final, with the replay also proving to be a tight affair, before the Norfolk outfit just squeezed through by a 3-point aggregate margin. Hackney Wick provided the opposition in final, having comfortably disposed of Leeds, prior to easing past Birmingham in the semi-final. The Firs Stadium subsequently hosted the first leg on 2 July, and Norwich made full use of their sweeping home circuit to rack up a 72-36 victory. Following that, it was always going to be an uphill struggle in the second leg for Hackney Wick, and so it proved exactly a week later, when they could only secure a 58-49 win, with the Stars taking all the plaudits by 121 points to 94 on aggregate. Having claimed their place alongside the Division One teams, Norwich continued their merry march when they grabbed a 58-50 home win over Harringay. The Stars duly progressed onto the semi-final stage, after the London side failed to stage the return leg and withdrew from the competition. Thus Norwich had created their own little piece of speedway history, by becoming the first side from a lower division to knock out a top-flight team in the National Trophy. Their fairytale run understandably came to an end in the semi-final, however, when Wembley registered a comfortable aggregate victory as previously mentioned.

The programme from the Yorkshire versus Dominions match at Leeds on 11 June 1938.

The English Speedway Trophy had actually kicked off the season, although the final didn't take place until August. The participating teams were split into two groups, with the northern section comprising a second Belle Vue side, along with Newcastle, Nottingham, Sheffield and, rather strangely, West Ham Hawks! Meanwhile, in the south, the six competing teams were Birmingham, Hackney Wick, Norwich, Southampton and the reserve sides of New Cross and Wembley. The two group winners subsequently met over a two-legged final, with Belle Vue II finishing on top in the north, whilst Southampton were the clear victors in the south. Throughout the competition, Belle Vue II had staged their 'home' matches on opponents' tracks (as indeed had West Ham II, New Cross Reserves and Wembley Reserves), and they duly held the first leg of the final at Sheffield on 25 August, running out victors by 47 points to 36. The Saints managed to gain revenge in the second leg six days later, winning 46-38, but it wasn't sufficient to prevent the Manchester outfit from collecting an aggregate 85-82 success.

As the season progressed, eight of the nine Second Division sides also partook in the Provincial Trophy, the exception being Lea Bridge. The competition had previously been run on a league basis in both 1936 and 1937, but with so many other trophies up for grabs, it was staged in a knock-out style, with each tie taking place over two legs. National Trophy giant-killers Norwich again fared well, progressing past the challenges of Hackney Wick and Birmingham to face Sheffield in the final – the South Yorkshire outfit having got there via victories over Newcastle and Southampton. On 20 October, the setting for the first leg was Sheffield's Owlerton Sports Stadium, and in a gripping encounter it was the home side who shaded the narrowest of wins by 54 points to 53. There was little doubt that Norwich were in the driving seat after that, and so it proved two days later, when they raced to a 74-32 success for an overall 127-86 triumph.

Finally, to complete what had been a jam-packed fixture schedule, an end-of-season mini-tournament saw Birmingham, Leeds, Newcastle and Sheffield face each other on a home and away basis for the Northern Cup. Despite the match between Birmingham and Newcastle not being run, the Brough Park based-Diamonds were decisive winners of this competition, having tasted victory in all five matches they raced.

The High Beech programme from 4 September 1938.

Marine Gardens Speedway programme, 1938.

Speedway could also be seen at a number of other arenas in 1938, with open licence racing again held at California (Longmoor Speedway), Crystal Palace, Dagenham, Eastbourne, High Beech, Holbeach, Middlesbrough, Ringwood, Rye House, Smallford, Staines and Workington (Lonsdale Park).

Aside from the usual open style meetings, Dagenham, Eastbourne, Rye House, Smallford and Romford also competed in the Sunday Dirt-track League, with the latter side riding their 'home' matches at Dagenham's Ripple Road circuit. Although full results and details of this league remain sketchy, it is known that the Championship was won by Eastbourne.

One addition to the list of operating tracks was Edinburgh's Marine Gardens, which re-opened on 14 May, when Belle Vue's Ernie Price was victorious in both the Edinburgh Scratch Race and the Scottish Silver Torch. It was the first time speedway had been seen at the venue since 1931, and a further 13 meetings (including a midget car event) were to prove successful enough to warrant continued racing at the circuit in 1939.

THE LEAGUE YEARS

1938 NATIONAL LEAGUE DIVISION ONE RESULTS

	Belle Vue	Bristol	Harringay	New Cross	Wembley	West Ham	Wimbledon
Belle Vue	XX	49-35	53-31	41-40	48-36	43-41	50-34
	XX	54-30	45-39	40-44	43-41	36-47	50-34
Bristol	40-41	XX	47-36	38-46	37-47	44-39	41-41
	45-38	XX	42-41	52-31	32-50	39½-44½	40-44
Harringay	51-30	41-42	XX	59-24	38-45	43-39	54-30
	52-32	45-39	XX	52-32	47-37	42-40	46-38
New Cross	55-28	51-33	56-28	XX	45-39	53-30	51-33
	55-29	48-34	54-29	XX	45-39	50-34	39-45
Wembley	54-30	57-27	50-34	37-46	XX	44-40	43-41
	47-36	54-28	49-35	35-48	XX	48-35	45-39
West Ham	46-38	55-29	55-28	41-39	40-34	XX	57-27
	56-28	54-30	50-33	42-42	50-34	XX	42-41
Wimbledon	48-36	53-31	41-41	44-39	42-42	49-34	XX
	51-31	47-35	48-35	43-39	47-36	45-39	XX

1938 NATIONAL LEAGUE DIVISION ONE TABLE

Team	Matches	Won	Drawn	Lost	For	Against	Points
New Cross	24	15	1	8	1072	925	31
West Ham	24	13	1	10	1050½	939½	27
Wembley	24	13	1	10	1043	953	27
Wimbledon	24	12	3	9	1005	996	27
Belle Vue	24	11	0	13	949	1052	22
Harringay	24	10	1	13	980	1018	21
Bristol	24	6	1	17	890½	1106½	13

Note: Matches were run over 14 heats, with a 3-2-1 scoring system.

1938 NATIONAL TROPHY

DIVISION TWO ROUND 1	Agg	DIVISION TWO SEMI-FINAL	Agg	DIVISION TWO FINAL	Agg
Norwich (75-33)	130				
Newcastle (53-55)	86				
		Norwich (77-31)	107		
		Southampton (76-30)	107		
Southampton	Bye				
		REPLAY			
		Norwich (37-17)	55	Norwich (72-36)	121
		Southampton (35-18)	52	Hackney Wick (58-49)	94
Hackney Wick (72-36)	122				
Leeds (56-50)	92				
		Hackney Wick (66-42)	115½		
		Birmingham (57½-49½)	99½		
Birmingham (77-26)	133				
Sheffield (51-56)	77				

DIVISION ONE QUARTER-FINAL	Agg	DIVISION ONE SEMI-FINAL	Agg	DIVISION ONE FINAL	Agg
Wimbledon (62-46)	119				
New Cross (50-57)	96				
		Wimbledon (78-29)	133		
		West Ham (53-55)	82		
West Ham (72-35)	128				
Bristol (50-56)	85				
				Wimbledon (58-49)	123
				Wembley (43-65)	92
Wembley (61-47)	109				
Belle Vue (60-48)	107				
		Wembley (38-15)	93		
		Norwich (53-55)	68		
Norwich (58-50)	58				
Harringay (Withdrew)	50				

Notes: (1) Most matches were run over 18 heats, with a 3-2-1 scoring system, the exceptions being both legs of the Norwich v Southampton replay, plus the meeting between Wembley and Norwich, which were staged over 9 heats; (2) Nottingham originally beat Hackney Wick by an aggregate score of 109-107 in the first round, but upon the track's premature closure, the result was cancelled by the ACU. Hackney Wick were subsequently reinstated in the competition to face Leeds, who had taken over the fixtures of Nottingham.

1938 ACU CUP

POOL ONE	Harringay	New Cross	West Ham		RACE POINTS		FINAL	Agg
Harringay	XX	57-51	42-64		166			
New Cross	75-32	XX	54-54		227			
West Ham	73-35	61-47	XX		252			
							West Ham (64-43)	122
POOL TWO	Belle Vue	Bristol	Wembley	Wimbledon			Wimbledon (50-58)	93
Belle Vue	XX	78-30	71-36	56-52	320			
Bristol	74-34	XX	44-64	53-55	283			
Wembley	67-40	61-47	XX	54-54	335			
Wimbledon	67-41	73-35	54-53	XX	355			

Notes: (1) Matches were run over 18 heats, with a 3-2-1 scoring system; (2) The finalists were determined purely on the basis of the highest aggregate race points scored in each group.

1938 LONDON CUP

ROUND ONE	Agg	SEMI-FINAL	Agg	FINAL	Agg
Wimbledon	Bye				
		Wimbledon (66-42)	127		
		Wembley (47-61)	89		
Wembley (60-44)	109				
Harringay (59-49)	103				
				Wimbledon (57-49)	109
				New Cross (55-52)	104
New Cross	Bye				
		New Cross (62-46)	114		
		West Ham (56-52)	102		
West Ham	Bye				

Note: Matches were raced over 18 heats, with a 3-2-1 scoring system in operation.

1938 NATIONAL LEAGUE DIVISION TWO RESULTS

	Birmingham	Hackney	Lea Bridge	Leeds	Newcastle	Norwich	Sheffield	South'pton	West Ham II
Birmingham (Hall Green)	XX	37-46	32-52	49-33	60-24	34-47	54-30	50-34	52-30
Hackney Wick	57-27	XX	51-33	59-24	58-26	48-35	59-25	47-37	54-29
Lea Bridge	59-24	37-46	XX	50-33	45-39	50-30	59-25	51-31	55-29
Leeds	0-70	27-54	46-36	XX	39-44	29-52	40-44	47-36	38-46
Newcastle	57-27	27-57	51-32	50-34	XX	41-43	52-29	45-39	42-40
Norwich	63-21	55-26	54-30	49-34	54-30	XX	63-21	56-26	41-36
Sheffield	47-35	44-40	49-34	48-35	52-31	32-50	XX	38-44	42-42
Southampton	52-29	58-26	51-33	54-29	63-21	58-24	58-26	XX	55-26
West Ham II	48-32	53-31	55-29	60-23	41-41	44-33	70-0	42-40	XX

1938 NATIONAL LEAGUE DIVISION TWO TABLE

Team	Matches	Won	Drawn	Lost	For	Against	Points
Hackney Wick	16	12	0	4	759	574	24
Norwich	16	12	0	4	749	560	24
Southampton	16	9	0	7	736	590	18
West Ham II	16	8	2	6	691	608	18
Lea Bridge	16	8	0	8	685	646	16
Newcastle	16	7	1	8	621	713	15
Sheffield	16	6	1	9	552	766	13
Birmingham	16	6	0	10	633	679	12
Leeds	16	2	0	14	511	801	4

Notes: (1) Matches were run over 14 heats, with a 3-2-1 scoring system; (2) Nottingham originally entered the Second Division, but closed before racing a single league match. Leeds subsequently stepped in to take over the defunct club's fixtures; (3) Aside from the main West Ham side, which operated in the First Division, a second team (known as West Ham Hawks) competed in Division Two; (4) The Leeds v Birmingham result was awarded after the original fixture had been rained off and not restaged; (5) The West Ham II v Sheffield result was awarded by the ACU, having originally ended in a 39-41 scoreline on track.

1938 PROVINCIAL TROPHY

ROUND ONE	Agg	SEMI-FINAL	Agg	FINAL	Agg
Norwich (75-33)	119				
Hackney Wick (62-44)	95				
		Norwich (72-34)	131		
		Birmingham (47-59)	81		
Birmingham (61-46)	119				
Leeds (48-58)	94				
				Norwich (74-32)	127
				Sheffield (54-53)	86
Sheffield (68-38)	115				
Newcastle (60-47)	98				
		Sheffield (58-49)	111		
		Southampton (53-53)	102		
Southampton (82-26)	125				
West Ham II (63-43)	89				

Note: Matches were raced over 18 heats, with a 3-2-1 scoring system in operation.

THE LEAGUE YEARS

1938 ENGLISH SPEEDWAY TROPHY (NORTH SECTION) RESULTS

	Belle Vue II	Newcastle	Nottingham	Sheffield	West Ham II
Belle Vue II	XX	59-24	48-34	41-35	30-54
Newcastle	36-45	XX	41-43	49-30	57-26
Nottingham	32-47	55-27	XX	35-47	50-34
Sheffield	41-42	55-29	46-35	XX	55-27
West Ham II	30-54	35-47	Not Run	39-44	XX

1938 ENGLISH SPEEDWAY TROPHY (NORTH SECTION) TABLE

Team	Matches	Won	Drawn	Lost	For	Against	Points
Belle Vue II	8	7	0	1	366	286	14
Sheffield	8	5	0	3	353	297	10
Nottingham	8	4	0	4	284	290	8
Newcastle	8	3	0	5	310	348	6
West Ham II	8	1	0	7	245	337	2

Notes: (1) Matches were run over 14 heats, with a 3-2-1 scoring system; (2) Both Belle Vue II and West Ham II staged their 'home' matches on their opponents tracks. There were two exceptions, however, with Belle Vue II v West Ham II raced at Sheffield, while West Ham II v Belle Vue II was run at Newcastle; (3) The match between West Ham II and Nottingham was not run; the return match was therefore raced for double league points.

1938 ENGLISH SPEEDWAY TROPHY (SOUTH SECTION) RESULTS

	Birmingham	Hackney Wick	New Cross Res	Norwich	Southampton	Wembley Res
Birmingham (H/Green)	XX	48-35	52-29	57-25	39-45	46-36
Hackney Wick	55-29	XX	45-36	60-22	38-43	54-30
New Cross Reserves	22-61	35-49	XX	38-46	33-47	52-30
Norwich	45-39	55-28	47-36	XX	46-36	40-44
Southampton	57-27	64-20	58-23	61-23	XX	53-29
Wembley Reserves	52-32	24-58	49-34	36-48	33-48	XX

1938 ENGLISH SPEEDWAY TROPHY (SOUTH SECTION) TABLE

Team	Matches	Won	Drawn	Lost	For	Against	Points
Southampton	10	9	0	1	512	311	18
Hackney Wick	10	6	0	4	442	386	12
Norwich	10	6	0	4	397	435	12
Birmingham	10	5	0	5	430	401	10
Wembley Reserves	10	3	0	7	363	465	6
New Cross Reserves	10	1	0	9	338	484	2

Notes: Matches were run over 14 heats, with a 3-2-1 scoring system; (2) Both New Cross Reserves and Wembley Reserves staged their 'home' matches on their opponents' tracks. There were two exceptions, however, with New Cross Res v Wembley Res raced at Hackney Wick, while Wembley Res v New Cross Res was run at Norwich; (3) The two group winners met in the final, with Belle Vue II winning the first leg (staged at Sheffield) 47-36. Southampton gained revenge in the second leg, winning 46-38, but it wasn't sufficient to stop Belle Vue II gaining an aggregate 85-82 success.

1938 NORTHERN CUP RESULTS

	Birmingham	Leeds	Newcastle	Sheffield
Birmingham (H/Green)	XX	60-24	Not Run	61-17
Leeds	44-39	XX	40-44	38-46
Newcastle	51-33	59-25	XX	47-34
Sheffield	53-31	44-40	35-44	XX

1938 NORTHERN CUP TABLE

Team	Matches	Won	Drawn	Lost	For	Against	Points
Newcastle	5	5	0	0	245	167	10
Sheffield	6	3	0	3	229	261	6
Birmingham	5	2	0	3	224	189	4
Leeds	6	1	0	5	211	292	2

Notes: (1) Matches were run over 14 heats, with a 3-2-1 scoring system; (2) The match between Leeds and Newcastle was staged at Sheffield.

1939

The First Division again ran with just seven teams, the only change from the previous year being Southampton exchanging licences with Bristol, who were happy to return to the lower sphere after a disastrous season in the top-flight. With an increased number of competitions to race for, there was a feeling of optimism as the tapes went up on the season, but that was to be shattered by the outbreak of the Second World War in September. The race for the Championship had reached a crucial stage by then, with Belle Vue holding a single point lead from Wimbledon at the head of the table, while third-placed Wembley were but a further point behind the Dons. Sadly, there was to be no conclusion as that was how things remained when racing was suspended at the end of August.

With the exception of Wembley, the Division One sides had earlier raced each other on a league basis for the British Speedway Cup. Thankfully, the fixtures were

The Belle Vue Reserves programme from their Union Cup encounter with Edinburgh on 9 August 1939.

THE LEAGUE YEARS

Harringay 1939. Back row, left to right: Alec Statham, Frank Dolan, Norman Parker, Dick Harris, Les Wotton, Lloyd Goffe. Front row, left to right: Charles Knott (Promoter), Jack Parker, Bill Pitcher, George Kay (Manager).

fully completed in this competition, which had an interesting way of awarding points. Teams who won their home matches still gained 2 league points, or 1 for a draw, however, in a change to normal, sides that won away from home gained 3 league points, or 2 for a draw. Belle Vue and West Ham set a really hot pace, both winning seven of their ten matches (five at home, and two away) to finish on 16 points, but it was the Aces who collected the trophy by virtue of a slightly better race points difference.

Due to Hackney Wick being a Second Division side, only five teams contested the London Cup, but the competition at least reached a conclusion. Just one first round tie saw Wimbledon bring Harringay's participation to a quick end, with the Dons subsequently booking a place in the final after a last-four win over Wembley. The other semi-final brought together New Cross and West Ham in a pulsating tie that went right down to the wire, before the Rangers grabbed aggregate victory by a single point. New Cross might have been buoyed by that success, but their smiles didn't linger when they hosted the first leg of the final on 5 July, suffering a 46-62 reverse. That Wimbledon would retain the cup they had won the previous season was never in doubt following that, and so it proved five days later as they stormed home by 72 points to 36 in the second leg, for an aggregate 134-82 success.

The National Trophy saw Belle Vue oust Wimbledon and New Cross to book their place in the final. There, the Aces would have met Wembley, who had knocked

A superb Wembley souvenir from 1939, featuring head-shots of the riders, together with their autographs.

out West Ham and Southampton, but unfortunately the mouthwatering showdown was never run because of the war.

Eight teams lined up in the Second Division, although only four survived from 1938, namely Champions Hackney Wick, plus Newcastle, Norwich and Sheffield. As mentioned earlier, these four sides were augmented by the inclusion of Bristol, with the other contestants being Crystal Palace, Middlesbrough and Stoke. It was a welcome return to league action for Crystal Palace and Middlesbrough, both of whom had been running open licence events since 1936. Meanwhile, Stoke (then known as Hanley) had only previously operated in the English Dirt-track League of 1929, when they withdrew after just five matches, prior to continuing with a series of open licence meetings.

This league was plagued by problems, however, with Middlesbrough resigning in June, having completed eight of their scheduled fixtures. Due to falling attendances, and with only ten matches under their belts, Crystal Palace then withdrew in July, leaving just six tracks remaining. The same month also saw the demise of Stoke, with a lack of support cited as the reason for the premature closure, although thankfully, Belle Vue Reserves were on hand to take over the Staffordshire outfit's remaining

The programme from Southampton's British Speedway Cup clash with Belle Vue on 17 May 1939.

The programme used at Sheffield for their Union Cup match against Edinburgh on 17 August 1939.

fixtures. The outbreak of war was to bring the Division Two programme to a halt, leaving the league table in a somewhat sorry state. With the results of Middlesbrough and Crystal Palace expunged, this was fully emphasized by the fact that leaders Newcastle had ridden fifteen matches, whilst third placed Sheffield had only completed eight of their fixtures!

The original eight starters in the Second Division had kicked off the campaign with the English Speedway Trophy, with the sides split into two groups of four. Separated only by race points, Newcastle pipped Middlesbrough at the head of the northern section, while Norwich came out on top in the south. The two regional winners subsequently met in the final, with the first leg held in Norfolk on 15 July, when the homesters were unable to shake off a dogged Newcastle team, mustering only a 42-40 win. The return match was equally tight, however, but the Diamonds did just enough to gain a 44-40 success, claiming overall glory by 84 points to 82.

Unlike the top-flight teams, the Division Two stage of the National Trophy was happily concluded, with Sheffield and Hackney Wick battling their way through for the right to meet in the final. On 8 July, the Londoners duly won the initial leg 67-39, and looked to have built up a substantial advantage to take up to South Yorkshire. It was to prove insufficient though, as the Tigers roared to a 75-33 success around their pacy Owlerton circuit five days later, giving them an aggregate 114-100 victory. This gave them a place in the First Division competition, but unlike Norwich the year before, Sheffield were unable to perform a giant-killing act, gallantly losing 114-97 on aggregate to Southampton.

A new competition saw the Second Division teams race for the Union Cup, with just Bristol, Hackney Wick and Norwich comprising the southern section. Meanwhile, in the north, Belle Vue Reserves, Newcastle and Sheffield were bolstered by the inclusion of Edinburgh (Marine Gardens) and Glasgow (White City), both of whom had been running open licence meetings. The Glasgow venue had actually re-opened in May, having not seen any speedway action since July 1931, when the side had pulled out of the Northern League after a couple of rained-off meetings had led to financial difficulties. Run in the same fashion as the English Speedway Trophy, with home and away matches against each of the other teams, the eventual group winners were due to contest a two-legged final, but the war sadly intervened to leave the competition unfinished. At the time, Newcastle headed Sheffield on race points difference in the northern section, but the South Yorkshire club did have a match in hand. The picture was also unclear in the smaller southern group, for although it threw up considerably fewer fixtures, the match between Bristol and Hackney Wick remained outstanding. That obviously would have had a bearing on the final table, as the London side was sitting in pole position, with the West Country boys two points behind.

The Provincial Trophy was again raced for in 1939, but with the fixtures not beginning until July, only the first-round matches were completed fully. Belle Vue Reserves then gained a first leg victory over Bristol in the semi-final, but the hostilities then saw to it that the competition was abandoned, with Sheffield and Newcastle not so much as turning a wheel in the other semi-final.

A Marine Gardens programme from 1939.

Glasgow's programme from their challenge match versus Middlesbrough on 13 May 1939.

On top of the venues already mentioned, other circuits running open licence meetings during the year were California (Longmoor Speedway), Dagenham, Eastbourne, High Beech, Holbeach, Ringwood, Rye House (Hoddesdon Stadium) and Smallford. Meanwhile, just one new track opened at Oxford on 8 April, when Roy Duke was triumphant in the Oxford Motorcycle Speedway Club Championship, with a number of other successful meetings following thereafter.

1939 NATIONAL LEAGUE DIVISION ONE RESULTS

	Belle Vue	Harringay	New Cross	Southampton	Wembley	West Ham	Wimbledon
Belle Vue	XX	46-35	54-30	61-23	57-27	45-39	44-40
	XX	54-30	56-27	Not Run	Not Run	63-21	Not Run
Harringay	Not Run	XX	43-40	53-31	36-48	44-40	48-36
	Not Run	XX	Not Run	55-29	Not Run	37-46	39-44
New Cross	42-42	34-50	XX	56-28	42-40	41-42	38-45
	Not Run	Not Run	XX	Not Run	Not Run	43-40	35-49
Southampton	38-45	39-45	48-35	XX	46-38	47-37	Not Run
	40-44	55-29	51½-32½	XX	Not Run	Not Run	Not Run
Wembley	50-34	42-42	52-31	57-27	XX	55-29	53-30
	43-41	Not Run	59-24	61-22	XX	58-26	39-45
West Ham	40-42	44-39	50-33	54-30	36-48	XX	44-39
	Not Run	Not Run	45-38	Not Run	53-31	XX	44-38
Wimbledon	50-34	46-37	52-32	53-31	51-33	48-36	XX
	Not Run	Not Run	41-42	56-26	44-40	Not Run	XX

1939 NATIONAL LEAGUE DIVISION ONE TABLE

Team	Matches	Won	Drawn	Lost	For	Against	Points
Belle Vue	16	12	1	3	762	575	25
Wimbledon	18	12	0	6	807	695	24
Wembley	19	11	1	7	874	716	23
West Ham	19	9	0	10	766	819	18
Harringay	16	7	1	8	662	674	15
Southampton	17	5	0	12	611½	811½	10
New Cross	19	4	1	14	695½	887½	9

Notes: (1) Matches were run over 14 heats, with a 3-2-1 scoring system; (2) Table as at 31 August, prior to the outbreak of war.

1939 NATIONAL TROPHY

DIVISION TWO ROUND 1	Agg	DIVISION TWO SEMI-FINAL	Agg	DIVISION TWO FINAL	Agg
Sheffield (69-38)	115				
Norwich (60-46)	98				
		Sheffield (75-32)	134		
		Bristol (46-59)	78		
Bristol (83-22)	148				
Crystal Palace (35-65)	57				
				Sheffield (75-33)	114
				Hackney Wick (67-39)	100
Hackney Wick (80-28)	119				
Stoke (68-39)	96				
		Hackney Wick			
		Middlesbrough (Withdrew)	W/O		
Middlesbrough (61-46)	109				
Newcastle (60-48)	106				

DIVISION ONE FIRST ROUND	Agg	DIVISION ONE SEMI-FINAL	Agg	DIVISION ONE FINAL	Agg
Belle Vue (67-40)	123				
Wimbledon (51-56)	91				
		Belle Vue (80-28)	144		
		New Cross (44-64)	72		
New Cross (57-51)	111				
Harringay (52-54)	103				
				Belle Vue	
				Wembley	
Wembley (63-45)	109				
West Ham (62-46)	107				
		Wembley (74-33)	120		
		Southampton (62-46)	95		
Southampton (68-36)	114				
Sheffield (61-46)	97				

Notes: (1) Matches were run over 18 heats, with a 3-2-1 scoring system; (2) The final was not staged due to the outbreak of war.

THE LEAGUE YEARS

1939 BRITISH SPEEDWAY CUP RESULTS

	Belle Vue	Harringay	New Cross	Southampton	West Ham	Wimbledon
Belle Vue	XX	65-31	58-38	63-33	59-36	53-43
Harringay	45-51	XX	58-37	72-24	54-42	56-39
New Cross	51-43	47-47	XX	68-28	60-36	59-37
Southampton	43-53	38-58	38-58	XX	42-53	45-50
West Ham	53-41	57-39	60-36	69-26	XX	66-30
Wimbledon	57-39	65-30	58-37	65-31	46-48	XX

1939 BRITISH SPEEDWAY CUP TABLE

Team	Matches	Won	Drawn	Lost	For	Against	Points
Belle Vue	10	7	0	3	525	430	16
West Ham	10	7	0	3	520	433	16
Harringay	10	5	1	4	490	465	13
New Cross	10	5	1	4	491	463	12
Wimbledon	10	5	0	5	490	464	11
Southampton	10	0	0	10	348	609	0

Notes: (1) Matches were run over 16 heats, with a 3-2-1 scoring system; (2) Teams who won their home matches still gained 2 league points, or 1 for a draw; however, in a change to normal, sides that won away from home gained 3 league points, or 2 for a draw.

1939 LONDON CUP

ROUND ONE	Agg	SEMI-FINAL	Agg	FINAL	Agg
Wimbledon (71-37)	113				
Harringay (64-42)	101				
		Wimbledon (59-49)	111		
		Wembley (55-52)	104		
Wembley	Bye				
				Wimbledon (72-36)	134
				New Cross (46-62)	82
New Cross	Bye				
		New Cross (57-50)	107		
		West Ham (56-50)	106		
West Ham	Bye				

Note: Matches were raced over 18 heats, with a 3-2-1 scoring system in operation.

1939 NATIONAL LEAGUE DIVISION TWO RESULTS

	Bristol	C.Palace	Hackney	Middlesbro'	Newcastle	Norwich	Sheffield	Stoke/BV II
Bristol	XX	Not Run	48-35	43-41	39-44	63-18	47-37	43-40 B
	XX	Not Run	42-39	Not Run	40-43	41-42	Not Run	Not Run
Crystal Palace	37-46	XX	Not Run	39-43	Not Run	Not Run	39-43	56-28
	Not Run	XX	Not Run	Not Run	Not Run	Not Run	Not Run	Not Run
Hackney Wick	53-29	Not Run	XX	44-40	46-38	Not Run	45-38	60-24
	45-39	Not Run	XX	Not Run	51-33	Not Run	Not Run	52-31
Middlesbrough	64-20	61-23	Not Run	XX	Not Run	47-37	Not Run	Not Run
	Not Run	Not Run	Not Run	XX	Not Run	Not Run	Not Run	Not Run
Newcastle	46-36	58-25	54-29	Not Run	XX	50-34	Not Run	59-25
	52-29	Not Run	Not Run	Not Run	XX	Not Run	Not Run	44-40 B
Norwich	47-37	50-34	46-35	44-40	33-51	XX	40-43	56-27
	Not Run	Not Run	Not Run	Not Run	Not Run	XX	Not Run	56-27 B
Sheffield	Not Run	41-40	Not Run	53-30	48-34	42-38	XX	54-29
	Not Run	63-21	Not Run	Not Run	Not Run	43-41	XX	Not Run
Stoke / Belle Vue Reserves	55-28	62-20	45-38	Not Run	32-52	45-38	28-56 B	Not Run
	Not Run	Not Run	45-39 B	Not Run	42-41 B	Not Run	Not Run	Not Run

1939 NATIONAL LEAGUE DIVISION TWO TABLE

Team	Matches	Won	Drawn	Lost	For	Against	Points
Newcastle	15	10	0	5	675	574	20
Hackney Wick	13	7	0	6	567	512	14
Sheffield	8	6	0	2	361	302	12
Norwich	12	6	0	6	501	493	12
Bristol	14	5	0	9	561	596	10
Belle Vue Res/Stoke	14	4	0	10	490	678	8
Middlesbro' (Expunged)	8	4	0	4	366	303	8
C. Palace (Expunged)	10	1	0	9	334	495	2
Stoke (Withdrew)	8	2	0	6	268	399	4

Notes: (1) Matches were run over 14 heats, with a 3-2-1 scoring system; (2) Table as at 31 August, prior to the outbreak of war; (3) The first Sheffield v Crystal Palace match was actually raced at Crystal Palace; (4) Middlesbrough resigned in June, having completed 8 matches, with their record expunged from the table; (5) Due to falling attendances, Crystal Palace withdrew in July after completing 10 meetings, with their record expunged from the table; (6) A lack of support also led to the closure of Stoke after 8 matches, with Belle Vue Reserves taking over their remaining fixtures. Results of meetings involving Belle Vue are indicated with a 'B'.

1939 PROVINCIAL TROPHY

ROUND ONE	Agg	SEMI-FINAL	Agg	FINAL	Agg
Sheffield (61½-32½)	115½				
Hackney Wick (41-54)	73½				
		Sheffield			
		Newcastle			
Newcastle	Bye				
Belle Vue Res (51-44)	99				
Norwich (48-48)	92				
		Belle Vue Res (66-29)			
		Bristol			
Bristol	Bye				

Notes: (1) Matches were raced over 16 heats, with a 3-2-1 scoring system in operation; (2) Due to the outbreak of war, the competition was not completed.

113

1939 ENGLISH SPEEDWAY TROPHY (NORTH SECTION) RESULTS

	Middlesbrough	Newcastle	Sheffield	Stoke
Middlesbrough	XX	42-41	57-26	49-34
Newcastle	41-42	XX	47-37	63-21
Sheffield	46-37	40-44	XX	46-35
Stoke	44-39	40-44	45-36	XX

1939 ENGLISH SPEEDWAY TROPHY (NORTH SECTION) TABLE

Team	Matches	Won	Drawn	Lost	For	Against	Points
Newcastle	6	4	0	2	280	222	8
Middlesbrough	6	4	0	2	266	232	8
Sheffield	6	2	0	4	231	265	4
Stoke	6	2	0	4	219	277	4

Notes: (1) Matches were run over 14 heats, with a 3-2-1 scoring system; (2) Newcastle v Middlesbrough originally ended 50-34, but the result was subsequently declared void and the match re-run.

1939 ENGLISH SPEEDWAY TROPHY (SOUTH SECTION) RESULTS

	Bristol	Crystal Palace	Hackney Wick	Norwich
Bristol	XX	51-32	22-59	40½-43½
Crystal Palace	33-46	XX	43-40	35-46
Hackney Wick	56-25	57-27	XX	65-19
Norwich	60-24	64-20	46-38	XX

1939 ENGLISH SPEEDWAY TROPHY (SOUTH SECTION) TABLE

Team	Matches	Won	Drawn	Lost	For	Against	Points
Norwich	6	5	0	1	278½	222½	10
Hackney Wick	6	4	0	2	315	182	8
Bristol	6	2	0	4	208½	283½	4
Crystal Palace	6	1	0	5	190	304	2

Notes: Matches were run over 14 heats, with a 3-2-1 scoring system; (2) The two group winners met in the final, with Norwich winning their home leg 42-40, prior to Newcastle gaining a 44-40 success in the return match to claim an 84-82 aggregate victory.

1939 UNION CUP (NORTH SECTION) RESULTS

	Belle Vue Reserves	Edinburgh	Glasgow	Newcastle	Sheffield
Belle Vue Reserves	XX	39-39	Not Run	52-32	39-45
Edinburgh	56-28	XX	56-27	39-44	46-37
Glasgow	Not Run	45-36	XX	29-53	41-43
Newcastle	40-43	42-37	58-22	XX	48-35
Sheffield	42½-40½	46-38	Not Run	46-38	XX

1939 UNION CUP (NORTH SECTION) TABLE

Team	Matches	Won	Drawn	Lost	For	Against	Points
Newcastle	8	5	0	3	355	303	10
Sheffield	7	5	0	2	294½	290½	10
Edinburgh	8	3	1	4	347	308	7
Belle Vue Reserves	6	2	1	3	241½	254½	5
Glasgow	5	1	0	4	164	246	2

Notes: (1) Matches were run over 14 heats, with a 3-2-1 scoring system; (2) With the eventual group winners due meet their southern counterparts in the final, several fixtures remained outstanding and the competition was not completed due to the outbreak of war.

1939 UNION CUP (SOUTH SECTION) RESULTS

	Bristol	Hackney Wick	Norwich
Bristol	XX	Not Run	44-39
Hackney Wick	51-33	XX	44-39
Norwich	Not Run	62-22	XX

1939 UNION CUP (SOUTH SECTION) TABLE

Team	Matches	Won	Drawn	Lost	For	Against	Points
Hackney Wick	3	2	0	1	117	134	4
Bristol	2	1	0	1	77	90	2
Norwich	3	1	0	2	140	110	2

Notes: (1) Matches were run over 14 heats, with a 3-2-1 scoring system; (2) The Hackney Wick v Norwich match originally ended 43½-39½, but was later amended by the ACU; (3) With the eventual group winners due to meet their northern counterparts in the final, several fixtures remained outstanding and the competition was not completed due to the outbreak of war.

THE LEAGUE YEARS

INDIVIDUAL CHAMPIONSHIPS

The London Riders' Championship was started at Crystal Palace, the competitors being drawn from the existing tracks in the capital. The inaugural 1930 title was taken by Wembley rider Jack Ormston, who later went on to become a racehorse trainer of some repute. In 1931, Crystal Palace teamster Joe Francis produced an exhilarating display to win the event on his home circuit, and as a result, the ever-smiling Joe was capped in several Test matches.

The competition wasn't staged in 1932/33, but was resurrected in 1934, when Tom Farndon produced a scintillating display to take the trophy. The brilliant New Cross racer repeated his success in 1935, but later that year, he tragically lost his life following a track crash at the compact 262-yard Old Kent Road venue. Wimbledon's Vic Huxley emerged as the victor in 1936, with the great American Jack Milne subsequently becoming a double Champion (1937 and 1939) prior to the outbreak

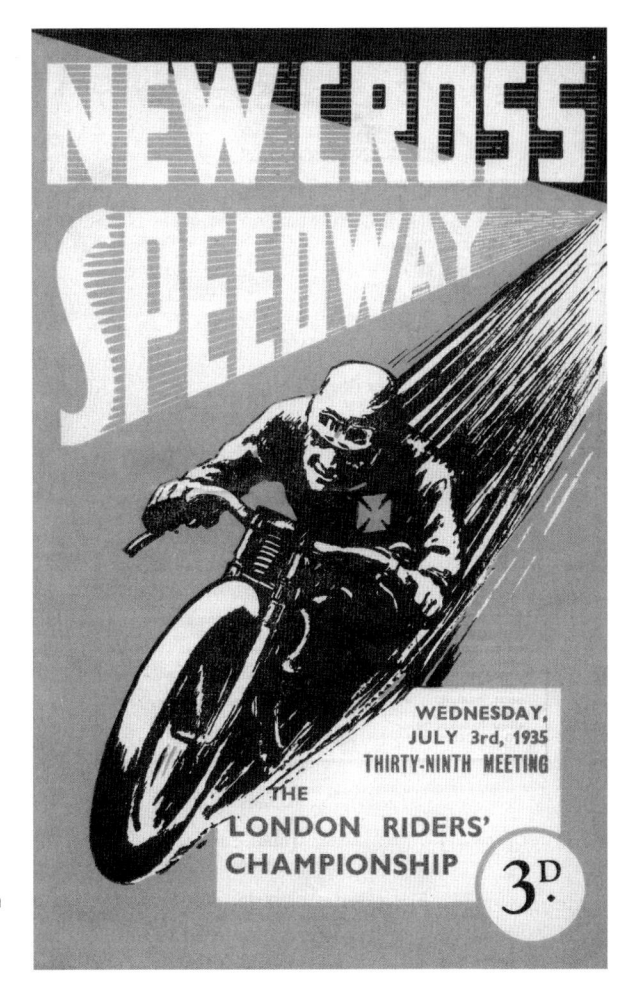

The programme from the London Riders' Championship, held at New Cross on 3 July 1935.

of war. In between Milne's brace of successes, West Ham's genial Canadian Eric Chitty claimed the coveted title in 1938. Before the war, these finals were almost always a sell out, with royalty, lords, Indian princes or film star celebrities persuaded to present the trophy, such was its prestige at the time.

Every track hosted its own individual championship of one style or another, whilst regional events were raced at selected circuits. All were important events, with the titles keenly contested by all eligible competitors.

LONDON RIDERS' CHAMPIONSHIP
PRE-WAR ROLL OF HONOUR

YEAR	VENUE	WINNER
1930	Crystal Palace	Jack Ormston
1931	Crystal Palace	Joe Francis
1932-3	Not Staged	
1934	New Cross	Tom Farndon
1935	New Cross	Tom Farndon
1936	New Cross	Vic Huxley
1937	New Cross	Jack Milne
1938	New Cross	Eric Chitty
1939	New Cross	Jack Milne

5
TEST MATCHES

1930

Following on from the success of league racing in 1929, fans were clamouring for Test matches involving England and Australia. Cricket had its Test matches and played annually to ever-increasing audiences, while football had inaugurated the World Cup, which had generated enormous interest and enthusiasm. Previous dirt-track efforts had been of a purely experimental nature, an early example of which saw England face Scotland over a series of match races at Crystal Palace on 14 July 1928, but it had clearly fired the public's imagination. With properly organized team competition being the order of the day, international matches were being considered by a consortium of leading speedway promoters, along with Lord Sempill, 'Sammy' Samuel and Norman Pritchard of *Speedway News* at a luncheon in early 1930. However, before general agreement had been reached on how and where the series should be run, Wimbledon actually announced their date for the first Test match as 30 June that year. Incidentally, this evening staging of the Australia *v.* England match was due to follow the Lord's Test at which a very youthful Don Bradman was billed to appear.

After a considerable advertising campaign of posters, sandwich-board men in South London, kites and flying banners at horse-racing courses, something more than 30,000 patrons turned up at Plough Lane. Quite a number could not get inside and had to be kept abreast of the proceedings whilst still in the car park. The nine-heat match was a trifle one-sided and resulted in a win for Australia by 35 points to 17. The England team and points from that historic event were as follows: Roger Frogley (6), Jim Kempster, captain (5), Wal Phillips (4), Jack Ormston (1), Jack Parker (1) and Frank Varey (0). Meanwhile, the victorious Aussies were represented as follows: maximum man Vic Huxley (9), Max Grosskreutz (6), Frank Arthur (6), Billy Lamont (6), Ron Johnson (5) and Dicky Case (3).

Four further matches were raced in 1930, but over sixteen heats instead of the inaugural nine. Australia were hampered due to the restricted numbers of riders available in this country, while on the other hand, an increasing number of English boys were becoming available, so a policy of 'horses for courses' was adopted in the selection of their team. Max Grosskreutz raced to a four-ride maximum in the

The programme from the England versus Scotland encounter, held at Crystal Palace on 14 July 1928.

Smiling Jim Kempster – England's very-first captain.

second Test at Belle Vue on 23 July, although the score-line favoured England 56-39. Jim Kempster (10) was England's top scorer, but he received solid support, particularly from Frank Varey (9), Squib Burton (9) and Eric Langton (8).

At Stamford Bridge on 20 August, England narrowly triumphed in the third Test by 49 points to 46, the top-scorers being Wal Phillips for England with a four-ride maximum, while Vic Huxley notched 11 for the Australians. That only tells part of the story, however, as at approximately 8.50 p.m. the lights failed for a period of 35 minutes – this was later described in *The Motor Cycle* as being a lapse on the part of the Gas Company. Prior to the enforced delay in proceedings, Frank Varey had hit the fence in the second heat, eventually departing from the track on board a stretcher. The light failure was to prove a blessing in disguise, for when the match restarted, the brave Varey took victory in heat six ahead of partner Arthur Warwick, thus hauling England back to within two points of the Aussies' 19-point total. Later in the match, Varey's heroics continued when he took the flag in heat fourteen to level the match at 42 points apiece. A 3-2 advantage then gave England the narrowest of leads, and with the match balanced on a knife-edge, the home nation finally secured victory when Syd Jackson and Tiger Stevenson combined to record a 4-2 in the final heat.

In the fourth Test match, again at Belle Vue on 3 September, the result was 51-45 in favour of the home country for whom Jack Parker and Frank Varey both netted 9 point tallies, whilst that man Huxley roared to a 12-point maximum for the battling

Aussies. The final match was staged at Wembley on 26 September and ended in another narrow win for the home nation by 49 points to 45. England's scoring was solid throughout with Jack Ormston and Colin Watson leading the way on 8 points apiece, whereas Vic Huxley again compiled a 12-point full-house for the losing side. So, despite suffering defeat in the first match, the series could be looked upon as being very successful for England with a 4-1 victory. The leading overall scorers in the series for England were Frank Varey (30) and Squib Burton (26), while the Australians were best served by the brilliant Vic Huxley (51), plus Max Grosskreutz (34).

Huxley was undoubtedly the man of the series as he amazingly crossed the line ahead in sixteen out of his total of nineteen races. Not only that, but after each Test match the riders competed for a special trophy, and Huxley won all five cups on offer! Concluding the story of a remarkable rider, Huxley actually broke the Wimbledon track record in the first-ever Test race on 30 June. Billy Lamont subsequently lowered it again in the seventh heat, only for that man Huxley to again clock the fastest time for the Plough Lane circuit in the second-half.

RESULTS

First Test	England 17 Australia 35
Second Test	England 56 Australia 39
Third Test	England 49 Australia 46
Fourth Test	England 51 Australia 45
Fifth Test	England 49 Australia 45
Series Result	England 4 Australia 1

1931

Strangely enough, England also won the 1931 series by four matches to one, with the Aussies' solitary success occurring at the 586-yard Leicester Super circuit on 20 July. Following a last heat 4-2 to the Australians, the match resulted in a narrow 47-46 score-line, but it was dogged by many false starts. In those days, push starts had been replaced by the almost equally dreaded procedure of rolling starts. This was fallible enough on ordinary quarter-mile tracks, but on the massive Leicester circuit, it led to numerous problems.

England had previously won the first match of the series by 55 points to 37 at Crystal Palace on 27 June, with Eric Langton bagging a super 12-point maximum, while both Squib Burton and Wal Phillips netted 10 points apiece. Meanwhile, with 9 points, Frank Arthur proved to be the best Australian on show, but the 18-point margin of defeat was an awfully bitter pill for them to swallow. It must have galvanized them, however, for they bounced back with the aforementioned success at Leicester Super, where future World Champion Lionel Van Praag topped their score-chart with 9 points to his name. On the night, both Wal Phillips and Squib Burton took heavy crashes, leaving the remaining English lads to produce a dogged performance to take the match to the wire, with 9 points being sufficient for Arthur Jervis to top the pile.

England quickly bounced back to win 53-43 at Wembley in the third Test with Jack Parker (11+1) and Reg Bounds (10) leading the way, whilst Frank Arthur scored 11 points for the Aussies. The fourth Test at Belle Vue on 5 September ended in another home win by 53 points to 41, with Jack Parker thundering through the card for a 12-point maximum, while Ginger Lees netted 11. Meanwhile, having scored but a single point in the previous match at Wembley, Vic Huxley got right back in the groove to top the Australian scoring on the 10-point mark. In a closely-contested final match at Stamford Bridge on 23 September, a last-heat share of the points left a 48-46 score-line in favour of England, for whom Jack Parker recorded another 12-point maximum, whilst Vic Huxley again grabbed 10 for the Aussies. A look at

The England versus Australia Test match programme, as issued at Crystal Palace on 27 June 1931.

Leicester Super's Test match programme from 20 July 1931.

the overall scoring in the series showed Jack Parker on top of the English chart with a 49-point tally, whilst a total of 41 was sufficient for Frank Arthur to head Australia's list. For Parker, it had been an incredible series, as he was undefeated by an opponent in no fewer than sixteen of his twenty rides.

RESULTS
First Test   England 55 Australia 37
Second Test   England 46 Australia 47
Third Test   England 53 Australia 43
Fourth Test   England 53 Australia 41
Fifth Test   England 48 Australia 46

Series Result   England 4 Australia 1

1932

For 1932, things were beginning to settle down a bit, and regular speedway patrons were following their favourite sport in very large numbers, with support for the Test matches being no exception. In the first match at Stamford Bridge on 4 June, England were victorious by 50 points to 41. The lively Tom Farndon netted 11+1 points and Wal Phillips 10 for England, while Max Grosskreutz topped the Australian scoring with a mere 7-point tally. Next, at Wembley on 23 June, the Australians ran riot, winning 59-35 with Dicky Case scorching to a 12-point maximum. Regular partner Billy Lamont provided tremendous support to follow Case home for 5-1 successes in each of their four rides together, thus gaining an unbeaten tally of 8+4 points himself. Solid scoring throughout was the key to their success, with Vic Huxley (9), Bluey Wilkinson (9) and Frank Arthur (8) providing great support to the dynamic Case/Huxley duo. Meanwhile, for England only George Greenwood stood out with an 8-point total.

The home country improved somewhat at Belle Vue on 16 July to gain a 53-43 success. Three English riders gleaned 11 points apiece, namely Tom Farndon, Frank Varey and Ginger Lees, whilst Dicky Case notched 10 for the visitors. On 6 August a huge crowd gathered at Crystal Palace to see Australia defeat England 49-45, with Dicky Case (10+2) and Eric Langton (10) being their respective countries' top scorers.

With the series level at 2-2, a massive attendance gathered at Wembley for the decider on 15 September, when England managed to eke out a 51-42 victory. Eric Langton and Ginger Less plundered 10-point tallies for the victors, whilst Vic Huxley scorched to a 12-point full-house for the defeated Aussie boys. The match had originally been allocated to Southampton, but with the series deadlocked, it was understandably switched to Wembley. At the time there was no longer any regular

Top Australian Dicky Case.

racing at Banister Court anyway, the league team having relocated to Lea Bridge (under the guise of Clapton) in June. With a huge public interest in the outcome, it was thought that the travelling distance would have been too great for most fans, and, of course, the accommodation too small. Newsreel cameras actually filmed the match, with the action and crowd scenes subsequently used to great effect in the speedway drama *Money For Speed*, which was released the following year. With an overall total of 34 points Eric Langton was man of the series for England, while the Aussies' scoring was led by 43 points from Dicky Case.

RESULTS
First Test   England 50 Australia 41
Second Test   England 35 Australia 59
Third Test   England 53 Australia 43
Fourth Test   England 45 Australia 49
Fifth Test   England 51 Australia 42

Series Result   England 3 Australia 2

The programme from the second Test at Belle Vue on 15 July 1933.

1933

With the universal introduction of electric starting gates in 1933, most of the original haphazard starting systems had become relics of the past. Meanwhile, individual scoring underwent a temporary change, which resulted in some rather large scores, with one or two riders even topping the 20-point mark on occasions. A prime example of this occurred in the first revamped 18-heat Test at Wembley on 29 June when England accumulated 76 points, of which Ginger Lees scored 20, Eric Langton 16, Syd Jackson 15 and Tiger Stevenson 13. Meanwhile, Australia totalled 47, with Vic Huxley amassing a round dozen points. Langton's performance was worthy of note as he actually won each of his first four rides, before suffering an exclusion for crossing the white line. As a result, he subsequently withdrew from the meeting, and the rest of the series! On a rather sad note, the match was marred by a broken leg suffered by Claude Rye, in what was actually his debut appearance for England.

Australia then won at Belle Vue by 65 points to 61 on 15 July, spearheaded by 16 points apiece from Vic Huxley and Bluey Wilkinson, while Dicky Case chipped in with 12. England's best performer was again Ginger Lees with a whopping 22 points, while Syd Jackson was next in line on 12. The match was a significant one in the career of Bill Kitchen, however, as after very little speedway experience, he rode as reserve in the English side. *Speedway News* commented on Kitchen's superb debut thus, 'He was brought in twice. The first time he finished second to his partner Lees, and on the other occasion he rode magnificently to win the seventeenth heat and give England a chance of saving the match.'

A close contest followed at Crystal Palace on 29 July, when the home nation just scraped home $63\frac{1}{2}$-$62\frac{1}{2}$, there being a dead heat for a minor position between Joe Francis and Vic Huxley in one race. Going into the final heat, England required a single point to ensure victory, and after Tiger Stevenson had pulled up with mechanical gremlins, his team-mate Joe Francis sensibly slowed down to make sure of the all-important third place. With a 17-point tally, Jack Parker was England's top man, while Ginger Lees (13), Tiger Stevenson (12) and Tom Farndon (11) provided solid backing. For the Aussies meanwhile, Dicky Case (15), Bluey Wilkinson (14) and Max Grosskreutz (13) were the principal scorers.

The fourth Test at Wimbledon on 21 August saw the visitors claim a narrow 64-62 success. The match again hinged on the final heat, but although Ginger Lees crossed the line ahead, it was Max Grosskreutz and Dicky Case who gave the Australians glory by filling the second and third positions respectively. The victorious side was led by Max Grosskreutz (18), Bluey Wilkinson (14), Vic Huxley (12) and Dicky Case (10), whilst England's best performers were Ginger Lees (17), Tiger Stevenson (13) and Tom Farndon (11). And so to the final and deciding Test, which was held before a large and enthusiastic crowd at West Ham's Custom House Stadium on 5 September. Cheered on by the partisan audience, a very determined England side took overall victory in the series with a convincing win by 74 points to 52. Here, Frank Varey (18), Tiger Stevenson (15), Squib Burton (12) and Tom Farndon (10) led the English charge, while

Bluey Wilkinson (16), Vic Huxley (13) and Dicky Case (12) did their utmost to keep the Australians in the hunt. In this series, scoring was maintained at the 4-2-1-0 system throughout, but returned to the more normal format of 3-2-1-0 for future seasons. Ginger Lees took full advantage of the scoring method that was operated to top the pile for England, garnering a staggering total of 72 points from the four matches he appeared in. Meanwhile, with 68 points from five matches, Bluey Wilkinson proved to be Australia's highest series scorer. One amazing fact was that no rider from either side managed to net a full or paid maximum throughout the whole series.

RESULTS
First Test	England 76 Australia 47
Second Test	England 61 Australia 65
Third Test	England $63\frac{1}{2}$ Australia $62\frac{1}{2}$
Fourth Test	England 62 Australia 64
Fifth Test	England 74 Australia 52
Series Result	England 3 Australia 2

1934

Australia took the Ashes for the first time in 1934, winning by three matches to two, courtesy of a dramatic 57-50 success in the final match at West Ham on 21 August. With a series total of 66 points, the consistent Ginger Lees hit double-figures in each and every one of the five Tests, while Eric Langton totalled 56 points and top-scored for England in each of the four matches he contested. Meanwhile, with an astounding 204 points between them, Max Grosskreutz (59), Ron Johnson (54), Bluey Wilkinson (46) and Dicky Case (45) formed a particularly potent Australian spearhead, which proved impossible to subdue in the final analysis.

The Aussies began the series in fine style, collecting a massive 69-38 success at Wembley on 7 June. No fewer than five riders hit double-figures for the victors, namely Max Grosskreutz (15), Dicky Case (13), Vic Huxley ($12\frac{1}{2}$), Bluey Wilkinson (12) and Ron Johnson (10). For England, Ginger Lees fought a valiant one-man rearguard action and had he not bagged 15 points, the Australians' huge margin of victory would have undoubtedly been greater.

England recovered well to win the second Test at New Cross by 58 points to 48, led by the high-scoring trio of Eric Langton (14), Ginger Lees (13) and Joe Abbott (13). On what was a somewhat disappointing night for Australia, their score-chart was headed by Dicky Case (13) and New Cross favourite Ron Johnson (10). The series then moved on to Wimbledon, where a closely-fought match finally resulted in a 54-51 triumph for the Aussies, the victory being garnered thanks to last heat 4-2 from Max Grosskreutz and Dicky Case. Leading light for the victors was final race hero Grosskreutz, who netted a total of 15 points, while team-mate Jack Sharp chipped in with a well-taken tally of 13. Meanwhile, Eric Langton (16), Ginger Lees (13) and Joe Abbott (11) performed gallantly for the narrowly defeated English side.

The series continued in its ding-dong fashion when the home nation levelled up the overall score to two victories apiece, courtesy of a $60\frac{1}{2}$-$45\frac{1}{2}$ success at Belle Vue on 21 July. Eric Langton (15), Ginger Lees (14), Frank Charles (13) and Joe Abbott (10) headed the points chart in the home camp, while Ron Johnson (15) and Max Grosskreutz (11) proved to be Australia's best. At the aforementioned decider at West Ham, Australia secured victory in the series with that 57-50 success. The visitors went into the match minus the services of the injured Vic Huxley, with Ron Johnson skippering the side. Going into the last heat, the score stood at 52-50 in

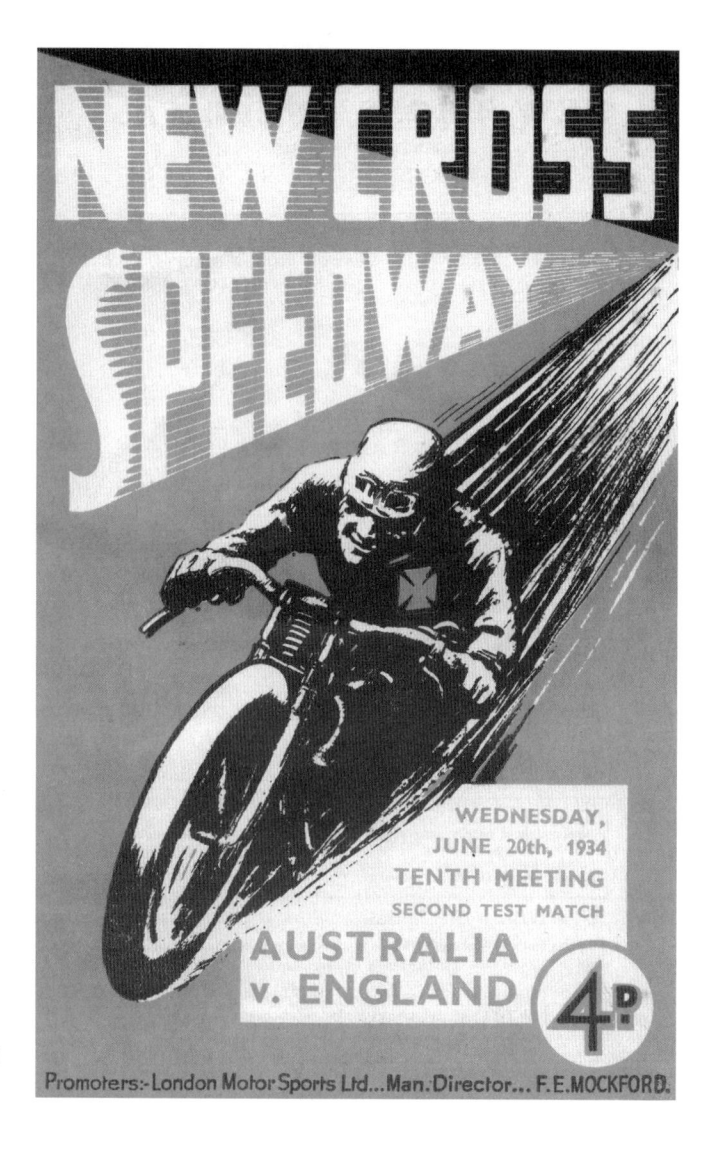

The Test match programme from New Cross, dated 20 June 1934.

favour of the Aussies, with Max Grosskreutz and Dicky Case combining for a 5-0 advantage after both home men had suffered misfortune, Tiger Stevenson being excluded, while Joe Abbott's machine gave up the ghost. The contributions of Bluey Wilkinson (16), Max Grosskreutz (15) and Ron Johnson (10) had swung the match in Australia's favour, with England generally being far too reliant on Eric Langton (13) and Ginger Lees (11). For a second successive series, not one rider from either side managed to register either a full or paid maximum!

RESULTS
First Test	England 38 Australia 69
Second Test	England 58 Australia 48
Third Test	England 51 Australia 54
Fourth Test	England $60\frac{1}{2}$ Australia $45\frac{1}{2}$
Fifth Test	England 50 Australia 57

Series Result: Australia 3 England 2

1934/35

After the British season had ended, Australia staged its first Test series in 1934/35, with the first of the nine heat matches staged at Sydney. Inspired by 8 points apiece from Max Grosskreutz and Lionel Van Praag, the Aussies opened up with a 35-19 success, with the remainder of their side made up by Bluey Wilkinson (7), Dicky Case (6), Clem Mitchell (4) and Wally Little (2). Meanwhile, England were represented by Tiger Stevenson (8), Eric Langton (5), Joe Abbott (3), Frank Varey (2), Wal Phillips (1), Dusty Haigh (0) and Cliff Parkinson (0).

Australia then moved into a 2-0 lead, courtesy of a 30-24 victory at Melbourne, with maximum man Max Grosskreutz (9) and Eric Langton (7) being the leading scorers for each side. A tremendous effort brought England their first-ever away win at Sydney in the third Test, albeit by a narrow margin (28-25). A maximum 9-point tally from Tiger Stevenson was the major contribution towards the victory, with Max Grosskreutz (7) being the top man for the homesters. The fourth match also took place at Sydney and led by seven points from Wally Little, the Aussies secured a narrow win by 29 points to 24. Joe Abbott proved to be England's main man with a super three-ride maximum, but he unfortunately lacked the necessary backing that might have brought a successive victory.

The fifth match was again held at Sydney and in a tense affair it was England who claimed a $27\frac{1}{2}$-$26\frac{1}{2}$ success, led by 8 points from Dusty Haigh. Going into the last heat, England held the lead by a single point, and although Bluey Wilkinson took the chequered flag, it was the team-riding tactics of Eric Langton (second place) and Wal Phillips (third place) that ensured victory for the tourists. Australia's scoring was topped by an unbeaten nine points from Bluey Wilkinson and they must have surely been relieved to have gained a 3-2 series victory over a spirited and hard-working England outfit. Overall, the main scorer for the host nation was Max Grosskreutz with 37 points, while Tiger Stevenson gleaned 28 points to lead the England totals.

RESULTS
First Test   Australia 35 England 19
Second Test   Australia 30 England 24
Third Test   Australia 25 England 28
Fourth Test   Australia 29 England 24
Fifth Test   Australia 26½ England 27½

Series Result   Australia 3 England 2

1935

Later on in 1935, England took a 4-1 victory in what was the sixth series on home soil, suffering their only defeat at West Ham on 30 July in the fourth Test. Eric Langton performed brilliantly throughout for the home nation, recording a total of 67 points, with Tom Farndon finishing next in the scoring stakes on 41. Meanwhile, despite their overall loss, the Australians boasted three men on 40-plus points in Max Grosskreutz (64), Bluey Wilkinson (44) and Ron Johnson (43).

The opening match of the series was held at Wembley on 6 June, with England taking a narrow 56-52 victory led by double-figure returns from Eric Langton (15), Bill Kitchen (12), Frank Charles (11) and Jack Parker (10). Victory was finally assured in heat seventeen, when Langton and Parker combined for a 5-1, thereby putting England into an unassailable 54-48 lead. With a final heat 4-2 in their favour, it was a case of so near and yet so far for the Aussies, for whom Max Grosskreutz (15) and Bluey Wilkinson (10) were the main contributors.

New Cross was the venue for the second match, with the homesters collecting a slightly more comfortable success by 59 points to 46. For England, the leading scorers in the match were Tom Farndon (14), Eric Langton (13) and Bill Kitchen (10), while the Aussies' points were topped by Dicky Case (12) and Max Grosskreutz (11). The third Test was then hosted by Belle Vue and saw England cruise into a 3-0 lead, courtesy of a 59-48 win. Eric Langton was top dog for the English with a mighty 17-point haul on his home circuit, while Joe Abbott (13), Tom Farndon (11) and Bill Kitchen (10) all made telling contributions. The Australians were by no means disgraced, however, with their leading individual performances coming from Bluey Wilkinson (13) and Ron Johnson (11).

The aforementioned solitary defeat for England occurred next, with the Aussies thundering to victory by 66 points to 40 at West Ham. Amazingly, not one of the home side reached double-figures, with a 9-point tally being sufficient for Tommy Croombs to head the chart. On the other side of the coin, however, in Max Grosskreutz (17), Ron Johnson (13) and Lionel Van Praag (12), the rampant Australians boasted a trio of big scorers.

England were obviously out for revenge in the final match at Harringay on 24 August and duly swept to a 63-44 success, their leading points being supplied by Eric Langton (14), Jack Ormston (14), Frank Charles (12) and Tom Farndon (10). It was an instantly forgettable meeting for the Aussies, with only Max Grosskreutz (12) and Vic Huxley (10) showing any resistance to England's impressive four-pronged attack. Once again, no rider registered any form of maximum throughout the series, although Max Grosskreutz set a new record for the most race wins, taking the victor's flag 18 times in 30 heats.

England versus Australia Test match programme from Wembley on 6 June 1935.

England 1935. Left to right: Jack Parker, Tommy Croombs, Eric Langton, Tom Farndon, Joe Abbott, Bill Kitchen, Tiger Stevenson, Bob Harrison.

RESULTS

First Test	England 56 Australia 52
Second Test	England 59 Australia 46
Third Test	England 59 Australia 48
Fourth Test	England 40 Australia 66
Fifth Test	England 63 Australia 44
Series Result	England 4 Australia 1

1935/36

The entire 1935/36 Australian series was staged at the Royal Agricultural Showground in Sydney, with the matches run over 12 heats. In the worst possible start, Frankie Elms was fatally injured in a race immediately prior to the first Test, with Billy Lamont unable to avoid the stricken rider and suffering an injury which ruled him out of the meeting. When the Test got underway, it was the host nation who kicked off in fine style with a comfortable 47-25 victory. Tiger Stevenson was England's leading man with 8 points, while Max Grosskreutz recorded what was the first in an amazing run of four successive

12-point maximums. The second Test resulted in another home win by 44 points to 28, with Vic Huxley (11+1) and Bluey Wilkinson (10) giving maximum-man Max Grosskreutz great support. The story wasn't so good from an English point of view, however, with 7 points being sufficient for Wal Phillips to head the scoring.

The third Test ended with an identical score to the second as the Australians moved into an unassailable 3-0 lead. Again, it was Vic Huxley (11+1) and Bluey Wilkinson (11) who formed a potent force alongside the irresistible Grosskreutz, while a seven-point total saw Nobby Key top the England score-chart. The Aussies managed to secure a 39-33 success in the fourth match and as the score suggests, they were made to work a lot harder by an England side inspired by Wal Phillips. In notching 10 points, the Wimbledon rider not only led the scoring for his country, but he also became the first Englishman to reach double-figures in an away Test match.

The much-improved fourth Test showing seemed to galvanize England and they ended the series with a morale-boosting 39-32 victory on 15 February. Wal Phillips again rode well to repeat his 10-point performance from the previous match, while Nobby Key backed him up with an 8-point tally. For Australia, Vic Huxley top-scored with 11+1 points (his third paid maximum of the series), while Max Grosskreutz finished on the 9-point mark, failing for the first time to hit a round dozen after suffering an exclusion for a tape-breaking offence. Looking back at the five matches, Grosskreutz was way out on his own with a total of 57 points out of a possible 60 (or put another way – 19 wins from 20 races), while Wal Phillips was England's best servant overall, having netted 33 points.

RESULTS

First Test	Australia 47 England 25
Second Test	Australia 44 England 28
Third Test	Australia 44 England 28
Fourth Test	Australia 39 England 33
Fifth Test	Australia 32 England 39
Series Result	Australia 4 England 1

1936

The 1936 series on home territory saw Frank Charles record no fewer than 68 points from five matches as England notched a 3-2 success. Eric Langton (44) and Bill Kitchen (40) were the winning nation's other main contributors, with Lionel Van Praag (57), Bluey Wilkinson (49) and Dicky Case (42) being the Aussies' best.

The series kicked off at Wembley on 28 May, with the host country scorching to a 65-43 success, led by the points-scoring prowess of George Newton (16), Frank Charles (13), Eric Langton (12) and Jack Parker (12). Meanwhile, the top end of

Australia's score-chart had a familiar look about it, with Max Grosskreutz (13) and Bluey Wilkinson (11) each hitting double-figures for the umpteenth time.

New Cross beckoned for the second Test and it was the turn of the Australians to gain a victory and level up the series. Inspired by Dicky Case (16), Max Grosskreutz (13) and Lionel Van Praag (12), the Antipodeans raced to a 57-49 victory, with England best represented by a quite brilliant 18-point maximum from Frank Charles. The English boys again moved ahead in the series, courtesy of a thumping 70-38 win in the next match at Belle Vue on 4 July. Continuing where he had left off at New Cross, Frank Charles weighed in with a 16-point tally, and together with regular partner Joe Abbott, the duo plundered five 5-1s and a 4-2. Abbott claimed a wonderful paid maximum (13+5 points), while Bill Kitchen netted an identical total to that of Charles. England's top trio received solid support from Eric Langton (13), while the beleaguered Aussie team was led manfully by Lionel Van Praag's 11-point total.

The great Vic Huxley of Wimbledon fame – certainly one of Australia's best.

134

England secured overall victory when they triumphed 58-47 in a hard-fought fourth Test at Wimbledon on 20 July. Eric Langton (15), Frank Charles (13) and Bill Kitchen (11) were the main contributors for the winning side, whereas Lionel Van Praag (15) and Vic Huxley (12) proved to be Australia's leading lights. Having lost the series, there was at least some consolation for the Aussie boys when they blitzed their way to a 73-35 success in the last match at West Ham on 18 August. Five members of the victorious team reached double-figure tallies, namely Bluey Wilkinson (16+2), Lionel Van Praag (15), Dicky Case (11), Vic Huxley (11) and Max Grosskreutz (10). It certainly was a dismal night for England, with 8 points being enough for Frank Charles and Bill Kitchen to share top spot on the score-chart. There was plenty for Charles to be happy about overall though, for having taken victory on 19 occasions (from 30 races), he equalled the series record set by Max Grosskreutz Down Under in 1935/36.

RESULTS

First Test	England 65 Australia 43
Second Test	England 49 Australia 57
Third Test	England 70 Australia 38
Fourth Test	England 58 Australia 47
Fifth Test	England 35 Australia 73
Series Result	England 3 Australia 2

1936/37

The Australian Tests for 1936/37 began at Sydney on 12 December, with the homesters claiming a narrow 29-25 success over the reinstated 9-heat formula. The match was evenly balanced at 24 points apiece following heat eight, before Bluey Wilkinson and Clem Mitchell teamed up to secure a match winning 5-1. The best performers in the meeting for the Aussies were the unbeaten duo of Wally Little (9) and the aforementioned Mitchell (8+1), while the English scoring was headed by 5 points apiece from Norman Parker and Tommy Croombs. Melbourne was the stage for the second meeting of the sides, with Australia chalking up another victory by 33 points to 21. Wally Little again plundered a three-ride maximum for the victorious hosts, as did team-mate Clem Mitchell, while 7 points was enough for Jack Parker to emerge as England's best performer.

All of the remaining matches were held at Sydney, beginning with the third Test on 18 January, when England caught their opponents on the hop to win 28-25. Amid great tension, the tourists went into the last heat with a three-point advantage, and although Vic Huxley raced to victory, Tommy Croombs and Wal Phillips remained cool to split the points, thereby securing England's success. Both Norman

Parker and heat nine hero Croombs netted 7 points for the victors, while Bluey Wilkinson weighed in with an unbeaten 9 point tally for Australia.

No doubt spurred on by the victory, England then edged to a narrow 28-26 success in the fourth Test to leave the series all-square at 2-2. The Aussies could have won the match had they gained a final race 5-1, but they were restricted to a 4-2 by a determined second place effort from Wal Phillips. Having netted a maximum in the previous match, Bluey Wilkinson continued where he left off and again recorded 9 points for the Aussies, but it was a greater all-round solidity that gave England the win, led by an 8-point return from Norman Parker. Unfortunately, England's joy was short-lived when the battling Wal Phillips broke a leg in a second-half scratch race, and was subsequently ruled out of the fifth Test.

The crucial decider took place on 6 February and it was the Australians who raised their game to take victory by 31 points to 22, thereby securing a 3-2 success overall. Wally Little (8+1) and Vic Huxley (8) were the main contributors to the Aussies' win, while a 7-point total put Jack Parker's name on top of the England list. The injury suffered by Wal Phillips after the fourth match undoubtedly had a bearing on the match as his replacement Eric Gregory unfortunately failed to get amongst the scorers. With a grand total of 36 points, Wally Little ended the series as the leading scorer for the hosts, while Jack Parker topped the English chart on 30.

RESULTS
First Test   Australia 29 England 25
Second Test   Australia 33 England 21
Third Test   Australia 25 England 28
Fourth Test   Australia 26 England 28
Fifth Test   Australia 31 England 22

Series Result   Australia 3 England 2

1937

Due to a subsequent injury suffered by Bluey Wilkinson, just one match took place between England and Australia in 1937. This occurred at Wembley on 27 May, when the home country swept to victory by 66 points to 41, led by tall scoring from Jack Parker (13), Eric Langton (12), Arthur Atkinson (12), Jack Ormston (11) and Bill Kitchen (10). It was a meeting to forget for the Australians, however, with only Bluey Wilkinson and Lionel Van Praag offering any resistance as they notched 17 and 12 points respectively. With Wilkinson breaking a collar-bone while riding for West Ham in a league match at Wimbledon four days later, the series was abandoned as it was felt the Australians no longer had a strong enough squad to be sufficiently competitive.

TEST MATCHES

RESULT

First Test   England 66 Australia 41

Series Result   England 1 Australia 0

Following the unfortunate abandonment of the series against Aussies, the first of five replacement matches pitched England against an Overseas team, which included American and Australian riders. The first meeting, staged at West Ham on 15 June, couldn't possibly have been closer, with England eventually just shading it by 54 points to 53. To all intents and purposes, it looked as though the home nation were heading for defeat as they trailed 45-33 after thirteen heats. However, amidst terrific crowd scenes a great fightback ensued, with Eric Langton and Bill Kitchen grabbing a couple of 5-1s, as did Arthur Atkinson and Tiger Stevenson. That gave the English a two-point lead after heat seventeen, with George Newton's second place finish in the final heat securing a brilliant victory. Top scorers for England were Eric Langton (13) and Bill Kitchen (12), while their opponents were best served by Cordy Milne (13), Wilbur Lamoreaux (13) and Jack Milne (10). The exciting tussle was subsequently described thus in *Speedway News*, 'Great success…reawakened the enthusiasm which marked the early Tests with Australia, but which had so obviously evaporated of recent seasons.'

The second Test was held at Belle Vue on 3 July, when another close encounter resulted in a 54-54 draw. England led by just two points as the riders lined up for heat eighteen, but a tremendous effort took Cordy Milne to victory on board Lionel Van Praag's spare machine. Meanwhile, filling second place for England was Joe Abbott, while the vital third place was occupied by Van Praag himself, who thereby gained a fighting draw for the Overseas. Top scorer Joe Abbott netted 15 points for the English, with superb backing supplied by Bill Kitchen (12), Eric Langton (11) and Frank Varey (11). Meanwhile, the leading points for the Overseas team were garnered by the powerful foursome of Eric Chitty (13), Jack Milne (11), Lionel Van Praag (10) and Wilbur Lamoreaux (10).

After two very close matches, it came as something of a surprise when the Overseas side then scorched to a 64-43 success in the third Test at New Cross on 21 July. The triumphant side were led home by 14 points from Jack Milne, while Eric Chitty (13), Bluey Wilkinson (13) and Lionel Van Praag (12) also scored heavily. For England, only Eric Langton revealed anything like his true form, fighting something of a lone-battle on his way to a 13-point total. If that was an impressive showing, then the Overseas side were absolutely stunning in the fourth Test at Wimbledon on 23 August, swamping England by 75 points to 32. A paid maximum (16+2 points) saw Jack Milne lead the victory charge, while Wilbur Lamoreaux (14), Lionel Van Praag (13), Eric Collins (12) and Cordy Milne (11) helped complete the rout. To be fair, England were handicapped by an injury to Eric Langton, which kept him out of action, with Bill Kitchen being the only team member to reach double-figures in netting 10 points.

That left England needing a result from the final match at Harringay on 11 September in order to square the series. It wasn't to be though, as the Overseas side clawed their way to victory by 57 points to 50, thereby wrapping up an overall 3-1 success. Jack Milne again led the Overseas scoring with 16 points, with Lionel Van Praag (15) and Wilbur Lamoreaux (12) once more lending solid support. Meanwhile, Eric Langton (14) and Joe Abbott (10) performed heroically to keep England in the hunt throughout, but they unfortunately lacked the necessary support. Man of the series for England was undoubtedly Eric Langton with a total of 51 points, while the Overseas side featured three men on 50-plus points, namely Jack Milne (67), Lionel Van Praag (56) and Wilbur Lamoreaux (54).

RESULTS
First Test   England 54 Overseas 53
Second Test   England 54 Overseas 54
Third Test   England 43 Overseas 64
Fourth Test   England 32 Overseas 75
Fifth Test   England 50 Overseas 57

Series Result   Overseas 3 England 1

One other match pitched England against the USA at Wimbledon on 30 August, with the Americans earning a 57-51 victory. Jack Milne was in top form for the victors with a full 18-pointer, while Wilbur Lamoreaux (15) and Cordy Milne (11) also scored heavily. Meanwhile for England, Bill Kitchen (13), Joe Abbott (11) and Jack Parker (10) were the main contributors.

RESULT
First Test   England 51 USA 57

Series Result   USA 1 England 0

Completing the story of 1937, a five-match series also took place between representatives of the Provincial League and Australia. To say the sides were unsuitably matched would be an understatement as the Aussies tracked the likes of Lionel Van Praag, Dicky Case, Vic Duggan and Bluey Wilkinson, so it was little surprise when they completed a 5-0 whitewash. The Provincial League side got closest in the first encounter at Nottingham on 13 July, going down narrowly by 53 points to 55. Sadly, it was downhill after that with defeats at Belle Vue, Southampton and Birmingham following the series low of a 29-79 reverse at Bristol in the second match. With 50 points overall, George Greenwood fought a valiant and lone battle for the Provincial League boys, whereas the Australian scoring was predictably led by Lionel Van Praag (61), Dicky Case (47), Bluey Wilkinson (46) and Eric Collins (43).

RESULTS

First Test	Provincial League 53 Australia 55
Second Test	Provincial League 29 Australia 79
Third Test	Provincial League 48 Australia 60
Fourth Test	Provincial League 43 Australia 64
Fifth Test	Provincial League 51 Australia 56
Series Result	Australia 5 Provincial League 0

1937/38

As had happened two years previously, the whole of the 1937/38 Australian series was run in Sydney, with England getting off to the best possible start when taking victory by 28 points to 26 in the first of the 9-heat matches. Les Wotton and Joe Abbott topped the England chart with 6 points apiece, while Bluey Wilkinson chalked up an unbeaten 9 points for the losing homesters. Wilkinson actually completed his maximum in the last race, but a share of the points from Arthur Atkinson and Les Wotton secured victory for the happy tourists. Australia quickly recovered to win the second Test 31-23, that man Wilkinson again netting a three-ride maximum, while Bill Kitchen was England's best representative on 6 points.

Having drawn level, the Aussies then moved ahead in the series, courtesy of a narrow 27-26 success in a hard-fought third Test. England needed a 5-1 to win in the last heat, but unfortunately their 4-2 advantage wasn't quite sufficient. For the third time, Wilkinson helped himself to another 9 points for the victors, as did teammate Clem Mitchell, with a three-way tie at the head of the England scoring as Les Wotton, Jack Parker and Joe Abbott each notched 7-point tallies. The fourth match went the way of Australia by 30 points to 24, thereby giving them an insurmountable 3-1 lead in the series. The amazing Wilkinson thundered to his fourth maximum on the trot for the hosts, with Clem Mitchell again matching his flying comrade's performance, while Joe Abbott's 6 points left him sitting pretty as top dog in the England camp.

There was bad news from the final meeting, when Joe Abbott was injured in his first race, and didn't ride again throughout the subsequent domestic season in 1938. Despite Abbott's misfortune, the tourists battled hard in the match, but they couldn't stop Australia from collecting a 29-25 win, courtesy of a last heat 4-2 advantage – nor could they end Bluey Wilkinson's dash to a fifth straight maximum! Meanwhile, with 7 points to his name, Bill Kitchen reached the head of the England scoring for the second time in the series. With a maximum 45 points from the five matches, Bluey Wilkinson had set a remarkable record for the Aussies at the head of the scoring stakes, while a total of 26 points saw Les Wotton finish in the number one position for England. Following Wilkinson's wonder showings, it was subsequently reported that he had taken his total scoring to 439 points from 42 Test matches, moving ahead of the 435 tally of fellow countryman Max Grosskreutz.

RESULTS
First Test   Australia 26 England 28
Second Test   Australia 31 England 23
Third Test   Australia 27 England 26
Fourth Test   Australia 30 England 24
Fifth Test   Australia 29 England 25

Series Result   Australia 4 England 1

1938

A five-match England versus Australia Test series returned to the British racing calendar for 1938, with Belle Vue hosting the first meeting on 28 May. The match was a close affair, but it was the Australians who emerged in front by 56 points to 52. Bluey Wilkinson (15+2) and Max Grosskreutz (15) were top men for the victorious side, with Bill Kitchen (13), Frank Varey (12) and George Newton (11) being England's leading performers. Incidentally, Grosskreutz had actually retired from racing in order to manage the affairs of Norwich Speedway the previous year, but was given permission to ride for Australia.

Revenge was quickly attained, however, when the English lads swept to a 63-44 win at Wembley in the second Test. Five riders netted double-figures for the triumphant home team, namely Frank Varey (13), Frank Charles (13), Bill Kitchen (11), George Newton (11) and Arthur Atkinson (10). In spite of their heavy loss, the Aussies included the two real stars of the match in Bluey Wilkinson and Lionel Van Praag, both of whom bagged brilliant 15-point returns.

The Australians hit back resolutely to win 61-47 in the third match at New Cross on 29 June, with the dynamic pair of Bluey Wilkinson and Lionel Van Praag each blasting to full six-ride maximums. Backing them up with 11 points was Ron Johnson, while England's leading players were Bill Kitchen (12), Arthur Atkinson (12) and Stan Greatrex (10). On 12 July, the fourth Test took place at West Ham and resulted in a narrow 55-51 success for the English, which squared the series at 2-2. After sixteen heats, the match was poised at 47 points apiece, with a 5-1 from Geoff Pymar and Arthur Atkinson proving decisive for the home country in the penultimate race. Top scorers for England were Arthur Atkinson (13), Bill Kitchen (11) and Tommy Croombs (10), while for the Aussies, Bluey Wilkinson showed up well on his home league circuit to plunder 14+1 points, with Max Grosskreutz notching 10.

The programme as used at Harringay on 27 August 1938 for the England & Australia versus America & Canada Test match.

It was the home country who dramatically claimed the series with a 58-49 triumph in the final match at Wimbledon on 25 July. England were spurred to victory by a good all-round team effort, with Geoff Pymar (13) and George Newton (12) being particularly impressive. With his second undefeated 18-pointer of the series, Australia's Bluey Wilkinson stood alone as the undisputed man of the meeting, while Lionel Van Praag lent him support on the 10-point mark.

Having accumulated 56 and 47 points respectively, Bill Kitchen and Arthur Atkinson were England's highest scorers over the five matches, but their totals were greatly overshadowed by the brilliant Bluey Wilkinson, who accumulated a mammoth 80-point haul for the Australians. Wilkinson actually won 24 out of 30 races, and followed a team-mate home on three occasions. Of his other three rides, mechanical gremlins had seen him fail to finish two of them, leaving a solitary series defeat at the hands of Bill Kitchen. Backing the man who was destined to become World Champion later in the year were Lionel Van Praag (52) and Max Grosskreutz (42).

RESULTS

First Test	England 52 Australia 56
Second Test	England 63 Australia 44
Third Test	England 47 Australia 61
Fourth Test	England 55 Australia 51
Fifth Test	England 58 Australia 49
Series Result	England 3 Australia 2

A further three-match series then pitched a combined England/Australia side against USA/Canada, with the opening meeting held at Bristol on 12 August. A crowd of 12,869 turned up at Knowle Stadium and were enthralled by the action, which saw the American and Canadian combination eke out the narrowest of victories by 54 points to 53. Their main scorers were Jack Milne (15), Wilbur Lamoreaux (15) and Cordy Milne (13), with the English and Australians' leading representatives being Bill Kitchen (14), Lionel Van Praag (13) and Bluey Wilkinson (12).

The second Test at Harringay also resulted in an American/Canadian victory by 64 points to 44, with the Milne brothers each romping to 18-point maximums, while also receiving great support from Wilbur Lamoreaux (16) and Benny Kaufman (10). Just 9 points were sufficient for Bluey Wilkinson to head the scoring for the losing side, but they did manage to salvage something from the series with a 63-45 success in the final match at Belle Vue on 17 September. That man Wilkinson was right back in the groove with an unbeaten 18 points to his name, while Belle Vue teamsters Eric Langton (14) and Bill Kitchen (12) used their vast knowledge of the circuit to good effect. Meanwhile, the opposition were again best represented by the Milne brothers, both of whom netted 14 points. Top scorers overall for England/Australia were Bluey Wilkinson (39) and Bill Kitchen (33), whereas the series winners were spearheaded by Jack Milne (47), Cordy Milne (45) and Wilbur Lamoreaux (39).

RESULTS

First Test	England/Australia 53 USA/Canada 54
Second Test	England/Australia 44 USA/Canada 64
Third Test	England/Australia 63 USA/Canada 45
Series Result	USA/Canada 2 England/Australia 1

Completing the summary of internationals staged in 1938, a seven-match series took place on National League Second Division circuits, which saw England square up to the Dominions, a team made up of riders from Australia, New Zealand, Canada and South Africa – although somewhat strangely Englishman Phil 'Tiger' Hart also rode for them! As with the previous year's Provincial League versus Australia series, this was an unfair contest. The Dominions comfortably moved into a 5-0 lead, before England gained a 65-43 success at Sheffield.

That they followed it up with a 58-48 win at Birmingham (Hall Green) in the final match was of little consolation either. Earlier defeats had occurred at Newcastle, Norwich, Southampton, Leeds and Hackney Wick, with George Greenwood being some way clear at the top of the English scoring on a total of 66 points. Meanwhile, the Dominions were led to their 5-2 success by the brilliant Bluey Wilkinson, who powered his way to a colossal $81\frac{1}{2}$ points. To emphasize the difference in the teams, other riders utilized by the Dominions over the course of the series included Bert Spencer, Wally Kilmister, Lionel Van Praag, Vic Duggan and Max Grosskreutz.

RESULTS

First Test	England 48 Dominions 58
Second Test	England 38 Dominions 69
Third Test	England 53 Dominions 55
Fourth Test	England 30 Dominions 77
Fifth Test	England 40 Dominions 67
Sixth Test	England 65 Dominions 43
Seventh Test	England 58 Dominions 48
Series Result	Dominions 5 England 2

1938/39

The Australian series of 1938/39 again saw the five meetings run at Sydney, with England claiming something of a surprise 32-22 victory in the opening 9-heat encounter, which was witnessed by a crowd of some 25,000. Alec Statham and Geoff Pymar sat nicely on top of the England scoring with 7 points each, while Bluey Wilkinson recorded what was actually his eighth three-ride maximum for the Aussies in Test matches on home soil.

The second meeting might have ended in the same 32-22 score-line, but this one was in favour of the Australians, for whom Bluey Wilkinson (8+1) and Lionel Van Praag (8) chalked up the highest tallies. Although Wilkinson recorded a paid maximum, it was almost another full house as he was beaten by a matter of inches by partner Bill Longley in one race. Meanwhile, Harringay's Alec Statham finished uppermost for the English on the 7-point mark. In a fighting display, England then roared back into a 2-1 lead after gaining a 31-23 success in the third match. They were unable to stop Wilkinson from darting to another three-ride maximum, but the English lads had the greater strength in depth, with Alec Statham again leading the way on 8 points.

Courtesy of a 28-24 victory in the fourth Test, Australia then levelled up the series at two wins apiece, with Bluey Wilkinson again romping to an undefeated 9 points. For England, it was a question of so near and yet so far, as a 5-1 from the last heat would have given them a draw, but unfortunately, from their point of view, the race ended in a share of the points. An 8-point tally put Jack Parker on top of the English score-chart, while a single point behind, Arthur Atkinson lent great support. As far as the tourists were concerned, the match was marred by injuries to Alec Statham and Geoff Pymar, which forced them to both miss the fifth Test a week later.

In front of a record audience of 38,000, the homesters made no mistake in the final match, winning comfortably by 35 points to 18 for an overall series victory of 3-2. Inevitably, it was Bluey Wilkinson who led them to success with his twelfth maximum (11 full, 1 paid) in Down Under Tests. England's cause wasn't helped by the fact that they could only track five riders due to the injuries suffered by Alec Statham and Geoff Pymar in the previous match – indeed, things were so bad that Jack Parker had to ride without a partner! In spite of this, Parker battled on gamely to lead England's scoring on the 7-point mark, with Arthur Atkinson also netting an identical total. Needless to say, Bluey Wilkinson was the leading scorer in the series with 44 points from a possible 45, while Jack Parker and Arthur Atkinson shared top spot for England on 28. It is impossible to conclude the review without harking back to the incredible Wilkinson, who at the conclusion of the series had remained undefeated in 10 successive Australian Test matches, dropping just one point along the way to partner Bill Longley. Spanning a nine-year period, he had also taken his career total to an amazing 540 points for the Aussies in 61 matches against England.

RESULTS

First Test	Australia 22 England 32
Second Test	Australia 32 England 22
Third Test	Australia 23 England 31
Fourth Test	Australia 28 England 24
Fifth Test	Australia 35 England 18
Series Result	Australia 3 England 2

1939

The 1939 home Test series began at New Cross on 7 June, with England producing a fine display to defeat the Australians by 62 points to 46. Victory was inspired by a brilliant 18-point full-house from Arthur Atkinson, with Bill Kitchen (15) and Jack Parker (11) also making telling contributions. For Australia, Vic Duggan (15) and Ron Johnson (12) were the main scorers in a side that featured several below-par contributions. The Australians put up a much better showing at Wimbledon in the second Test on 26 June, however, with the English boys having to strain every sinew in order to eke out a 55-53 success and move into a 2-0 lead overall. The tourists could have forced a draw had they gained a last heat 5-1, but a 4-2 was all they could muster. Bill Kitchen (14), Jack Parker (10) and Eric Langton (10) were the main men for the home nation, with Lionel Van Praag (17) and Vic Duggan (16) leading the way for the battling Aussies.

The third Test was hosted by Harringay on 15 July, and in what turned out to be their only success of the series, Australia triumphed 58-48. Powerhouse performances from Ron Johnson (16), Lionel Van Praag (14) and Vic Duggan (12) took them to victory, while the defeated English were kept in the hunt by spirited efforts from Arthur Atkinson (12) and Bill Kitchen (10).

England then gained further wins at Belle Vue (65-42) and Wembley (71-36) to wrap up overall victory by four matches to one. The meeting at Belle Vue saw Bill Kitchen head England's score-chart with a paid maximum (16+2 points), while Jack Parker (15) and Arthur Atkinson (10) provided great backing. With a dozen points, the Aussies' best man was the speedy Vic Duggan, while Lionel Van Praag chipped in with a tally of 8. At Wembley, England boasted some very impressive scoring, with Bill Kitchen again recording a paid maximum (15+3), while Eric Langton (14), Jack Parker (11), Arthur Atkinson (11), plus Malcolm Craven (11) all netted big returns. Meanwhile, for the second match running, Vic Duggan headed the way for Australia, with Lionel Van Praag also joining him on the 11-point mark.

Man of the series for the victorious home country was Bill Kitchen with 70 points, while Jack Parker (55), Arthur Atkinson (51) and Eric Langton (46) all recorded significant totals. For the disappointed Australians, Vic Duggan (66) and Lionel Van Praag (58) performed best, despite lacking consistent top-end support throughout.

The England versus Australia Test match programme from Belle Vue on 12 August 1939.

TEST MATCHES

RESULTS
First Test	England 62 Australia 46
Second Test	England 55 Australia 53
Third Test	England 48 Australia 58
Fourth Test	England 65 Australia 42
Fifth Test	England 71 Australia 36
Series Result	England 4 Australia 1

As with the previous year, England took on the Dominions on Second Division circuits, the series being cut back from seven matches to five. Interestingly, having represented the Dominions in 1938, Tiger Hart was part of the England squad in 1939. This turned out to be a much more competitive contest, but it was still the Dominions who emerged victorious by a 3-2 score-line. The first match at Hackney Wick resulted in a 40-66 reverse, but England quickly levelled things up with a comfortable 64-41 success at Newcastle.

The Dominions then won the third Test by 63 points to 44 at Bristol, with both Eric Chitty and Eric Collins thundering to 18-point maximums. The home nation again came back to grab a 59-49 victory at Norwich; however, hopes of an overall English triumph soon disappeared in the final match at Sheffield as the Dominions sprinted to a 65-42 win. Top man in the series for England was Jim Baylais with 34 points, while the victorious Dominions squad was headed by George Pepper (61), Eric Chitty (60) and Ernie Evans (46).

RESULTS
First Test	England 40 Dominions 66
Second Test	England 64 Dominions 41
Third Test	England 44 Dominions 63
Fourth Test	England 59 Dominions 49
Fifth Test	England 42 Dominions 65
Series Result	Dominions 3 England 2

Two matches were also staged between Scotland and England, both held north of the border, with the first at Glasgow's White City Stadium on 12 August. An 11-point tally was sufficient for George Greenwood to head the scoring for the home country as they collected a 45-38 success, with George Pepper in pole position on the England score-chart, having amassed the same total. The second meeting took place ten days later at Marine Gardens, Edinburgh, and it was the Scottish side who again took victory by 51 points to 32. Oliver Hart and Cecil 'Gruff' Garland recorded 11 points apiece for the victors, while Ernie Evans raced to a 12-point maximum for the defeated England team. The team line-ups seemed to be rather strange for these matches, as the homesters didn't track a single Scot. Aside from Australian Gruff Garland, the remainder of their representatives were English, namely George Greenwood, Harold Jackson, Oliver Hart, Will Lowther, Jack Hyland, Bob Wells, Leo Lungo and Jack Chapman. Meanwhile, the English side included Australians Reg Hay and Syd Littlewood!

RESULTS

First Test   Scotland 45 England 38
Second Test   Scotland 51 England 32

Series Result   Scotland 2 England 0

One further international was staged prior to the outbreak of war, when England faced a combined USA/Canada side at Southampton on 16 August. The meeting ended all-square at 54-54, with the home nation's leading scorers being Frank Goulden (14), Jack Parker (11) and Arthur Atkinson (10). With honours even, the American/Canadian team was best represented by Cordy Milne (17), Wilbur Lamoreaux (12) and Eric Chitty (11).

RESULT

First Test   England 54 USA/Canada 54

Series Result   England 0 USA/Canada 0

TOP SCORERS

ENGLAND V. AUSTRALIA 1930-39

ENGLAND	TESTS	POINTS	AUSTRALIA	TESTS	POINTS
1. Eric Langton	34	338	1. Bluey Wilkinson	38	359
2. Jack Parker	33	257	2. Max Grosskreutz	38	327
3. Bill Kitchen	23	227	3. Vic Huxley	34	285
4. Ginger Lees	19	197	4. Lionel Van Praag	38	270
5. Frank Charles	21	179	5. Ron Johnson	44	269
6. Tom Farndon	20	138	6. Dicky Case	32	254
7. Frank Varey	16	120	7. Frank Arthur	15	92
8. Joe Abbott	17	119	8. Vic Duggan	6	66

TEST MATCHES

9. Arthur Atkinson	11	116	9. Billy Lamont	12	58
10. Tommy Croombs	20	96	10. Eric Collins	11	43

AUSTRALIA V. ENGLAND 1934-39

AUSTRALIA	TESTS	POINTS	ENGLAND	TESTS	POINTS
1. Bluey Wilkinson	23	181	1. Jack Parker	15	82
2. Clem Mitchell	20	106	2. Tiger Stevenson	14	65
3. Max Grosskreutz	10	94	3. Arthur Atkinson	16	63
4. Vic Huxley	11	81	4. Wal Phillips	13	57
5. Lionel Van Praag	13	73	5. Cliff Parkinson	17	$47\frac{1}{2}$
6. Wally Little	10	51	6. Les Wotton	10	44

ENGLAND V. AUSTRALIA 1930-39 (IN BOTH COUNTRIES COMBINED)

ENGLAND	TESTS	POINTS	AUSTRALIA	TESTS	POINTS
1. Eric Langton	39	364	1. Bluey Wilkinson	61	540
2. Jack Parker	48	339	2. Max Grosskreutz	48	421
3. Bill Kitchen	27	249	3. Vic Huxley	45	366
4. Ginger Lees	19	197	4. Lionel Van Praag	51	343
5. Frank Charles	21	179	5. Dicky Case	39	279
=5. Arthur Atkinson	27	179	6. Ron Johnson	48	276
7. Joe Abbott	26	162	7. Clem Mitchell	26	137
8. Tiger Stevenson	26	$151\frac{1}{2}$	8. Frank Arthur	15	92
9. Tom Farndon	20	138	9. Vic Duggan	13	85
10. Frank Varey	20	128	10. Billy Lamont	15	59

6
STAR CHAMPIONSHIP AND WORLD FINALS

1929

1929 saw the introduction of a competition sponsored by *The Star*, a popular London evening newspaper of the time. This is widely regarded as the forerunner of the World Championship, with the event being run on a match race basis. A total of twenty riders associated with ten of the Southern League teams were selected for the Star Riders' Trophy, with the two Birmingham tracks at Perry Barr and Hall Green omitted, presumably on the basis of geographical location. In that initial year there were two contests, one for home riders and one for the overseas boys, the reason for this being because in those far off times, it was considered that the raw British racers would be no match for the more experienced Australian and American aces. The match races were run on a home and away knock-out basis, with each leg decided over three races.

It is worth recalling the names of those original track legends, with the British lads being Ivor Creek (West Ham), Tommy Croombs (Lea Bridge), Buster Frogley (Wembley), Roger Frogley (Crystal Palace), Jimmy Hayes (Southampton), Jim Kempster (Wimbledon), Gus Kuhn (Stamford Bridge), Jack Parker (Coventry), Eric Spencer (Harringay) and Colin Watson (White City, London). The teams shown in brackets relate to each rider's league club, although Tommy Croombs, Roger Frogley and Jack Parker didn't actually make any official appearances for the tracks they were associated with.

Meanwhile, Australia were represented by crack riders Frank Arthur (Harringay), Stan Catlett (Wembley), Alf Chick (Coventry), Billy Galloway (Southampton), Max Grosskreutz (Lea Bridge), Vic Huxley (Wimbledon), Ron Johnson (Crystal Palace) and Billy Lamont (White City, London), with but two Americans competing in Sprouts Elder (West Ham) and Art Pechar (Stamford Bridge).

As touched upon in the section on league racing, riders of international repute weren't initially permitted to appear in domestic racing, therefore the teams shown in brackets relate to the track with whom each was associated. There were a couple

Australian Frank Arthur – Overseas Star Champion in 1929.

of exceptions though, for Alf Chick did actually ride in the league for Wembley prior to joining Coventry, while Stan Catlett also appeared for Wembley in the Southern League.

After beating Gus Kuhn in the first round, Roger Frogley went on to defeat Ivor Creek and Jack Parker, thus becoming the first Star Home Riders' Championship winner, while the overseas title went to Frank Arthur following victories over Max Grosskreutz, Billy Lamont and Vic Huxley.

RESULTS

HOME RIDERS

ROUND ONE
Buster Frogley bt Jim Kempster
Ivor Creek bt Tommy Croombs
Jack Parker bt Jimmy Hayes
Colin Watson bt Eric Spencer
Roger Frogley bt Gus Kuhn

ROUND TWO
Roger Frogley bt Ivor Creek
Colin Watson bt Buster Frogley
Jack Parker bye

SEMI-FINAL
Jack Parker bt Colin Watson
Roger Frogley bye

FINAL
Roger Frogley bt Jack Parker

OVERSEAS RIDERS

ROUND ONE
Sprouts Elder bt Billy Galloway
Billy Lamont bt Art Pechar
Vic Huxley bt Ron Johnson
Frank Arthur bt Max Grosskreutz
Stan Catlett *v.* Alf Chick not raced

SEMI-FINAL
Vic Huxley bt Sprouts Elder
Frank Arthur bt Billy Lamont

FINAL
Frank Arthur bt Vic Huxley

Speedy Australian Vic Huxley, winner of the Star Championship in 1930.

1930

In 1930, when all speedsters contested the one championship, an excellent twelve-rider field was in place for the final at Wembley on 12 September. The qualifiers were selected on the basis of being the highest point scorers from the first 15 Southern League matches per track, and the superb line-up read thus: Frank Arthur (Stamford Bridge), Squib Burton (Leicester), Tom Farndon (Coventry), Roger Frogley (Crystal Palace), Vic Huxley (Harringay), Syd Jackson (Leicester), Jim Kempster (Wimbledon), Jack Ormston (Wembley), Triss Sharp (Crystal Palace), Tiger Stevenson (West Ham), Harry Taft (Hall Green) and Colin Watson (Wembley).

Sadly, just prior to the event, in a match race with Lea Bridge skipper Jimmy Stevens, the Crystal Palace captain Triss Sharp broke his leg in a nasty spill. He was sidelined for the remainder of the season and his chance of Star glory had gone. Sharp's place was subsequently filled by Geoff Taylor of Southampton, who had previously ridden for Halifax. After making his way through to the final, the flying Australian Vic Huxley duly sealed success, speeding to victory by two races to nil over his compatriot Frank Arthur.

RESULTS
Heat 1: Arthur, Taylor, Stevenson (fell)
Heat 2: Taft, Frogley (fell), Jackson (fell)
Heat 3: Huxley, Watson, Kempster
Heat 4: Ormston, Burton (ret), Farndon (ret)
Semi-final: Arthur, Taylor, Taft
Semi-final: Huxley, Ormston, Watson
Final (1st leg): Huxley, Arthur
Final (2nd leg): Huxley, Arthur

1931

A further change in 1931 saw the introduction of an eliminating round at each track, prior to the grand finale at Wembley Stadium on 18 September. The field was increased to twenty for the final, with sole American contestant Ray Tauser eventually coming out on top from Vic Huxley and England's Tommy Croombs. Twenty assorted riders from England, Australia and the USA contested the final, namely Les Patrick and Syd Jackson from Coventry, Harry Shepherd and Ron Johnson of Crystal Palace, Syd Edmonds and Phil Bishop representing High Beech, Charlie Spinks and Harold Hastings of Lea Bridge, the Nottingham duo of Fred Strecker and Nobby Kendrick, Southampton's Ernie Rickman and Jack Parker, Stamford Bridge twosome Frank Arthur and Arthur Warwick, the Wembley pair of Col Stewart and Colin Watson, West Ham's Tommy Croombs and Bluey Wilkinson, plus Vic Huxley and Ray Tauser of West Ham. Both Squib Burton (Lea Bridge) and Billy Ellmore (Nottingham) had actually qualified for the big event, only for injury to unfortunately rule them out. No fewer than thirteen of the finalists were making their debut, but amazingly it was the little-fancied American who emerged to take the title ahead of his club team-mate Vic Huxley.

RESULTS
Heat 1: Watson, Tauser, Shepherd, Bishop
Heat 2: Parker, Rickman, Jackson, Stewart
Heat 3: Warwick, Edmonds (fell), Hastings (fell), Wilkinson (ret)
Heat 4: Croombs, Huxley, Kendrick, Strecker
Heat 5: Arthur, Spinks, Patrick, Johnson
Semi-final: Huxley, Rickman, Watson
Semi-final: Tauser, Arthur
Semi-final: Parker, Croombs
Final: Tauser, Huxley, Croombs, Parker (ex)

To confuse matters a little, also in 1931, members of the Association of Motor-Cycle Track Racing Promoters' declared Vic Huxley to be the world's best, due to his phenomenal performances throughout the previous season. Needless to say, not everyone was of the same opinion, and it was eventually decided that Huxley should meet Colin Watson over two legs in a match race series, and the winner would be considered the world's undisputed Champion. Huxley went on to record a 2-0 victory in the first leg at West Ham, before Watson gained revenge with a 2-0 success of his own in the second leg at Stamford Bridge. That necessitated a decider, which was held at Wembley, and resulted in a 2-0 win for Huxley. The competition caught the imagination of the public – so much so that the promoters of the time organized a series of match races in a knock-out style, under a World Championship banner.

The competition was run on a regional basis, with Eric Langton defeating Ginger Lees in the northern final, while Jack Parker beat Tommy Croombs in the south. The two section winners then faced each other for the right to challenge Vic Huxley, and it was Parker who conclusively won both legs 2-0. The so-called World Championship Match Race Contest followed, and although it went to three legs after the first had been drawn, Parker was a comfortable winner overall. Although Parker was duly declared World Champion, the ACU refused to give their approval of the title as Huxley had not held an official title in the first place!

American Ray Tauser, who took victory in the 1931 Star Championship.

The Star Championship programme from 1932.

1932

With the governing Association of Motor-Cycle Track Racing Promoters folding and the National Speedway Association taking over, the renamed Star National Championship was run in 1932, with the top northern-based riders further enhancing the competition. A total of eighteen contestants took part in the event at Wembley on 22 September, namely the Belle Vue duo of Eric Langton and Frank Varey, brothers Norman and Jack Parker representing Clapton, Roy Dook and Syd Jackson of Coventry, the Crystal Palace pairing of Ron Johnson and Tom Farndon, Plymouth's Bert Spencer and Bill Clibbett, Stamford Bridge twosome Frank Arthur and Wal Phillips, Wembley's Gordon Byers and Ginger Lees, West Ham's Les Wotton and Tommy Croombs, plus the Wimbledon pair Vic Huxley and Dicky Case. Three other contestants should have graced the big event, but unluckily missed out through injury, these being Joe Francis (Crystal Palace), Eric Collins (Plymouth) and Bluey Wilkinson (West Ham). It was no real surprise when the meeting resulted in a popular victory for Eric Langton, with Aussie Vic Huxley claiming second place ahead of his fallen compatriot Dicky Case.

RESULTS
Heat 1: Byers, Dook, Arthur
Heat 2: Case, N. Parker (ret), Johnson (fell)
Heat 3: Langton, Wotton, Jackson (ret)
Heat 4: Huxley, Spencer, Phillips
Heat 5: J. Parker, Varey, Croombs
Heat 6: Lees, Farndon, Clibbett
Semi-final: Case, Langton, J. Parker
Semi-final: Huxley, Byers, Lees (fell)
Final: Langton, Huxley, Case (fell)

1933

Further alterations in 1933 saw twenty riders line up at Wembley for what was considered by many as one of the most thrilling meetings ever seen at the great venue. The Star line-up was packed with class and featured Eric Langton and Frank Varey from Belle Vue, Norman Parker and Phil Bishop of Clapton, the Coventry pair Stan Greatrex and Dicky Case, Crystal Palace twosome Tom Farndon and Ron Johnson, Nottingham's Jack Chapman and Les Wotton, the Plymouth pairing of Frank Goulden and Jack Sharp, Sheffield's Eric Blain and Chun Moore, Wembley duo Colin Watson and Harry Whitfield, West Ham's Tommy Croombs and Bluey Wilkinson, plus Vic Huxley and Syd Jackson representing Wimbledon. An appre-

The Star Championship programme from 1933.

ciative audience duly watched spellbound as the talented Tom Farndon gave a scintillating display to triumph, with fellow Crystal Palace ace Ron Johnson grabbing second place ahead of Bluey Wilkinson.

RESULTS
Heat 1: Wotton, Case, Huxley, Croombs
Heat 2: Farndon, Moore, Varey, Parker
Heat 3: Blain, Whitfield, Bishop, Sharp
Heat 4: Wilkinson, Langton, Chapman, Greatrex
Heat 5: Johnson, Jackson, Goulden, Watson
Semi-final: Farndon, Wotton, Whitfield
Semi-final: Wilkinson, Jackson
Semi-final: Johnson, Bishop, Moore
Final: Farndon, Johnson, Wilkinson

1934

The 1934 Star Championship was staged at Wembley on 23 August, and once again a tremendous field was assembled for the prestigious event, comprising Eric Langton and Bob Harrison (Belle Vue), Les Wotton and Jack Chapman (Hall Green), Jack Parker and Frank Arthur (Harringay), Ron Johnson and George Newton (New Cross), Jack Sharp and Mick Murphy (Plymouth), Dicky Case and Dusty Haigh (Walthamstow), Ginger Lees and Colin Watson (Wembley), Tommy Croombs and Bluey Wilkinson (West Ham), plus Claude Rye and Syd Jackson (Wimbledon). Sadly as had happened in 1932, Joe Francis of New Cross had qualified for the event, only for injury to prevent his participation. Having only run a third place in his opening ride, Jack Parker recovered well to take victory in his semi-final, prior to racing to glory from Eric Langton and Ginger Lees in the final.

RESULTS
Heat 1: Langton, Johnson, Parker, Sharp
Heat 2: Jackson, Wilkinson, Arthur, Watson
Heat 3: Lees, Case, Rye, Wotton
Heat 4: Newton, Haigh, Harrison
Heat 5: Croombs, Chapman, Murphy
Semi-final: Langton, Jackson, Case
Semi-final: Lees, Johnson, Newton
Semi-final: Parker, Croombs, Harrison
Final: Parker, Langton, Lees

The programme as used for the Star Championship at Wembley in 1934.

1935

The 1935 Star Championship was run on completely different lines, with qualifying rounds and a Wembley final taking place in a similar format to what would be utilized for the first official World Championship the following year. Twenty-three top riders competed in the preliminary round, each participating in four meetings, with the highest sixteen scorers progressing to Wembley for the big meeting on 29 August. A 51-point tally was sufficient for West Ham's Bluey Wilkinson to lead the way, with the other qualifiers being Tom Farndon of New Cross (48 points), Jack Parker (Harringay, 47), Dicky Case (Hackney Wick, 45), Max Grosskreutz (Belle Vue, 45), Ron Johnson (New Cross, 43), Bill Kitchen (Belle Vue, 36), Vic Huxley (Wimbledon, 35), Tommy Croombs (West Ham, 32), Frank Charles (Wembley, 31), Wally Kilmister (Wembley, 30), Eric Langton (Belle Vue, 28), Tiger Stevenson (West Ham, 28), Jack Ormston (Harringay, 25), Jack Sharp (Wimbledon, 25) and Lionel Van Praag (Wembley, 24).

Unfortunately, the night before the final, tragedy struck at New Cross, when Tom Farndon and Ron Johnson were involved in a terrible track crash in the second-half

1935 Star Champion Frank Charles.

scratch race final. Geoff Pymar and Norman Parker stepped in to replace the injured riders, but with Farndon in a critical condition, the accident cast a huge black shadow over the prestigious event.

The meeting soon developed into a battle between Frank Charles, Jack Ormston and Max Grosskreutz, each of whom thundered to victory in their first three rides. The crunch came in heat fourteen, when Grosskreutz jumped ahead from the gate, with Charles in close attendance behind. The Australian, who was affectionately known as 'Grasshopper', held the lead until the third lap, when he over-cooked a bend and fell. That allowed Charles to charge on and win from Ormston, while Grosskreutz remounted to claim a point. With four wins under his belt, Charles was in charge of the meeting and he subsequently completed a brilliant maximum with a win over Eric Langton in heat seventeen.

The Wembley man was the happy recipient of £100 and a Silver Star at the conclusion of the meeting, while Ormston collected the runner-up prize of £50 and a Bronze Star after taking his tally to 14 points with a heat twenty victory. Meanwhile, the unlucky Grosskreutz ended up a point behind Ormston in third place, having bounced back with a win in his final ride. There was great sadness the day following the Wembley showdown though, when Tom Farndon died at the Miller General Hospital in Greenwich, having failed to regain consciousness. The news on Ron Johnson was better, however, for he escaped without serious injury, although he was badly bruised and had severe arm lacerations.

RESULTS

		POINTS				TOTAL
Frank Charles	3	3	3	3	3	15
Jack Ormston	3	3	3	2	3	14
Max Grosskreutz	3	3	3	1	3	13
Eric Langton	0	3	2	3	2	10
Bluey Wilkinson	2	2	3	1	2	10
Jack Parker	2	2	0	3	3	10
Vix Huxley	3	1	1	2	2	9
Dicky Case	1	2	2	3	R	8
Tommy Croombs	2	1	2	1	1	7
Norman Parker	2	1	1	2	0	6
Bill Kitchen	1	2	1	R	R	4
Tiger Stevenson	0	0	2	1	1	4
Geoff Pymar	1	1	0	0	1	3
Lionel Van Praag	1	0	2	0	0	3
Jack Sharp	0	0	1	0	R	1
Wally Kilmister	F	-	-	-	-	0

1936

History was made on 10 September, 1936, when the first World Speedway Championship Final was staged at Wembley Stadium. There were sixteen finalists, and the field included representatives from Australia, USA and Denmark; however, with nine participants, host nation England had the most entries.

The qualifying rounds of the tournament were of a varied international flavour, with an initial entry of sixty-three riders from not only the previously mentioned nations, but also from Sweden, Canada, New Zealand, Germany, Spain, France and South Africa. The top twenty-eight riders from the qualifying rounds went on to partake in the championship round, which subsequently took place on the seven National League circuits. It was quite an arduous schedule as each competitor then faced a further four meetings, with the top sixteen riders going on to Wembley for the final itself.

A complicated bonus point system was operated and this was best described by the late Ron Hoare, former secretary and treasurer of the Veteran Speedway Riders' Association, thus: 'Bonus points were calculated on a percentage performance basis. Each rider's percentage of possible points was calculated over the first two sets of qualifying rounds, and the percentage was then divided by seven. The reason for this being that there were a total of seven meetings in the championship round, thus the bonus points represented an award on overall performance. For example, top qualifier Eric Langton accumulated 66 points over his qualifying rounds, which gave him 91.7 per cent of the total points possible. This figure was then divided by seven, meaning that the Belle Vue rider therefore went to Wembley with a bonus of 13.'

One major disappointment was the fact that Belle Vue's Max Grosskreutz, who had been almost unbeatable, was prevented from participating in the qualifying rounds by injury. As mentioned, Eric Langton headed the qualifiers with 66 points, with the other leading scorers being Frank Charles (Wembley, 59 points), George Newton (New Cross, 59), Jack Parker (Harringay, 59), Lionel Van Praag (Wembley, 58), Morian Hansen (Hackney Wick, 48), Bob Harrison (Belle Vue, 48), Vic Huxley (Wimbledon, 48), Bluey Wilkinson (West Ham, 48), Dicky Case (Hackney Wick, 47), Jack Ormston (Harringay, 47), Jack Milne (New Cross, 45), Cordy Milne (Hackney Wick, 43), Ginger Lees (Wembley, 37), Wal Phillips (Wimbledon, 37) and Joe Abbott (Belle Vue, 36). Unfortunately, in the event, both Jack Parker and Joe Abbott were ruled out by injury. First reserve Arthur Atkinson of West Ham replaced Parker on the big night, whilst Abbott's replacement was New Cross favourite Ron Johnson, however, in the event, he too suffered injury and was replaced in turn by Harringay's Bill Pitcher.

Each rider carried the all-important bonus points forward to the final thus: 13 Langton; 12 Charles, Newton and Van Praag; 10 Hansen, Harrison, Huxley and Wilkinson; 9 Case, Ormston and the Milne brothers; 7 Lees and Phillips; 6 Atkinson and Pitcher. In addition to these, the meeting reserves Norman Parker and Balzer Hansen carried 6 and 5 points forward respectively. It was the bonus points that were

Australian Lional Van Praag, the sport's first World Champion.

to cause much controversy, especially where Bluey Wilkinson was concerned. The flame-haired Australian rode unbeaten for a 15-point maximum, but was not crowned Champion since he had accumulated fewer bonus points than overall winner and fellow Australian Lionel Van Praag.

Some 65,000 fans turned up to watch the final, from which the winner received £500 in cash plus a World Trophy replica. £250 went to the runner-up and the ACU Gold Medal, while the third placed man received £100 and the ACU Silver Medal, and the fourth placed rider got £50 and the ACU Bronze Medal. When one compares the value of money in those days to the present, it is fair to say that all three men on the rostrum were richly rewarded.

The World Final itself produced some fine racing, and it needed a run-off to establish the winner on the night. Having tied on 26 points apiece (including bonus), Lionel Van Praag, mounted on an Excelsior JAP, met Englishman Eric Langton in the run-off, with Langton breaking the tapes at the first time of asking. When the two contestants finally got away at the second time of asking, it was the Englishman made the start to lead, only for Van Praag to sweep past near the finishing line, and take victory by less than the length of a bike.

It was the American Cordy Milne who caught the eye and was definitely one of the best of the foreign contingent, scoring 11 points to take the fourth position. The Hackney Wick representative was in great form, but blew his chances when only finishing third in heat thirteen, a race won by Bluey Wilkinson. After his success in the previous years Star Championship, Frank Charles had been expected to do well, but it just didn't pan out that way. After winning his opening couple of races with ease, including the establishing of a new track record in heat one, Charles ran a last when up against Van Praag, Danish ace Morian Hansen and Arthur Atkinson in heat nine. A second place behind Langton followed in heat eleven, before Charles disappointingly ended the night with another last place in heat seventeen.

There was no doubt that the man of the evening was Wilkinson, who raced to as fine a maximum as one is ever likely to see, mounted incidentally, on board a machine loaned to him by Max Grosskreutz. Outstanding wins for Bluey in heats thirteen and fourteen saw him beat both the title protagonists, however, only when he had completed his maximum in heat seventeen, was it was realised he was just one point short of the overall totals of Van Praag and Langton. That unfortunately meant he would only finish in third place, but the sporting Aussie reacted brilliantly, shrugging his shoulders and accepting the fact he was the victim of cruel luck.

Perhaps the biggest disappointment for the fans was the fact that Vic Huxley failed to win a heat. Vic scored 7 points, but was just a shadow of the rider who had done so well in the early Star Championships. Sadly, this World Final was to be the only time Vic would make it to the big night. For Wal Phillips, Bill Pitcher, Dicky Case and Bob Harrison, it would also prove to be their only World Final appearance, although Harrison did qualify in 1937, but didn't ride through injury.

Bill Pitcher set an unenviable record, when he was excluded by ACU Steward J. O'Neill for a tapes offence, thus becoming the first rider to suffer this fate in a World Final. This occurred in heat twelve, with Norman Parker taking his place in the re-run. It was interesting to note that when the meeting was covered in the *Speedway News*, the correspondent commented that it had been against the rules to bring in a reserve after a rider had been excluded for tape breaking! Looking back at this some sixty-seven years later, it is also particularly odd that Pitcher should have been excluded and yet Langton was permitted to take part in the title run-off, having fouled the tapes at the first attempt!

Van Praag, as a result of his success, went into the speedway history books as the initial winner, with Wilkinson becoming the only rider in history to win every race on the night and not take the World crown.

RESULTS

	POINTS					TOTAL	BP	TOTAL
Lionel Van Praag	3	3	3	2	3	14	12	26
Eric Langton	3	3	3	2	2	13	13	26
Bluey Wilkinson	3	3	3	3	3	15	10	25
Cordy Milne	2	2	1	3	3	11	9	20
Frank Charles	3	3	0	2	0	8	12	20
Dicky Case	2	0	3	1	2	8	9	17
Jack Ormston	1	1	2	3	1	8	9	17
Vic Huxley	1	2	0	2	2	7	10	17
George Newton	F	0	3	1	0	4	12	16
Jack Milne	1	2	1	0	2	6	9	15
Bob Harrison	0	0	2	0	3	5	10	15
Morian Hansen	2	1	2	F	0	5	10	15
Wal Phillips	1	1	0	2	1	5	7	12
Ginger Lees	2	0	1	0	1	4	7	11
Arthur Atkinson	0	2	1	0	0	3	6	9
Bill Pitcher	0	1	T	X	1	2	6	8
Norman Parker (res)	1	-	-	-	-	1	6	7
Balzer Hansen (res)	-	-	-	-	-	-	5	5

1937

The 1937 World Final, held at Wembley Stadium on 2 September, was a triumph for America, with their riders dominating the event and finishing in the first three positions. Jack Milne was the winner, riding to a fine 15-point maximum and, happily, with enough bonus points to ensure he took the title. Meanwhile, Wilbur Lamoreaux was runner-up, and Cordy Milne, brother of the new Champion, took third position.

Prior to the big meeting, qualifying rounds had been held, although there were considerably less participants than the previous year. Each rider contested two meetings in a preliminary round, with the highest twenty-eight scorers going forward to the championship round, where they then had to record as many points as possible from a further four meetings apiece. The tallies from the preliminary and championship rounds were then added together, with the sixteen qualifiers being Jack Milne (New Cross, 83 points), Eric Langton (Belle Vue, 78), Wilbur Lamoreaux (Wimbledon, 74), Cordy Milne (Hackney Wick, 71), Eric Chitty (West Ham, 70), Lionel Van Praag (Wembley, 70), Jack Parker (Harringay, 69), George Newton (New Cross, 67), Frank Charles (Wembley, 64), Ginger Lees (Wembley, 61), Frank Varey (Belle Vue, 51), Joe Abbott (Belle Vue, 49), Arthur Atkinson (West Ham, 49),

Morian Hansen (Hackney Wick, 45), Bob Harrison (Belle Vue, 45) and Bill Kitchen (Belle Vue, 45). Unfortunately, injuries prevented Bob Harrison from taking part, and he was replaced by West Ham's Tommy Croombs, who had gleaned 39 points from the qualifying rounds. The controversial bonus point system remained in place, meaning that Jack Milne had a head start on his rivals with 13 points on the board, while nearest challengers Eric Langton and Wilbur Lamoreaux began with 12 each. One slight amendment, which was of little significance, meant that the reserve riders did not carry bonus points forward to the final.

Sadly, from the West Ham fans' point of view in particular, unlucky Australian Bluey Wilkinson, who had ridden unbeaten in the 1936 World Final, was not on parade, having suffered a broken wrist which prevented him from taking part in the qualifying rounds. Although riding on his home circuit, defending Champion Lionel Van Praag had a poor meeting. After winning his first race, Lionel suffered from mechanical gremlins in his second outing and was subsequently replaced by reserve Alec Statham of Harringay in his third programmed ride. Returning to normal form, Van Praag took victory in his fourth ride, but unfortunately in the final race of the evening, he trailed in last behind Frank Charles, Jack Parker and Frank Varey.

American ace Jack Milne, who was crowned World Champion in 1937.

A huge crowd of some 85,000 people gathered to watch Jack Milne's triumph, and on board his super quick Excelsior JAP, he did not let them down. He had enjoyed a fantastic season for New Cross and was undoubtedly the best rider on the night. He was never in trouble, winning all his races with ease, starting with a convincing triumph over Joe Abbott in the opening race. Jack then beat Morian Hansen in heat five, before seeing off the challenge of brother Cordy in heat nine. In his third outing (heat eleven), the man on a mission nullified the threat of fellow countryman Wilbur Lamoreaux, while Bill Kitchen brilliantly squeezed into second place ahead of 'Lammy'. It was this heat when Jack should also have met Lionel Van Praag, but the Australian had pulled out due to the aforementioned machinery problems. The race format was obviously different at the time, for the super-charged American had completed four rides and the meeting was only at heat eleven! Jack had a long wait until his final ride in heat seventeen, but he remained focussed to make sure of his place in the record books with a good win from ever-pressing New Cross team-mate George Newton.

England's best rider was Jack Parker, who finished in fourth position with 10 points (plus 11 bonus), but even he had no answer to the outstanding American trio. One Englishman who had been expected to do well was the aforesaid Georgie Newton, the pint-sized rider with the spectacular leg-trailing style. Indeed, he started well, securing a tremendous win over Cordy Milne in heat two, only to then suffer three successive falls, prior to following Jack Milne home in that title deciding heat seventeen.

Ginger Lees was another man riding on his home circuit and although he didn't trouble the leading lights, he was involved in one of the best races of the night, when he fought a wheel-to-wheel duel with Bill Kitchen in heat eighteen, just coming through to take victory on the line. On the other hand, major disappointments on the night were the form Danish ace Morian Hansen, who scored just 8 points, and 1936 runner-up Eric Langton, whose efforts yielded only 4 points. Both riders did manage one win apiece, however, with Hansen defeating Bill Kitchen in heat twelve, while Langton saw off the challenge of Jack Parker in heat fourteen.

All in all, the meeting was a grand event, with some top-class racing enjoyed by the huge Wembley audience. By comparison to the first World Final, this was a quieter affair though, with ACU Steward Alfred Pickering not having to make any difficult decisions.

RESULTS

	POINTS					TOTAL	BP	TOTAL
Jack Milne	3	3	3	3	3	15	13	28
Wilbur Lamoreaux	3	3	3	1	3	13	12	25
Cordy Milne	2	3	2	3	2	12	11	23
Jack Parker	2	3	1	2	2	10	11	21
Ginger Lees	1	1	2	2	3	9	10	19
Frank Charles	0	0	1	3	3	7	10	17

Lionel Van Praag	3	R	3	0	–	6	11	17
Bill Kitchen	1	2	2	2	2	9	7	16
George Newton	3	F	F	F	2	5	11	16
Eric Langton	1	R	0	3	0	4	12	16
Morian Hansen	1	2	3	1	1	8	7	15
Eric Chitty	0	2	0	1	1	4	11	15
Joe Abbott	2	1	1	2	0	6	8	14
Arthur Atkinson	2	0	2	1	1	6	8	14
Frank Varey	0	1	1	0	1	3	8	11
Tommy Croombs	0	2	0	0	0	2	0	2
Alec Statham (res)	0	–	–	–	–	0	0	0
Ron Johnson (res)	–	–	–	–	–	–	–	–

1938

The 1938 World Championship Final, staged at Wembley Stadium on 1 September, was the occasion when it was said, and quite correctly too, that justice was done, as it was West Ham's Bluey Wilkinson who captured the major title. Wilkinson had scored an unbeaten 15-point maximum in the first World Final of 1936, but didn't take the crown due to insufficient bonus points, and in the 1937 event, he was sidelined with a wrist injury. Finally, even though he was carrying a shoulder injury, the small Australian performed brilliantly on his Grosskreutz JAP machine, collecting the title that had eluded him in the previous two seasons.

The Championship had seen the qualifying rounds extended to include Second Division riders, with the initial phase featuring fifty-six competitors. Only six riders went through from that stage to join the First Division aces in another round, which was subsequently whittled down to the top twenty-eight scorers, who then took part in the championship round. Ultimately, the best sixteen went forward to the World Final itself, led by the aforementioned Wilkinson, who netted 53 points. Meanwhile, the other star names who also made it through to the final were Wilbur Lamoreaux (Wimbledon, 52 points), Cordy Milne (Bristol, 50), Jack Milne (New Cross, 49), Lionel Van Praag (Wembley, 47), Bill Kitchen (Belle Vue, 40), Eric Langton (Belle Vue, 37), Alec Statham (Harringay, 37), Benny Kaufman (Wimbledon, 35), Geoff Pymar (Wimbledon, 35), Arthur Atkinson (West Ham, 34), George Newton (New Cross, 34), Jack Parker (Harringay, 31), Tommy Croombs (West Ham, 29), Frank Varey (Belle Vue, 29) and Tommy Price (Wembley, 27).

The unpopular bonus point system was still in place, however; so that there wouldn't be quite as much disparity as before, these were calculated on the championship round only. That, therefore gave Bluey Wilkinson an 8-point start, whereas Wilbur Lamoreaux, Lionel Van Praag and the Milne brothers had 7 points each.

Arthur 'Bluey' Wilkinson, a brilliant Australian rider who lifted the World Championship in 1938.

It was mighty unfortunate, but no less than three of the finalists went into the meeting carrying injuries or illness. Bluey Wilkinson, the man who would ultimately triumph, picked up the previously mentioned shoulder injury the very night before the big meeting, while racing at New Cross. Such was the state of his shoulder that Wilkinson spent a good deal of World Final day actually undergoing treatment at Tottenham Hotspur Football Club. This undoubtedly helped his condition, but even so, when he arrived at Wembley, the diminutive Australian was still far from being 100 per cent fit. The other two riders with problems on the day were 1936 World Champion Lionel Van Praag, who was carrying a leg injury, and Jack Milne, who had a bad dose of 'flu.

A crowd of close on 93,000 witnessed ACU Steward (and former Stamford Bridge rider) Alan Day release the tapes on the opening heat and Van Praag showed that, despite his injury, he was still a force to be reckoned with, as he sped home from Jack Parker. Then, Jack Milne ignored his problems to take a good win from compatriot Benny Kaufman in heat three. Fellow American Wilbur Lamoreaux had also thrown his hat into the ring, with a stirring victory in the second race ahead of Alec Statham and Cordy Milne. So, the pressure was already on, when Wilkinson appeared for two rides on the trot in heats four and five. Despite the obvious discomfort from his injury, Bluey won them both in brilliant style. His heat five success was particularly important, as he had shown a clean pair of heels to both Van Praag and Lamoreaux.

Jack Milne won heat eight to keep the pressure on the Australian, but Lamoreaux did Wilkinson a huge favour when he subsequently beat the reigning World Champion in the tenth heat. Jack Milne hit straight back, however, with a victory over Eric Langton in heat eleven, before Bluey held off the challenge of Arthur Atkinson to take heat twelve. Wilkinson increased his grip on the proceedings with a fine win from Kaufman in heat fourteen, before Lamoreaux kept an outside chance alive by taking the very next race. 'Lammy', however, must have long since realised that his dropping of two points to Wilkinson in the fifth heat was going to cost him dear. In a similar vein, Van Praag must have regretted his failure to improve on a third position in the eleventh heat, won of course by Jack Milne.

While the top boys were battling for glory, Bill Kitchen was proving to be the best of the British contingent, but whilst he was quietly picking up points, he wasn't winning any races. Back to the title chase, and Van Praag let everyone know he was still interested in the outcome, when he won heat seventeen, ahead of meeting reserve Jack Ormston, who was taking one of Frank Varey's rides. Harringay rider Ormston, had already replaced Varey in the previous race, when he took a splendid victory from Tommy Price. It is interesting to note that Price, who was making his World Final debut, would go on and take the British Riders' Championship in 1946, and the World title itself in 1949.

It was crunch time in the penultimate heat, when Jack Milne and Bluey Wilkinson met, with Cordy Milne and Jack Parker also in the showdown. Some race it proved to be too, as Jack Milne went away from the gate like a rocket, closely followed by his brother. Wilkinson, who must have been going through the pain threshold by that stage, somehow managed to get ahead of Cordy, but seemed content to just sit behind Jack Milne, knowing that a second place would ensure he took the coveted title. Cordy Milne rode a hard race, worrying Wilkinson all the time, but the West Ham ace held him out and when he crossed the finishing line, the stadium simply erupted. The reaction of the crowd was no surprise, since Bluey was one of the most popular riders ever to grace British speedway.

A final look at the score-chart showed that both Bluey Wilkinson and Jack Milne had finished level on 14 points, but the World Championship belonged to the gritty Australian by virtue of the single bonus point advantage he had going into the meeting. Nevertheless, no one denied Wilkinson his crown, he was in great form on the night and his success must surely have made up in some small way for the disappointment suffered in 1936.

RESULTS

	POINTS					TOTAL	BP	TOTAL
Bluey Wilkinson	3	3	3	3	2	14	8	22
Jack Milne	3	3	2	3	3	14	7	21
Wilbur Lamoreaux	3	1	3	3	3	13	7	20
Lionel Van Praag	3	2	2	1	3	11	7	18
Bill Kitchen	2	2	1	2	2	9	6	15
Cordy Milne	1	3	3	0	1	8	7	15
Alec Statham	2	3	0	0	3	8	5	13
Eric Langton	1	2	2	3	0	8	5	13
Benny Kaufman	2	1	0	2	2	7	5	12
Jack Parker	2	2	2	0	0	6	4	10
Arthur Atkinson	1	0	2	1	1	5	5	10
Tommy Price	1	0	1	2	0	4	4	8
Tommy Croombs	0	1	1	1	1	4	4	8
George Newton	0	1	0	1	0	2	5	7
Geoff Pymar	0	0	1	0	1	2	5	7
Jack Ormston (res)	3	2	-	-	-	5	0	5
Frank Varey	0	0	0	-	-	0	4	4
Jimmy Gibb (res)	-	-	-	-	-	-	-	-

1939

The 1939 World Speedway Championship, which should have been raced for at Wembley Stadium on 7 September, became the final that never was. All the qualifying meetings to establish the final sixteen contestants had taken place, the riders were known, and the bonus points were allocated. However, just four days before the final was due to be held, there was the declaration of the Second World War and the event was cancelled.

Qualifying had been run along the same lines as the previous year, with the 16 finalists emerging from the twenty-eight competitors in the championship round. With 53 points from his 4 meetings, Southampton's great American ace Cordy Milne headed the scoring and received 8 bonus points. Meanwhile, the other fifteen speedsters who had done enough to qualify were: Eric Langton (Belle Vue, 51 points), Wilbur Lamoreaux (Wimbledon, 50), Bill Kitchen (Belle Vue, 47), Vic Duggan (Wimbledon, 45), Lionel Van Praag (Wembley, 44), Arthur Atkinson (West Ham, 40), Jack Milne (New Cross, 40), Alec Statham (Harringay, 36), Jack Parker (Harringay, 34), Benny Kaufman (Southampton, 33), Eric Chitty (West Ham, 32), Ron Johnson (New Cross, 32), Frank Varey (Belle Vue, 31), Eric Collins (Wimbledon, 30) and Aub Lawson (Wembley, 30). The next two in line qualified as the meeting reserves, namely Malcolm Craven (Wembley, 26) and Frank Goulden (Southampton, 24).

So, aside from Cordy Milne, the bonus points carried forward showed Langton, Lamoreaux and Kitchen with 7 apiece, while Duggan, Van Praag, Atkinson and Jack Milne each had 6. On the 5-point mark were Statham, Parker, Kaufman, Chitty and Johnson, with remainder of the 16 finalists having 4 points each, namely Varey, Collins and Lawson.

As ever, speedway patrons were really looking forward to the event, but like other sports which attracted vast crowds, the cinder-shifting game suffered as the Government of the day were concerned about the possibility of air raids from the enemy, which could have resulted in heavy casualties.

The occasion, if it had been raced, could well have given Britain a first World Champion, since a popular choice for the title was Arthur Atkinson, who had been in tremendous form in the National League with West Ham. Reigning Champion Bluey Wilkinson had retired in order to manage Sheffield, so the real favourite was Cordy Milne, who would have started with a bonus point advantage over his rivals and was confident of improving on the third place he had taken in 1937. Following the success of Bluey Wilkinson in 1938, the Australians confidently expected great things from Wembley starlet Aub Lawson and the up-and-coming Wimbledon rider Vic Duggan. As previously mentioned, Malcolm Craven was one of the reserves for the 1939 final, but unfortunately, like everyone else, he didn't get to ride and sadly, this turned out to be the only time he actually qualified for speedway's night of nights. On the other hand though, it would have been Aub Lawson's first final, and he would still be qualifying and performing in World Finals, right up until 1960.

7
THE RIDERS

A lack of sufficient space prohibits details on every rider who appeared during the early days of the sport in Britain, but the following is a glossary of the greats who undoubtedly left an indelible mark on the history of speedway racing, along with a number of other particular crowd favourites and real characters.

Joe Abbott was a very gallant rider, who suffered a great many broken bones through track accidents and thus acquired the nickname of 'Iron Man'. Born in Burnley on 12 April 1902, he first appeared for his hometown track in 1929, before joining Preston that same year. Joe then spent a further two seasons at Preston, prior to linking with Belle Vue in 1932. He was to remain with the Aces until the outbreak of war, although injuries forced him to sit out the domestic campaign in 1938, following a crash in the fifth Test match at Sydney early in the year. After the end of hostilities, he returned to the sport with Harringay in 1947, before moving to Odsal later in the year. Joe then remained with the West Yorkshire side until 1950, when he was tragically killed in a crash at the stadium on 1 July. He represented England in six home series versus Australia (1930-31, 1934-36 and 1939), plus two tours Down Under (1934/35 and 1937/38). On top of that, Joe raced for his country against USA (1937), and the Overseas (1937). He also qualified for two World Finals (1936 and 1937), although unluckily he missed the first through injury.

Tommy Allott started out as a member of the Barnsley outfit in the 1929 English Dirt-track League, and remained at the ill-fated venue until they resigned from the Northern League the following year. Tommy then spent 1931 at Sheffield, and could still be identified with the South Yorkshire side at the start of 1932, prior to joining West Ham later in the season. Two full years with the London club followed, before he returned north to ride for Belle Vue in 1935. For the 1936 campaign, Tommy started out at Belle Vue, but later appeared for both Bristol and Nottingham in the Provincial League. He stayed with Nottingham throughout 1937, and then rejoined Sheffield in 1938, prior to riding for Stoke/Belle Vue II in 1939.

On the international front, Tommy represented the Provincial League against Australia in 1937, and England versus the Dominions a year later. Tommy was quite a star of the immediate post-war years, being a tall-scorer for Sheffield from 1946-49, before starting the 1950 campaign with Edinburgh. His stay in Scotland was shortlived, however; he returned to Sheffield later in the year, before finally ending his elongated shale-shifting career with Liverpool (1951-53). On the individual front, his career highlight was appearing in the British Riders' Championship final at Wembley Stadium in 1946. During the latter part of his career, Tommy also rode for Britain in two series against the Overseas in 1950 and 1951.

Born in Lismore, New South Wales on 12 December 1907, **Frank Arthur** went on to become the sport's leading rider/promoter. He received a number of £100 appearance money cheques, and was one of the three real superstars in this country during 1928/29 – the others being Vic Huxley and Sprouts Elder. Even when aged just twenty-one, he was an astute businessman, being responsible for bringing Max Grosskreutz to England in 1929, and then fielding a team of six in 1930, including Dicky Case and Ray Tauser. Frank supplied the riders with machines and back-up in return for 50 per cent of their winnings. Dubbed 'The Wizard', he represented Stamford Bridge between 1930-32, but his riding ability declined after the closure of his tricky, narrow home circuit. He then missed a year of British racing, for after taking an English party to his homeland for the 1932/33 season, he linked up with Johnnie Hoskins on a failed mission to interest Canadians and New Yorkers in the sport.

Frank was a reliable scorer for Harringay in 1934, but nothing more, and a single appearance in 1935 convinced him that his riding days were over. Back in Australia, he promoted at the Speedway Royale track in Sydney, until being outbid for the lease in 1938. Undaunted, Frank built the famous Sports Ground track on a football field next door to the Royale! He promoted there for two years after the outbreak of war, with Cordy Milne, Lionel Van Praag, Max Grosskreutz and Vic Duggan being his star riders. During his army service, the track's lease expired and after hostilities ended, a consortium of riders took over the rights. Lionel Van Praag and Max Grosskreutz offered Frank a share of the promotion on the condition that he rode. Unsurprisingly, he was reluctant to don his racing gear again and declined the offer, but he did manage to secure a weekly racing date from the Sports Ground's trustees. He then took over the Royale arena after the army vacated it, having already re-opened the Exhibition Speedway in Brisbane. The rival promotions in Sydney fueded quite bitterly for a few years, until Frank finally secured the Sports Ground again for the 1948/49 season. Completing a brief summary of his racing career, he represented Australia against England in the Test match series of 1930-32 and 1934. Frank enjoyed quite a run in the Star Championship too, the high spot being crowned Champion in the overseas section of 1929. The following season saw him finish as overall runner-up in the revamped competition, while he also appeared in the finals of 1931, 1932 and 1934.

Arthur Atkinson originally began with Halifax in 1929, prior to joining Leeds later that same year. Aged just eighteen, he then took one of the first Rudge machines to Australia, and 'cleaned-up' everywhere, winning the Australian Two-Mile

Arthur Atkinson, a formidable English rider.

Championship and the West Australian Championship. Arthur continued this excellent form with Wembley in 1930, until the final league match, when he crashed heavily and was left unconscious. In dispute with Wembley, he missed the 1931 season, but returned to the track with West Ham in 1932. Having previously lost a brother (Dennis), following a track accident at Middlesbrough in July 1929, and mindful of his own injuries, 'Akko' seemed content to be a solid second-string for several seasons. However, he gained a taste for success when winning the prestigious Coronation Cup best pairs competition alongside Bluey Wilkinson in 1937. He was to remain with West Ham until the outbreak of the war, usually supplying good support to skipper Tiger Stevenson, who also spent many seasons with the Custom House-based outfit.

Arthur was a great experimenter with engines, and this greatly contributed to the upsurge in his form – one being a super-charged single-cylinder effort, and he later used 350cc motors when all others were mounted on normal 500cc equipment. Indeed, his 1939 machine included much use of aluminium, which made his bike 70lb lighter than the conventional machines. He was a Test match regular for England

176

against the Australians (1936-39) and appeared in all-three pre-war World Finals from 1936-38, as well as qualifying for the aborted 1939 event. From Arthur's point of view, it was certainly a great shame that the event didn't take place as he had been a popular choice to lift the title. Getting back to the international scene, he also represented his country versus the Overseas (1937) and USA/Canada (1939), as well as appearing in four Test series in Australia (1934/35, 1935/36, 1937/38 and 1938/39). Being extremely busy on the international front, Arthur also raced for the combined England/Australia side against USA/Canada in 1938.

Following the war, he managed the sport alongside Stan Greatrex at West Ham from 1946-49, prior to promoting at Rayleigh with his wife Tippy from 1950-56. Whilst running Rayleigh, Arthur returned to the saddle to ride for West Ham once again in 1951. This didn't prove to be too successful as he had been away for a long time and he ended the year with 93 points to his name from 25 league matches. In 1952, Arthur moved to Harringay for a transfer fee of £80 and fared better, scoring 176 points from 33 meetings. The following year, he again rode for the Racers, but after only attaining 43 points from 15 matches, he wisely decided to finish riding for good.

Leg-trailing Londoner **Phil Bishop** earned the nickname 'King of Crash' and first appeared on the scene at High Beech in 1930, spending two seasons of Southern League activity at the venue before a move to Southampton in 1932. He then moved with the club to Lea Bridge in mid-season, where the side completed the campaign under the banner of Clapton Saints. Phil remained with the Clapton team the following year, prior to linking with Harringay in 1934. The Green Lanes circuit was

Phil Bishop in thrilling leg-trailing action.

his home base until mid-way through the 1936 campaign, when a move to West Ham beckoned, and he was to stay with the Hammers until war broke out in 1939. As far as individual highlights go, he twice made it through to the Wembley-staged Star Championship final, in 1931 and 1933, while internationally he represented England against the Dominions in 1938. After the war, he joined New Cross in 1946, but was back with West Ham a year later, remaining at the Custom House track until 1948. Phil then spent his final two seasons of league racing with Southampton (1949-50).

After several years out of the saddle, he made a one-off appearance for Southampton in 1955, netting 3 points, and then in 1959, he rode for Belle Vue at Wimbledon, but failed to score. Amazingly, Phil once again donned his leathers at New Cross in 1963, when he defeated Ron Johnson in a series of second-half match races. In 1966, he became team manager of West Ham and was still happily engaged in the post when the Hammers undertook what turned out to be an ill-fated racing trip to Holland in 1970. Having ridden in meetings at Tilburg and Amsterdam, the tour party were on their way to Ostend for the ferry home on 14 July, when their mini-bus was involved in a road smash with two lorries and a petrol tanker, just outside the Belgian town of Lokeren. Tragically, Phil lost his life in the accident, along with four young riders, Gary Everett, Peter Bradshaw, Martyn Piddock and Malcolm Carmichael.

Eric Blain began his career in the north, racing for Liverpool (1930) and Sheffield (1930-31). He remained on board with the South Yorkshire team in 1932, prior to journeying south for a stint with Crystal Palace later in the season. Eric was back at Sheffield for 1933, but then embarked on something of a yo-yo spell, representing Lea Bridge/Walthamstow (1934), Belle Vue (1935), Liverpool (1936), Liverpool/Belle Vue (1937) and Sheffield (1938). He made his one and only appearance in the Star Championship final in 1933.

Les Blakeborough was one of the sport's pioneer riders in 1928. He had a job as minor civil servant and was later asked to resign if he wished to continue racing. His real name was Bottomley, so in order to carry on riding, he took his mother's maiden name of Blakeborough. He appeared for Stamford Bridge from 1929-31, prior to riding for Clapton in 1932, and Coventry in 1933. Les was a fearless rider, but sadly died in tragic circumstances later in 1933, after contracting diptheria.

Hoddesdon-born **Les Bowden** was another pioneer racer in 1928, whose first league appearances were made for Crystal Palace the following year. He disappeared from the scene after 1929, but returned with Wembley in 1934. Les continued to be based with the illustrious London side until a move to Plymouth mid-way through the 1936 season. Birmingham was his next port of call in 1937, prior to stints with both Leeds and Wembley Reserves in 1938 – his final year of league racing in Britain. On the international stage, Les appeared for the Provincial League versus Australia in 1937, and represented England against the Dominions in 1938.

Ted Bravery was one of the sport's original journeymen, having begun his career in open licence events at Portsmouth in 1930. From the Copnor Gardens venture, he moved on to make his league debut with Wimbledon later that year, prior to joining Stamford Bridge in 1931. Ted remained with the Pensioners the following season, but then linked with Plymouth for two years at the beginning of 1933. Regular moves followed thereafter, with the Bristol-born rider representing no fewer than seven more teams before the outbreak of war, namely West Ham (1935), Cardiff and Nottingham (1936), Hackney Wick and Nottingham (1937), Sheffield (1938) and Stoke/Belle Vue II (1939). International calls saw Ted ride for the Provincial League versus Australia (1937), as well as representing England against the Dominions (1938-39) and also Scotland (1939). Following the war, his career followed a much more settled pattern as he joined Norwich in 1946, and spent the rest of his racing days with the Stars before a compound fracture to the leg forced him to hang up his leathers in 1950.

Born on 16 January 1908, **Cyril 'Squib' Burton** was another of the pioneer boys in 1928, prior to racing for Rochdale in the English Dirt-track League of 1929. The following season was spent with Leicester (Stadium), a year which saw him billed as the English Vic Huxley. He had a stint with Lea Bridge at the start of the 1931 campaign, prior to rejoining Leicester (Stadium), but unfortunately it turned into a year to forget after he broke an arm in the second Test match at Leicester Super. Squib then joined Sheffield in 1932, but suffered another nasty knock at Wimbledon, which left him nursing a broken leg. He resumed with Sheffield the following season, but the injuries effectively finished him as a star man, and he was to see out his career with Lea Bridge/Walthamstow (1934) and Hackney Wick (1935). He reached the Star Championship final on two occasions in 1930 and 1931, although he unfortunately missed the latter event through injury. Squib also represented England in three Test series versus Australia in 1930, 1931 and 1933. After the war, he was installed as the speedway manager at Leicester in 1950.

Gordon Byers began at Newcastle (Brough Park) in 1929, and after a year of inactivity in 1930, he returned to league racing with Leeds in 1931. He subsequently joined Wembley in 1932, remaining with the famous club until his retirement at the end of 1936. Gordon reached his only Star Championship final in 1932, and also represented England against Australia from 1932-34 inclusive.

Born on 7 June 1910, **Dicky Case**, who was actually christened Ray George Arthur Case, hailed from Toowoomba in Queensland, Australia. In January 1930, when working as a waiter, he served a meal to Frank Arthur on a train in Australia. He told Frank that he fancied being a speedway rider, and six months later, thanks to Arthur, who signed him on, Dicky was riding for Australia in the first-ever Test match at Wimbledon! Prior to that, he had first appeared in league racing on these shores for Wimbledon, and showing sensational form the following year, he actually out-scored his skipper Vic Huxley, being undefeated in 18 out of 34 league matches. In all, he plied his trade at Plough Lane for three full seasons, prior to representing Coventry (1933) and Lea Bridge/Walthamstow (1934). Three years of activity followed at Hackney Wick (1935-37), before Dicky spent the 1938 campaign with Wembley. Unfortunately, he struggled with injuries and endured a mediocre season, scoring just 48 points from 13 league matches. He subsequently called it a day, but came back for one meeting in 1939, the World Championship round at Hackney Wick on 3 June; however, after just two rides he retired for good.

Next to Vic Huxley, he was probably the most consistent of the Aussies in the early years, but he never won a major trophy and was defeated by Tom Farndon in his only challenge for the British Individual Championship in 1935. Despite the lack of individual honours, he had a great record in the Star Championship, finishing third in 1932, and also reaching the subsequent finals from 1933-35, while in the World Final, he made his only appearance in the 1936 staging, recording an 8-point tally. On the Test match scene, Dicky raced for the Aussies against England in all the series of 1930-37 inclusive, and represented the Overseas side in 1937. On top of that, he raced for his country against the Provincial League in 1937. Back in his homeland, he also represented the Australians against England in two series (1934/35 and 1936/37). Under the banner of 'Dick Case's Speedway', he later ran open licence meetings at Rye House during the war and continued at the venue for several years after the cessation of hostilities, being handily placed as he was the manager of the public house right next to the circuit!

Born on 10 March 1908, **Frank Charles** first appeared in league racing at Burnley in 1929, later riding for Preston that same year. The following season saw him represent a further two teams in Northern League circles, namely White City (Manchester) and Belle Vue. In yet another move, Frank began 1931 at Leeds, but after Harringay had resigned from the Southern League part-way through the season, he saw out the rest of the campaign with their replacements Manchester, alias Belle Vue Reserves. In 1932, he moved into the main Belle Vue side and was to remain with the mighty Aces for three full seasons, before linking with Wembley in 1935 for a reputed £1,000 fee – the first four-figure speedway transfer. Frank had been a top-class rider until 1931, but faded quite badly in 1932 and 1933, although he surprised everyone by winning the Empire Cup at Wembley in the latter year. Wembley proved more to his liking though, and he won the track's three major trophies in 1935, including the Star Championship, courtesy of a 15-point maximum in what was his only appearance in the final of the prestigious event. However, it must be said that he was a tad fortunate, as he wasn't among the twenty-four riders chosen to compete in the preliminary rounds – an injury to team-mate Ginger Lees gave him a place.

He was to spend the rest of his pre-war racing days with the London club until tragically being killed in a gliding accident at Great Hucklow, Derbyshire on 15 July 1939. Frank also appeared in the first two World Finals (1936 and 1937), and had been a regular international, first representing England versus the Australians in 1930, and then every year from 1934-39 inclusive, as well as racing against both USA and

Frank Charles, who was also an excellent accordion player as well as speedway star.

the Overseas in 1937. Multi-talented Frank was an excellent accordion player too, and often entertained the crowds with his music. He also featured in an amusing incident when, with rain falling heavily at one meeting, he toured around in last position holding an umbrella over his crash helmet, with the Steward finally taking the hint and deciding to abandon the meeting!

Born in Toronto in 1909, **Eric Chitty** linked with West Ham in 1936, spending four great seasons with the Hammers prior to the outbreak of war, during which time he won the London Riders' Championship in 1938. He was shown as Eric 'Rickey' Chitty on his advertising photocards, sporting a dinner jacket on the front as a 'crooner', while publicising his motorcycle business on the back. He also sometimes 'doubled-up' as the announcer at Hackney Wick, as like all North Americans, Eric knew the value of publicity. During the hostilities, Eric was a regular competitor at Belle Vue, where he took victory in the first three British Individual Championships from 1940-42, and showing a great level of consistency, the brilliant Canadian also shared second place with Tommy Price in the 1945 contest. The following year, he rejoined West Ham and continued to give sterling service until suffering a double leg fracture in a track crash involving Dennis Parker at Brisbane in mid-February 1949. The accident happened just before he was due to leave for this country, and he was to miss much of the season, eventually returning to the West Ham side for a league match at Belle Vue on 20 August.

Back on board with the Hammers at the start of 1950, Eric was a big scorer throughout the year, and indeed the one that followed. Unfortunately, he was on the receiving end of more misfortune following the completion of the 1951 campaign, when he fell from a horse, badly breaking a leg. He was still recovering from the injuries at the start of 1952, and was advised not to ride. Sadly, that was to bring a premature end to what had been a wonderful career in the saddle. Although he qualified for two World Championship finals, Eric only ever rode in the 1937 event, with the 1939 staging having to be aborted. He did, however, qualify and ride in the three British Riders' Championship events from 1946-48, his best performance being a 10-point tally in the middle year. As far as Test matches are concerned, he appeared for the Overseas team in the series against England in 1937, and for the Dominions versus England in 1939. He also represented the combined USA/Canada side in the one-off match versus England at Southampton in 1939, and again rode for the Overseas side versus England in 1948.

Bill Clibbett began his racing days at non-league Portsmouth in 1930, later gaining Southern League experience with Harringay that same year. He began the following season with the Green Lanes outfit, before switching to Wimbledon part-way through the campaign. His career then settled as he spent the next three seasons at Plymouth (1932-34). Bill's next port of call was Hackney Wick from 1935-37, with the rider subsequently based at Bristol for the two years immediately prior to the outbreak of war. His one and only appearance in the Star Championship final occurred in 1932. On the international scene, Bill represented England in the Test series Down Under in 1934/35, and again raced for his country versus the Dominions in 1939.

Australian **Eric Collins** first appeared for Harringay in 1931, prior to joining Lea Bridge later in the season. He then spent 1932 racing for Plymouth, although his season unfortunately ended prematurely through injury. Eric did not return to league racing in this country until 1935, when he linked with Wimbledon. Although he remained with the Plough Lane club in 1936, he also assisted Bristol, proving to be quite a star in the Provincial League with 126 points from 15 matches for the Bulldogs. Eric again lined up for Wimbledon in 1937, and indeed went on to entertain at the London venue until the outbreak of the war. On the world stage, he was dogged by cruel luck as his 1932 injury kept him out of the Star Championship final, while the only time he made it through to the World Final was in 1939, when the event was cancelled! He did, however, represent his country versus England in four Test match series (1936-39), as well as racing for the Aussies against the Provincial League in 1937. On top of that, Eric also rode against England for both the Overseas in 1937, and for the Dominions in 1938 and 1939.

Malcolm Craven first appeared on the scene at Belle Vue in 1937, before also racing for Wembley, Norwich and Birmingham in that same year. His pre-war career was more settled thereafter, as he was to remain with Wembley throughout 1938-39. During 1937, he represented the Provincial League in a Test series against Australia, prior to first riding for England versus the Dominions the following year. Malcolm also rode for England in the 1939 Test match series versus the Australians, as well as qualifying for the aborted World Final at his home circuit. Following the hostilities, Malcolm joined West Ham in 1946, where he was a leading performer until retiring at the close of the 1954 season. Aside from the World Final that never was in 1939, he sadly never made it to the big night again, although he twice rode in the British Riders' Championship (1946 and 1948), his best score being 10 points on the former occasion. Internationally, he again rode for England against Australia in four home series (1947-48 and 1950-51) and two away series (1947/48 and 1951/52), while he also represented his country versus Scotland in 1952.

Tommy Croombs, born in New Malden, Surrey on 13 December 1906, was one of the pioneer riders in Britain, prior to being associated with Lea Bridge in 1929 – although he didn't make any league appearances for Leyton-based outfit. Following that, he became a loyal West Ham member, remaining at the Custom House venue from 1930 to 1939. Tommy was a frequent Test match choice for England versus the Aussies from 1931-39 inclusive, although he never really did himself full justice. He always tried to establish a winning lead early on in a race, as he found the final lap hard going due to a slight, but permanent, hand problem. Continuing with a summary of his international record, he appeared in the series versus the Overseas in 1937, also partook in one Australian Test series (1936/37), and represented England v. USA (1937), England/Australia versus USA/Canada (1938), as well as racing for England against USA/Canada (1939). Renowned as a superb 'white-liner', Tommy rode in the Star Championship final on six occasions (1929 and 1931-35), his best effort being a third place finish in 1931. Continuing on the individual theme, he later made two World Final appearances in 1937 and 1938, with 4 points being his best effort in the latter event. Tommy subsequently rejoined West Ham in 1947, when he netted 124 league points after coming out of retirement to assist his former club. He continued with the Hammers in 1948, again topping 100 league points, prior to retiring for good, and emigrating. On the international front, he represented his country for one last time in the 1948 Test series versus Australia.

Billy Dallison could reasonably be described as having an unsettled career in British speedway as he raced for no fewer than six teams between 1929 and 1934, before putting roots down for any real length of time at Harringay. Prior to that, he had started out for White City (Manchester) in the 1929 English Dirt-track League, with moves subsequently linking him with Hall Green (1930), High Beech (1931), Southampton/Clapton (1932), Clapton (1933) and Birmingham (1934). He might have started 1934 at Birmingham, but after finishing the year with Harringay, Billy was to remain based at the Green Lanes venue until the end of 1937. During his latter two seasons with the Tigers, he also 'doubled-up' with Provincial League side Southampton, and eventually joined the Hampshire outfit on a full-time basis in 1938, staying on board until the Second World War. Internationally, Billy represented the Provincial League against Australia in 1937, prior to racing for England versus the Dominions the following season.

Jack 'Broncho' Dixon – a tough competitor and always a game trier.

Jack 'Broncho' Dixon had a spell with Middlesbrough in the English Dirt-track League of 1929, but was to make no further official appearances until racing for Sheffield in 1931. Jack again lined up for the South Yorkshire team in 1932, but joined Belle Vue part-way through the season. He then remained with the glamorous Manchester club until a move to Wembley in 1934. A further change saw him link with West Ham later that year, but he was back with Wembley for 1935. Broncho then made the trip across London to Hackney Wick in 1936, only to return to West Ham later in the year. After familiarising himself with the surroundings at Custom House for the best part of three seasons, another change saw him spend the final year of regular pre-war activity back with Sheffield. That 1939 season also saw him ride for England in Test series against both the Dominions and Scotland.

As well as being a pioneer rider in 1928, **Roy Dook** was another of the sport's frequent travellers. After beginning his league career at Lea Bridge in 1929, he spent 1930 at West Ham, prior to resuming at Lea Bridge the following season. He then joined Coventry for two years, before making New Cross his home in 1934. Roy stayed with the Old Kent Road outfit until 1936, a year that also saw him help out at Provincial League Bristol. He was to ride on a full-time basis for the West Country side in 1937, remaining with the Bulldogs upon their elevation into the National League Division One in 1938, and subsequent quick return to the Second Division the following season. Roy's one and only appearance in the Star Championship final occurred in 1932.

Following the war, he joined Birmingham in 1946, racing for them in the Northern League and heading their scoring with 145 points. Roy remained with the Brummies for a further two years and then went into management, being identified with Rayleigh in 1949. He later moved on to act as technical adviser at Newcastle in 1951, and when things were tough for his team, he again donned his leathers to help out. Roy accumulated 24 points from the league matches he appeared in, but his efforts couldn't help the club from avoiding the wooden spoon in the Division Two table, or indeed from closing down after the season had ended. At international level, Roy made appearances for the Provincial League against Australia in 1937 and for England versus the Dominions two years later in 1939.

The brilliant Australian **Vic Duggan** came from the much-vaunted birthplace of the sport at West Maitland. His first British side was Hackney Wick in 1937, and he went on to race for both Bristol (1938) and Wimbledon (1939). In his homeland, he raced against England in two Test series (1936/37 and 1937/38), inbetween again racing for his country against the Provincial League in Britain. In 1938, Vic appeared for the combined England/Australia side in two matches against USA/Canada, while also racing for the Dominions against England. In 1939, as well as representing the Aussies in the Test series against England, he also qualified for the World Final that never was. In 1947, Harringay re-opened for speedway and Vic came over, along with his brother Ray and fellow Australian Frank Dolan to form the backbone of the Racers side. Vic enjoyed a brilliant season too, plundering 275 points (plus 2 bonus) from 24 league matches for an astounding 11.54 average, and recorded no less than 16 full maximums along the way! In the British Riders' Championship, he didn't drop a point in the preliminary round and though a hot favourite for the title, could only muster 8 points in the big event.

He made up for his disappointment the following year, however, when taking victory with 14 points, being beaten only by Alec Statham of Wimbledon. Still based at Harringay in 1948, he notched up another 229 points in the league, and this highscoring form continued in 1949 (326 points) and 1950 (269 points). Surprisingly, his only appearance in the World Final occurred in 1950, when he recorded a 4-point tally. The death of his brother in a track accident at the Sydney Showground earlier that year on 20 January had an obvious effect on him and at the end of the season, Vic returned home to his native land and retirement. On the international front, he accumulated many caps after the war, riding in four Test series against England in this country (1947-50), plus one on home soil (1947/48), as well as representing the Overseas side versus England in 1948.

Born in Fresno, California on 4 August 1904, one of the first real track legends was **Lloyd 'Sprouts' Elder**, a lanky American with some experience in his own country, prior to showing up in Australia in 1926. On arrival in England in 1928, he became one of the real big money riders. Appearance fees were his strong point and he seldom rode unless he received at least £100, plus his other winnings at each track. He is variously reported to have had at least five such meetings per week.

Altogether, he is alleged to have earned the best part of £50,000 during his three-year stint in this country. Sadly, things were to go wrong for him when he later invested his money in a silver mine and lost the lot. Further tragedies saw him struck by a car, prior to him committing suicide following the death of his wife in the mid-1950s. During his days in Britain, he was associated with West Ham in 1929, and also appeared in the overseas section of the Star Championship that same season. Then in 1930, he linked with Belle Vue, although he didn't actually make any appearances for the Aces, prior to racing in the Southern League with Southampton.

Mike Erskine took his first steps as a novice at Coventry in 1933, before appearing in the Reserve League with New Cross in 1934. He then took some open licence outings at Luton in 1935, also making his full league debut with New Cross later that year, and was to remain with the Old Kent Road side in 1936, while also helping out at Provincial League Bristol. Either side of a stint with Southampton in 1938, Mike had a quiet time of it, making no official appearances whatsoever! He subsequently joined Wimbledon in the post-war period and was a consistent scorer for them until 1951. His best season on track for the Dons was 1949, when he recorded 261½ points in league matches alone, and his efforts were recognized internationally when he was one of the reserves for England in the second Test match

Old Etonian Mike Erskine – a good, steady rider and a fine engineer.

versus Australia at Birmingham, although in the event he failed to get a ride. Mike didn't make a World Final proper, although he was reserve in 1950, actually taking one ride in which he failed to score. After his retirement, he concentrated on his business, being an outstanding engineer. His so-called 'Erskine Staride' became famous in speedway circles, with Freddie Williams mounted on one of the steeds when claiming victory in the World Finals of 1950 and 1953. Mike also assisted in the management of Southampton when Charlie Knott re-opened the club to Southern League racing in 1952, playing an important part in the the re-establishment of the Saints.

Middlesbrough-born **Norman 'Pansy' Evans** started out with his hometown club in 1929, but really found fame when riding for the London teams. He made no official appearances in 1930, but joined Wembley a year later and was to remain with the Empire Stadium team for three seasons. A move to Harringay followed in 1934, and although Norman started the 1935 campaign at the Green Lanes venue, he ended the season with spells at both New Cross and back at Wembley. Throughout 1936/37, Norman again appeared for New Cross, prior to another hop across the Metropolis to Wimbledon in 1938. The merry-go-round continued in 1939, when after beginning the season with the Dons, he once more moved to New Cross part-way through the campaign. After the war, Norman linked up with Newcastle in the Northern League and became a leading scorer. He stayed with them until 1949, when he moved with the whole team, lock, stock and barrel, to Ashfield (Glasgow) under the promotion of Johnnie Hoskins. Unfortunately, a badly broken leg in a track accident caused him to retire prematurely and in his only season with the Giants, he recorded 118 league points. Throughout his career, Norman was famous for two things, namely wearing a beret and his 'Pansy' nickname.

Born in Coventry in 1910, **Tom Farndon** represented his hometown track from 1929-30, before going to Crystal Palace, where he became the uncrowned king of South London. He remained at the Palace until its closure before the 1934 season, when he moved along with the whole operation to New Cross. Sadly, Tom died two days after being involved in a track crash with team-mate Ron Johnson at the 262-yard circuit in August 1935. Tom had previously won the Star Championship in 1933, as well as making it to the finals of both 1930 and 1932. He had qualified for the 1935 final, but the tragic accident happened the very day before the final and the sport lost one of its most popular riders of all-time. He also won the British Individual Championship from Vic Huxley in 1934, and successfully defended the title against Ron Johnson, Dicky Case and Max Grosskreutz (twice) prior to his fatal crash. The competition was then abandoned as a mark of respect, to be subsequently revived post-war as the Match Race Championship. Continuing his list of achievements, he took victory in the London Riders' Championship in both 1934 and 1935. Tom also appeared for England in five consecutive Test series against the Australians from 1931 to 1935 inclusive.

Double London Riders' Champion Tom Farndon – one of England's greatest.

Pioneer rider and man of Kent **Joe Francis** was born on 3 October 1906, and rode for Crystal Palace from 1929-33 inclusive, prior to representing both Plymouth and New Cross in 1934. Showing great loyalty, he was to then continue with the Old Kent Road club right the way through to the start of the hostilities. Always a popular rider, he represented England in four Test series against Australia from 1931-34. After being crowned London Riders' Champion in 1931, Joe also qualified for the Star Championship final in 1932 and 1934, but he was unfortunately ruled out on both occasions through injury.

Former TT racer **Arthur Franklyn** represented Belle Vue from 1929 to 1931, before appearing for the famous Manchester club's second side, which took over the prematurely closed Harringay's Southern League fixtures during the latter of the three years. Sadly, his career was rather shortlived due to injury and he subsequently became a pilot in the RAF. He returned to speedway as part of the company who got the go ahead to introduce the sport at Foxhall Heath Stadium, Ipswich in 1950. He was such a successful manager/promoter at the Suffolk venue that the track was allocated a junior Test match 1951, whilst still a non-league set-up. That was due, in no small way, to the outstanding crowds enjoyed at the circuit and it came as no surprise when Ipswich subsequently joined the Southern League in 1952. Arthur was to remain with the club until they were truly established, prior to going into retirement.

Roger Frogley – Home Star Champion in 1929.

Roger Frogley was another of the pioneer men of 1928, being one of the first English star riders, who later made his league debut with Crystal Palace in 1930. He remained at the Sydenham circuit until 1932, but then retired in order to pursue business in the Herts and Essex Aero Club, founded by him with his brother Buster, the former Wembley captain. Roger returned to the track to assist New Cross late in 1935, following the death of Tom Farndon. In 1936, he signed for Wembley, but didn't appear in the Lions side at all, only actually riding in scratch race events, while also training novices at High Beech. Roger twice took part in the prestigious Star Championship in 1929 and 1930, defeating Jack Parker in the final on the first occasion to win the home riders' section of the event. Roger also represented England in the 1930 Test match series against Australia.

Having first practised at California in 1934, **Lloyd 'Cowboy' Goffe** made his league bow with West Ham in 1936. He was actually christened Kenneth, but he was more often known by his middle name of Lloyd or his popular 'Cowboy' nickname. Although he began the 1937 campaign at Custom House, he was also to have some outings in the Provincial League with Leicester. Lloyd again started out at West Ham in 1938, but he was later to appear for both Harringay and Lea Bridge that same year. After something of an unsettled start to his career, there was at least some stability in 1939, when he spent the whole time with Harringay, scoring 68 points prior to the outbreak of war. Lloyd was a very active man in the post-war period, riding for Wimbledon (1946 and 1947) and Harringay (1948 and 1949), prior to switching to West Ham part-way through the 1950 campaign.

Remaining with the Custom House club, he started the 1951 campaign with the Hammers, but later joined Odsal in a £500 transfer, only for a nasty injury to curtail his season just as he was beginning to settle in at the northern circuit. He resumed in 1952 with Odsal, but after struggling to find any form, he was given special dispensation to join St Austell in the Southern League. However, despite being in a lower level of racing, Lloyd still found the going hard, actually scoring just 29 points from 8 league matches for the Gulls. He subsequently retired to concentrate on his business interests, but when Reading opened for speedway in 1968, being a local man he was often to be seen enjoying the racing in the newly-formed Second Division. As far as individual highlights go, he was a non-riding reserve in the British Riders' Championship of 1946, but rode in the 1948 event, scoring 5 points. The following year, Lloyd made his only appearance in a World Final, recording 2 points in the Wembley showpiece. Lloyd was also recognized internationally in two series, although there was a considerable time span between his appearances, representing England versus the Dominions in 1938, and then against Australia in 1948.

Frank Goulden began his career at Southampton in 1930, and remained with the Banister Court outfit until joining Plymouth part-way through 1932. He then spent a similar amount of time based at Pennycross Stadium, before moving on to West Ham during the 1934 campaign. After missing an entire year, he returned to the saddle with Harringay in 1936, later 'doubling-up' to also help out at Provincial League Southampton. The 1937 campaign proved to be an exact copy of the previous year, as Frank was again identified with both Harringay and Southampton. He made a full-time return to his old stamping-ground at Banister Court in 1938, however, and remained at the Hampshire track until the outbreak of war. He made his only appearance in the Star Championship final in 1933, while the one time he qualified for the World Final was as reserve in 1939, when the event was scrapped. On the Test match front, he represented the Provincial League against Australia (1937), and England versus both the Dominions (1938), and the combined USA/Canada side (1939). Following the war, Southampton didn't re-open until 1947, when they joined the National League Division Three. Quite naturally, they hoped to again utilize the services of Frank, but were prevented from doing so by a ruling that would not permit pre-war Division One riders from racing in the Third Division. Frank therefore became team manager of the Saints, and did very well too, leading his charges to promotion after third place finishes in both 1947 and 1948.

Stan Greatrex was actually born in St Petersburg, Russia (with the slightly different surname of Greatorex), and first came to England when his family fled the revolution in 1917. As far as dirt-track racing is concerned, he initially appeared in the Southern League with Leicester in 1931, but his stint with the side only lasted into April as the Blackbird Road operation ended up in the hands of a liquidator. Coventry stepped in to take over Leicester's remaining fixtures, with Stan also moving his home base to Brandon. He was to stay with Coventry until the end of 1933, prior to linking with New Cross, where he remained until the war. Stan raced for England in three Test matches series versus Australia (1936, 1938 and 1939), plus the one against the Overseas in 1937. He also made it to the Star Championship final just once in 1933. After the war, he managed the sport alongside Arthur Atkinson at West Ham from 1946-49.

Yorkshire-born **George Greenwood** was originally a Leeds team-man in 1929, but subsequently joined Wembley the following season. He proved to be a great rider, remaining with the mighty London side until the end of 1932. He then joined Nottingham in 1933, before a return to Wembley the folowing season. After missing a year, he was back with Wembley in 1936, a term which also saw him represent both Cardiff and Nottingham in the Provincial League. Capping a fine season back in the saddle, George took victory in the prestigious Provincial League Riders' Championship. Again, he was to have three clubs in 1937, firstly resuming with Wembley, before linking with Hackney Wick in an early season move. His stay with the Wolves lasted just five league matches, however, after which he joined Nottingham for the rest of the year, netting 104 points from 11 Provincial League fixtures. George opted to stay with Nottingham in 1938, but after they had completed their English Speedway Trophy matches, the side pulled out of the league. Leeds subsequently stepped in to take over the defunct club's fixtures, with George taking his place in the Yorkshire side and racing to a tally of 140 points. Keeping himself particularly busy, George joined Middlesbrough in 1939, and also enjoyed a spell with Edinburgh (Marine Gardens), racing in seven Union Cup matches for the Scottish side. George appeared in two Test series against the Austraslians, representing England in 1932, and the Provincial League five years later in 1937. He also rode for England against the Dominions in two series (1938 and 1939), as well as racing for Scotland versus England in 1939. After hanging up his leathers, he later maintained an interest in the sport when running a JAP agency in North London. During their time together at Wembley, George and colleague Harry Whitfield became the sport's first great exponents of team-riding. They remained close friends after quitting the game, and George died just a few weeks after Harry in 1988.

Born on 25 April 1906, the diminutive Australian **Max Grosskreutz** (or Maximillian Octavius Grosskreutz to give him his full name) hailed from Proserpine in Queensland and after lifting the Australian Championship, he first came to England in 1929, under contract to Frank Arthur. After being associated with Lea Bridge and failing to live up to his reputation that season, his league career subsequently began the following year with White City (Manchester), prior to joining Belle Vue upon their withdrawal. In 1931, Max continued with Belle Vue in the Northern League, and later took some rides for Manchester (alias Belle Vue Reserves), who had replaced Harringay in the Southern League.

In 1932, he switched back to the main Belle Vue side, but the following season he tried promoting/riding alongside Dicky Case in Germany, with financially disastrous results, before rejoining Belle Vue in June. He was then to remain with the illustrious Hyde Road side until the end of 1936, a year which saw him almost unbeatable mounted on board frames he had designed himself. Unfortunately, injury prevented his qualification for the first World Final; however, he loaned his machine to Bluey Wilkinson, who went on to score maximum points, but failed to take the crown due to the bonus point system in operation at the time. Before that, Max twice challenged for Tom Farndon's British Individual Championship crown, but lost in both 1934 and 1935. He was again crowned Australian Champion in 1935, and during his time at Belle Vue, the partnership he formed with Bill Kitchen was probably the best of the 1930s. Having completed his racing days as far as he could see it at the time, Max was installed as speedway manager of Provincial League Norwich in 1937.

Still working in the same capacity in 1938, he was later to make a return to the saddle for his country, and then with Norwich, but it was back to the other side of the fence the following year, when he assumed the role of team manager of the Norfolk outfit. He twice rode in the Star Championship final, the first occasion being the overseas section of the competition in 1929, with his other appearance resulting in a third place finish in 1935. Max raced on many occasions for his country, taking part in eight pre-war Test series versus England (1930-36 and 1938), while also riding for the Dominions against England (1938). Meanwhile, Down Under, he raced in another two series against England in 1934/35 and 1935/36.

In the post-war period, he again donned his leathers to join Odsal in June 1947, netting 75 points from a dozen league matches. Max returned to Odsal in May the following year, but after revealing good form, his riding days were prematurely ended by a bad knock after only eight league fixtures. His comeback had at least allowed him to make more international appearances for his country against England in the two series of 1947 and 1948, while in his homeland, he also raced in the series of 1947/48. During his early racing years in this country, Max was unpredictable, sometimes absolutely brilliant, with a wonderful Test record, but all the same, often disappointing. One thing was sure though – he had a unique style, which once seen was never forgotten.

Leeds-born **Herbert 'Dusty' Haigh** made his league debut for Halifax in 1929, prior to racing for a couple of other northern tracks in Belle Vue (1930) and Sheffield (1931). In something of a yo-yo start to his domestic career, he returned to Belle Vue in 1932, prior to again teaming up with Sheffield in 1933. The following year saw Dusty begin the campaign at Lea Bridge, but upon their mid-season closure, he moved with the side to Walthamstow. In 1935, what turned out to be his final career move saw him link with Hackney Wick. Sadly, on 15 May 1936, while riding in an ACU Cup match against visiting West Ham, he was to lose his life at the Waterden Road venue, after a heat fifteen track crash had left him with a fractured skull. Aside from representing England against the Australians in two home Test series (1931 and 1932), Dusty also appeared in two away series (1934/35 and 1935/36). He made his one and only appearance in the Star Championship final in 1934.

Having been born in Copenhagen on 10 January 1905, **Morian Hansen**, whose real name was actually Jens Henning Fisker Hansen, can rightly be described as speedway's original 'Great Dane'. He first appeared on these shores in an international meeting at Belle Vue in 1930, before joining West Ham the following season, and although he again represented the London team in 1933, he did not ride in the middle year. Morian then missed the 1934 season, but again returned to complete three years with Hackney Wick (1935-37). Bristol was his next home base in 1938, prior to him spending the final year of pre-war activity with Wembley. Aside from appearing in the first two World Finals (1936 and 1937), the Danish racer also represented the Overseas side in the second Test match against England at Belle Vue in 1937. When the Second World War broke out, he was enlisted in the Air Force as a Flying Officer, and his courage later saw him decorated with the George Medal and the DFC.

Bob Harrison made his debut for Belle Vue in the English Dirt-track League of 1929, remaining with the side in 1930, when he also appeared for White City (Manchester) later in the year. In 1931 he again represented two teams, firstly racing for Belle Vue, and then for Manchester (alias Belle Vue Reserves), who had stepped in to take over the Southern League fixtures of the closed down Harringay. Bob subsequently returned to the main Belle Vue team in 1932, and was well into an eighth consecutive season for the Aces when the war brought proceedings to an abrupt halt. On the individual front, Bob made it to the Star Championship final in 1934, and again qualified as reserve the following year, although as things turned out he was unable to travel to Wembley Stadium.

Bob subsequently rode in the 1936 World Final, prior to again qualifying the following year when injury unfortunately prevented his participation. He was a regular international, representing England in six Test series against Australia (1930, 1933, 1935-36 and 1938-39). Completing his Test record, aside from appearing in the 1938/39 series Down Under, Bob also rode for the combined England/Australia side versus USA/Canada in 1938. After the war, he was allocated to West Ham in June 1946, and continued to serve the Hammers until the opening league match of 1949, after which he saw out the rest of the season and his riding career back at Belle Vue

Wigan-born **Oliver Hart** soon became renowned for his leg-trailing technique, having made his Provincial League debut for Liverpool in 1936. He again lined up for the Merseysiders in 1937, and although the operation was switched from Liverpool to Belle Vue part-way through the season, Oliver remained on board for the re-titled Belle Vue Merseysiders. He reverted to the main Belle Vue side in 1938, and stayed in place for the final season of pre-war racing, a year which also saw him ride for Stoke in the Second Division, as well as appearing in the Union Cup for Edinburgh. When league racing resumed in 1946, Oliver was allocated to Wimbledon, where he became a leading scorer and one of the most thrilling riders in the sport with his spectacular leg-trailing style.

In 1947, a three-way transfer involving Messrs Longley, Hart and Wotton saw him move to Odsal, which was much nearer his home and business. Oliver qualified for both the 1947 and 1948 British Riders' Championship finals, but injury prevented his riding in the first, although he subsequently rode well in the second, scoring 9 points. He qualified as reserve for the 1949 World Final, subsequently taking three outings for a single-point return. Oliver continued to ride well for Odsal, but in July 1952, he suffered serious back injuries in a track crash at Sheffield, which sadly ended his racing days. Whilst he was still riding, he had interests in the promoting side at Wigan Speedway during 1947, along with his wife Anne, and Hughie Alker. During his racing days, Oliver made several appearances at international level, representing England against Australia in the home series of 1948 and 1949, as well as the away series of 1947/48 and 1949/50. He also raced for his country against the Dominions (1939) and Overseas (1948), while somewhat bizarrely, he rode for Scotland versus England in 1939, prior to reversing the roles and riding against the Scots in 1951!

Phil 'Tiger' Hart first appeared in open licence events at Portsmouth's Wessex Stadium in 1930. From there, he moved on to make his league bow with High Beech in 1931, prior to a series of moves between West Ham and Plymouth. Initially, he made Custom House Stadium his base in 1932, before switching to Pennycross Stadium the following season. He was back at West Ham part-way through the 1933

Phil 'Tiger' Hart was a fine rider, whose career was sadly cut short by a broken leg.

campaign, however, with exactly the same thing happening in 1934, when he started at Plymouth, only to end up back at West Ham! After missing out completely in 1935, he returned to the sport with Hackney Wick in 1936, also spending part of the season helping out at Provincial League Nottingham. Another change of track followed in 1937, when he linked with Birmingham (Hall Green) and although Phil remained with the Bulldogs in 1938, he also had a spell in the Sunday Dirt-track League with Eastbourne. One further pre-war move saw him re-join Hackney Wick for a season of Division Two racing in 1939.

On the international front, he represented the Provincial League against Australia in 1937, prior to riding for the Dominions versus England in 1938. However, a quick switch of allegiance then saw him identified in an England race-jacket against the Dominions in the last year of pre-war activity! Immediately after the hostilities, Phil lined up for Northern League Birmingham at the Alexander Sports Stadium, where he was a leading scorer throughout 1946 and 1947. The following year, he actually signed for Wimbledon, but broke a leg in the Dons' first challenge meeting and retired from active racing. He subsequently took over as team manager at Tamworth, where he remained until the club closed at the end of 1950. Later on, when Birmingham re-opened at Perry Barr Greyhound Stadium in 1971, he was identified as the Clerk of the Course.

South African **Keith Harvey** was born in Verulam, Natal and having joined Stamford Bridge in 1930, his first three seasons in British racing were spent with the London side. In 1933, he initially moved to Nottingham, but returned to the capital later in the year with West Ham. Keith was again based at Custom House Stadium in 1934, but then missed the whole of the 1935 campaign. He was back the following year, however, when linking with Cardiff in the Provincial League. Moving on again, Keith then joined Birmingham (Hall Green) in 1937, where he was to stay for two full seasons, prior to racing for both Crystal Palace and Norwich in 1939. Away from the domestic scene, internationally he represented the Dominions in the Test series versus England in 1938. Following the war, he linked with New Cross in 1946, and subsequently retired after spending two seasons with the Rangers.

Frank Hodgson arrived on the scene at Hackney Wick in 1936, and was to remain with the Waterden Road side until the outbreak of war. During his time with the London side, he also had stints assisting at Nottingham in the Provincial League (1937) and Dagenham in the Sunday Dirt-track League (1938). On the international scene, Frank represented England in both series against the Dominions of 1938 and 1939. After the war, Frank was one of the most able competitors in the Northern League and was not only a high-scorer for Middlesbrough, but an inspirational captain. He qualified for the British Riders' Championship final in 1946, and was excellent value for an 8-point tally. As one of the reserves, he again made it through to the prestigious event in 1948, only to unfortunately finish the meeting without a point to his name. In 1949, when the Middlesbrough promotion moved everything up to Newcastle, Frank was quick to settle at Brough Park, recording 307 points in the league for the re-titled Magpies. In 1950, after starting the campaign with Newcastle, he was transferred to Glasgow (White City), where he remained until his retirement at the end of 1952. Always popular and well-liked, Frank was one of the sport's most respected riders.

Walter 'Wally' Hull first arrived on the scene in the English Dirt-track League with White City (Manchester) in 1929, and he remained with the club the following year, prior to linking with Belle Vue upon their withdrawal from the Northern League in mid-season. He stayed with the Hyde Road outfit in 1931, but transferred to Wimbledon a year later. Another change occurred in 1933, when he spent a season in South Yorkshire representing Sheffield. A further move then saw Wally link with Lea Bridge in 1934, with him subsequently becoming a Walthamstow rider when the Leyton track closed down in mid-season. After returning to Belle Vue in 1935, he provided the Aces with five years of great service leading up to the outbreak of war. In 1939, he also appeared in two Second Division matches for Belle Vue Reserves, who had taken over the fixtures of Stoke upon the Staffordshire track's closure part-way through the season. On the international front, Wally made just two appearances for England against Australia in 1930. After the war, Wally resumed in the Belle Vue side in 1947, remaining with the Aces until his retirement at the close of the 1948 campaign.

Vic Huxley was born in Brisbane on 23 September 1906, and it didn't take him long to set the British tracks on fire upon his arrival in 1928. He was a regular in the Star Championship final, appearing six times between 1929-35, with 1934 being the only year he missed out. Having finished as runner-up to fellow countryman Frank Arthur in the overseas section of 1929, Vic bounced back to emerge as Champion in 1930, before again having to settle for second position in both 1931 and 1932. He actually won thirteen major trophies in 1930, including his victory in the Star Championship, plus the Track Championships of five London circuits. In fact, so brilliant was he that he was appointed World Champion at the start of the 1931 season. As it was the promoters' decision, the ACU withheld official recognition of the title, although they did allow the competition to be billed as 'World' throughout the year, prior to making their ruling! Going back to the actual contest, Vic defeated his first challenger Colin Watson, but then lost to Jack Parker, who had won through the preliminary rounds. He again took victory in the renamed British Individual Championship when beating Tiger Stevenson in 1934, prior to losing to Tom Farndon later in the same year.

His league career was based entirely in London, initially with Harringay (1930-31), prior to a six-season stint with Wimbledon (1931-36). He was a regular Test match rider, captaining Australia in 26 of his 34 Test appearances in England from 1930-36, including the first-ever match in 1930. Vic also appeared in three series Down Under (1935/36, 1936/37 and 1938/39), and took part in the first World Championship final at Wembley Stadium in 1936, netting a 7-point tally. Prior to that he won the

London Riders' Championship at New Cross on 20 May, but having carried an injury throughout the year, he rode in some pain, so decided to retire after the 1936/37 Australian season. As mentioned in his Test record, he did ride again in one further Down Under series against England, and much later reappeared briefly for fun at the Exhibition Speedway, Brisbane on 17 May 1947, when he failed to break the one-lap flying start record by just 0.6 seconds.

Having previously been a TT rider, **Syd Jackson** first represented Leicester (Stadium) in 1929, prior to linking with Coventry upon the track's premature closure in April 1931. He remained at Brandon the following year, before joining Wimbledon for a five-year spell (1933-37). Syd made it to the final of the Star Championship on five successive occasions from 1930-34, while also appearing for England in four Test series versus Australia from 1930-33 inclusive.

Ron Johnson (real name Johnston) was born at Duntocher, Scotland on 24 February 1907, but emigrated with his parents to Australia when he was just a child. He returned to Britain as one of the original pioneer riders in 1928, having begun racing at Claremont Speedway in Perth, Western Australia the previous year. Ron subsequently joined promoter Fred Mockford at Crystal Palace and he was the idol of their fans with his swashbuckling leg-trailing style between 1929-33 – although he didn't actually make any official appearances in his first term with the club as riders of international repute weren't initially permitted to appear in domestic racing. During those early years he qualified for the Star Championship on four occasions (1929, 1931-1933), his best finish being second place behind Tom Farndon in 1933. However, Ron did manage to win the British Individual Championship in 1933, after it had been relinquished by Eric Langton, defeating Claude Rye in one leg, with the Wimbledon rider unable to contest the second leg, having broken a leg during a Test match. He then beat off Syd Jackson's challenge to retain the title, before losing out to Tiger Stevenson. He was also to lose out in a later challenge against Tom Farndon. As well as modelling for men's trilby hats and promoting Ovaltine, Ron also doubled for John Mills in the speedway scenes for the 1933 film *Britannia of Billingsgate*.

Ron moved with the entire Crystal Palace promotion to New Cross in 1934, where he was to stay for the rest of the 1930s as the darling of the crowd. The highlights of this period were another appearance in the Star Championship final in 1934, and making it through as reserve to the first World Final in 1936. Ron's services were required to replace the injured Joe Abbott for the big night, but in the event, he unluckily suffered injury himself and was replaced in turn by Bill Pitcher. In between, Ron had again qualified to participate in the 1935 Star Championship final. However, a terrible accident in the second-half scratch race final at New Cross the night preceding the event ruled out both himself and the also qualified Tom Farndon. Sadly, Ron's team-mate at the mini 262-yard circuit never regained consciousness and died the day following the Star final.

Continuing with his individual record, Ron also qualified for the World Finals of 1937 and 1939, although he didn't ride in either as he was an unused reserve in the

Ron Johnson, a fabulous Australian rider who was actually born in Scotland.

former, while the latter was cancelled due to the war. On the international front, he represented Australia in the Test match series against England from 1930-39 inclusive, as well as riding in the series Down Under of 1937/38. In 1937, having changed to the neater and slightly faster foot-forward style of riding, Ron also raced for the Overseas side versus England, as well as appearing for Australia against the Provincial League, while in 1938, he raced for the Dominions versus England, and also represented the combined England/Australia team against USA/Canada. He was triumphant in the London Riders' Championship in both 1945 and 1946; the latter year also saw him return to New Cross for the resumption of league racing after the war. Ever-loyal to their cause, Ron was to remain with the Rangers until mid-way through 1951, when, after a loss of form, he linked with Second Division Ashfield (Glasgow). During this time, he made it through to all three stagings of the British Riders' Championship (1946-48), his best effort being runner-up to Vic Duggan in 1948, having garnered a 13-point total. He also appeared in four more Test series against England in this country (1947-50), as well as representing the Overseas side versus England in 1948.

In his latter years with the Rangers, he sustained a fractured skull in 1949, and then served a rather harsh prison sentence for a motoring offence at the end of 1950. After his stint with Ashfield in 1951, 'Johnno' then went back to Australia, but returned to England in 1955, when he had a trial with West Ham, eventually riding in just one match for the Hammers. He then disappeared from the scene again, only to suddenly reappear at Provincial League Edinburgh in 1960, where he was given the title of rider/coach. Sadly, at the age of fifty-three, his superb timing of old had diminished by then and the comeback turned into a disaster. Amazingly, he attempted another, albeit short-lived, comeback at New Cross in 1963, when he raced against Phil Bishop in a series of second-half match races. This proved a step too far as he was well-beaten by his opponent, who had also previously represented High Beech, as well as Harringay, Southampton and New Cross among others.

Many years later, after he had returned to Australia, and following an accident which left him wheelchair-bound, he died and his unmarked grave was discovered in Karrakatta Cemetery, Perth, Western Australia. Led by Bob Buckingham, several former New Cross supporters and other fans then got together and paid for a very fine stone to be placed over his grave, with a short ceremony being attended by a number of ex-riders. Ron lived his life like an old-time Hollywood star and when he was at the top of his game, earning lots of money, he lived permanently at the Dorchester Hotel in London, travelling from track to track by taxi.

At the age of twenty-seven, **Jim Kempster** (full name: Ernest Arthur David Kempster) was one of the oldest riders to take up the sport in 1928. Despite this, he became the first English rider to beat the overseas stars, when he won a Golden Helmet event from Vic Huxley and Frank Arthur at Wimbledon in August that year, and he was subsequently carried shoulder-high from the track for his achievement. In league racing, Jim enjoyed three years of fame with Wimbledon (1929-31), appearing in the Star Championship final in each of the first two seasons of the competition. Although Jim only represented England on four occasions, each time in the 1930 series versus Australia, he has the distinction of being his country's first captain in the initial Test match at Wimbledon on 30 June that year. He later rode for Clapton in 1933, and in the mid-1930s, he popped up alongside Don Durant as a coach at Luton, which was primarily run as a training track for Wembley riders. After retiring, Jim ran a haulage business, but he closed it during the Second World War in order to become a First Officer with the Air Transport Auxiliary. Sadly, on 29 June 1945, aged just forty-four, he was killed when his aircraft flew into communication wires over Rhine Gorge at Bingen in Germany.

Having been another of the pioneer riders in 1928, **Walter 'Nobby' Key** first had league spells with Wembley (1929) and Nottingham (1930-31), prior to arriving at Crystal Palace later in 1931. He then remained at the Sydenham circuit until the end of 1933, before a move to New Cross. Nobby continued to entertain the masses at the Old Kent Road until linking with Wimbledon part-way through 1937, where he was to remain until the war. He represented England in Test matches against Australia in 1932 and 1934, as well as appearing in the Down Under series of 1935/36. Despite an impressive record, he somewhat surprisingly never made it to a Star or World Final. He subsequently retired from the sport to concentrate on a large tyre business in Epsom.

Walter 'Nobby' Key – a star man at Crystal Palace, New Cross and Wimbledon among others.

New Zealander Wally Kilmister, who made his name with Wembley.

Having first ridden for the club in 1930, **Wally Kilmister** made his name at Wembley, remaining with the Lions right the way through to 1938. A change of scenery then saw the New Zealander spend the final season of pre-war racing at Banister Court with Southampton. Wally made a solitary appearance in the Star Championship final, his career highlight occurring in 1935, when he unfortunately fell in his first ride and took no further part in the meeting. Internationally, Wally was recognized in 1938, when he appeared for the Dominions against England.

After gaining experience on the grass, and in TT racing, Lancashire's **Bill Kitchen** emerged on the dirt-track scene with Belle Vue in 1933, although he had dabbled at the sport since 1929, appearing at Burnley and Preston among other tracks, as well as racing in some junior events at the Manchester venue. He was to remain with the famous Aces all the way through to the outbreak of hostilites, and subsequently appeared in many war-time events at Hyde Road – the highlight of which was his winning of the British Individual Championship in 1945, having previously finished as runner-up in both 1941 and 1943. He was a regular in the England side, representing his country against the Australians in seven successive Test series from 1933-39 inclusive, while also riding versus both the Overseas and USA (1937). On top of that, he rode in one away series against Australia (1937/38), and additionally appeared for the combined England/Australia side against USA/Canada (1938). Bill once made it through to the Star Championship final in 1935, prior to qualifying for all three World Finals from 1937-39, scoring 9 points in each of the first two, while the latter wasn't staged.

After the war, Bill moved to Wembley in 1946, where he was quickly made skipper of the famous Lions and topped the side's scoring in league matches with a total of 205 points. Bill subsequently repeated this achievement in 1947, when he raised his tally to $238\frac{1}{2}$ points in National League racing. He qualified for the final of the British Riders' Championship in both 1946 and 1947, finishing second on each occasion with 13 and 14-point tallies respectively. In 1949, Bill suffered a broken arm in a track accident and whilst recovering, he helped out Third Division Plymouth in a coaching capacity. However, after missing a considerable chunk of the season, he was back in the saddle with Wembley, later making one last appearance in the World Final and netting 9 points. Bill was to remain with Wembley until his retirement at the end of 1953. He officially remained in place as non-riding captain the following year, but still made the odd appearance when required. Skipper of the Lions from 1946 until he finally hung up his leathers, Bill was one of the old-fashioned star riders to whom team riding and captaincy really meant something. He remained active on the international scene in the post-war period, representing England in home Test series against Australia (1947) and Scotland (1951), while also appearing in away tours of Australia (1949/50), New Zealand (1952/53) and South Africa (1953/54).

Another of the early riders from 1928 was Birmingham-born **Gus Kuhn**, a former TT racer who made his name at Stamford Bridge (1929-32), where he was captain of the very first league-winning side. Upon the closure of the Stamford Bridge circuit, he subsequently spent four years with Wimbledon (1933-36), and although he started the 1937 season with the Dons, he was to end the campaign with a stint at Wembley. In 1938, he dropped down to Division Two racing with Lea Bridge, while also representing Wembley Reserves in the English Speedway Trophy, prior to retiring and running his Stockwell motor-cycle emporium. Gus rode in the home riders' section of the 1929 Star Championship final and also represented England against Australia in 1930, 1931 and 1936.

Billy 'Cyclone' Lamont was actually christened Wilfred Spencer Lamont and hailed from Newcastle in New South Wales, Australia. He was another of the pioneer men, and was initially associated with White City (London) in 1929, although he didn't make any league appearances for the side. His first league outings were taken the following year later with Wimbledon, prior to a season out of the sport in 1931. Billy then returned to Wimbledon in 1932, before linking with Clapton for 1933. A further year away followed in 1934, with the Aussie returning to the domestic scene when joining Wembley in 1935. He remained with the famous London club in 1936, while also assisting at Provincial League Plymouth. In 1937, a full year in the lower league saw him line-up at Nottingham, while additional moves also took him to Sheffield (1938) and Newcastle (1939) before the outbreak of war. Billy appeared in the overseas section of the Star Championship final in 1929, while on the international front, he represented his country against England in four Test series in this country (1930-32 and 1936), plus two in his homeland (1935/36 and 1936/37). He also raced for the Aussies against the Provincial League in 1937, and was identified sporting a Dominions race-jacket versus England the following year.

American **Wilbur Lamoreaux** didn't arrive on these shores until linking with Wimbledon in 1937, and he was to remain with the Plough Lane outfit until the outbreak of hostilities. He also qualified for the three World Finals during that time, finishing as runner-up in 1937, prior to filling third spot in 1938, while the 1939 event never took place. 'Lammy' represented both the Overseas and the USA in the 1937 Test series against England, as well as racing for the combined USA/Canada side in matches versus England/Australia (1938) and England (1939). In 1946, Wilbur took victory in the American National Championship, prior to making a return to the British scene two years later after Wembley had suffered a number of injuries to key riders. This was after a bid for Frank Hodgson had failed, with the Wembley management subsequently persuading Wilbur to come over after special dispensation had been granted for the speedy American to assist them. He quickly slipped into a heat-leader role, scoring 100 league points, with the year also seeing him race for the Overseas against England.

His efforts over the season clearly proved he was still a force to be reckoned with, so much so in fact, that when Birmingham were promoted to the First Division in 1949, their management were given permission to sign Wilbur in order to take their side up to the required strength. He responded brilliantly to score 303 league points, but his return to regular racing was to end abruptly when he retired from the British

Wilbur Lamoreaux, the great American who was runner-up in the 1937 World Championship.

scene at the end of the campaign. Individually, he raced in the final of the British Riders' Championship in 1948, scoring 6 points, while in 1949 he appeared in the World Final and ended up with a 9-point tally. 'Lammy' did suffer cruel luck in the latter meeting, however, when an engine failure robbed him of a certain victory in the twelfth heat. Had he won that race, the outcome of the World Championship could have been so very different indeed.

TT racer and Leeds-born **Eric Langton** began his dirt-track career in 1928, making his league debut for his hometown team the following season. From there he moved on to Belle Vue in 1930, remaining loyal to the Manchester outfit thereafter and was still to be seen setting the Hyde Road circuit alight when war broke out. He was considered by many, including Jack Parker, to be the best rider of the 1930s. Indeed, he took Jack's British Individual Championship from him in 1932, but relinquished it the following year, when, due to a clash of dates, he chose to ride for Belle Vue rather than defend the coveted title. Eric made it through to the Star Championship final on four successive occasions (1932-35), winning the coveted title in 1932, and finishing second in 1934. He also finished as runner-up in the 1936 World Final, as well as qualifying for the other three pre-war events. In fact, he came very close to winning the World crown in 1936, but lost to Lionel Van Praag in a run-off for the

Eric Langton, one of England's finest riders and a loyal servant to Belle Vue.

Championship. Just before Van Praag died, he disclosed that he and Eric 'arranged' the run-off, so that the leader at the first bend would be allowed to win. In the event, Eric was ahead at the first turn, only for Van Praag to sweep past near the finishing line and take the title. Eric, who for many years wouldn't talk about the meeting, confirmed this story and said that he never spoke to Van Praag again. For his part, Van Praag defended his action by saying that the arrangement was voided by Eric breaking the tapes, but still being allowed a second chance in the re-run.

Eric was a regular international as well, representing his country in all ten Test match series versus the Aussies from 1930-39 inclusive, while also appearing in the 1934/35 series Down Under. Again representing England, he took part in the 1937 series against the Overseas side, while in 1938, he also rode for the combined England/Australia team versus USA/Canada. Following the war and having announced his retirement, Eric had a change of heart and resumed racing with Belle Vue in May 1946. He did well too, notching 153 points in the National League. Due to an internal operation, Eric was again a late starter the following year, but when he returned to the saddle in June, he soon slipped back into a high-scoring groove, and again appeared for his country in the Test series versus Australia. He did, however, retire from racing for good at the end of the campaign, later being associated in an off-track capacity with both Odsal and Halifax, the latter side when they were invited to join the Third Division in 1949. Individual highlights after the cessation of hostilities saw Eric twice reach the final of the British Riders' Championship in 1946 and 1947, his best performance being 11 points in the former. First and foremost, he was very much a team man, and didn't enjoy the tensions of individual championships, although actually being very successful in them.

The career of **Oliver Langton** followed a very similar pattern to that of his brother Eric. He initially began with TT racing in 1926, prior to appearing in the pioneer dirt-track year of 1928. His team debut subsequently occurred for Leeds in the English Dirt-track League in the first season of official club competition the following year. Oliver then went to Belle Vue in 1930, remaining on board with the famous Manchester side until 1932. He completely missed both 1933 and 1934, before returning to the saddle with the Aces in 1935, where he was to remain until the war. Oliver represented his country just once, in the second Test match against Australia in 1930.

Born in New South Wales, Australia, **Aub Lawson** made his league debut in Division Two with Middlesbrough in 1939, prior to seeing out the season in the top-flight with Wembley. He qualified for that year's World Final as well, and although the event was cancelled, the amazing Aub still made it through to speedway's big night on many more occasions, right up to 1960 in fact!

He made his Test match debut for the Aussies in the 1938/39 series against England in his homeland, prior to again representing them throughout the entire 1939 series in this country, a year which also saw him race for the Dominions versus England. It would be fair to say that Aub was a star for the whole of his post-war riding career. He returned to the UK in 1947, and having linked with West Ham, he was to remain a high-scoring Hammer until 1951. Aub then remained in his native land for the whole of 1952, returning the following season to join Norwich, where he was to stay until his retirement at the end of 1960. Aub qualified as reserve for the British Riders' Championship in 1947, but failed to trouble the scorers. However, his amazing run in the World Final was just around the corner, which saw him reach the big night on nine occasions (1949-51, 1953-54 and 1957-60). Additionally, he also qualified for the major event in 1955, but was ruled out through injury. His best performance occurred in 1958, when after winning a run-off, he finished in third place behind the awesome duo of Barry Briggs and Ove Fundin.

Whenever he graced a World Final, Aub was usually regarded as a 'spoiler', but he really ought to have won the title at least once as there was no doubting he had the ability. He will be remembered in the sport for a real piece of history that saw his 'smoothing the way' through the Speedway Riders' Association to allow Ove Fundin to ride regularly in Britain from 1955 onwards. Undoubtedly, he was one of Australia's finest riders of all-time, winning numerous Test match caps in six post-war series against England in this country (1947-51 and 1953), as well as another six in his homeland (1947/48, 1949/50-1952/53 and 1958/59). Concluding a brief run-down on a truly wonderful career, Aub also represented Australasia in six series versus England (1954-56 and 1958-60), and in three Test tours of Sweden (1957-59). On top of all that, whilst riding for Norwich, he also managed to find time to have a spell as promoter at Ipswich in 1959, his side riding under the name of Foxhall Heath in the Southern Area League.

Former TT rider **Harold 'Ginger' Lees** first appeared in the English Dirt-track League for Burnley in 1929. He then spent the following two years at Liverpool and Preston respectively, before linking up with Wembley in 1932. Ginger then remained with the famous London club until retiring at the end of the 1937 campaign. He was always one of the top six riders from 1932, until a bad accident ruined his career as a superstar in 1935. Ginger was a very self-confident rider, however, despite still scoring fairly heavily in 1936 and 1937, he retired having dropped out of the higher echelons of the sport. On the individual front, he finished third in the Star Championship of 1934, having previously made his only other final appearance in 1932. Ginger also reached the World Final on two occasions (1936 and 1937) and represented England in six Test series against the Australians (1931-34 and 1936-37 inclusive), plus one series each versus both the Overseas and USA in 1937. Ginger had a good sense of fun, which showed in his small role in the speedway feature film *Money For Speed*, released in 1933.

Jeff Lloyd, the younger brother of Wally, initially learnt the business as a Wembley Cub in 1936, prior to representing the famous London side's reserve team in the English Speedway Trophy of 1938. Later that same year, he also made his Second Division debut with his hometown club Birmingham (Hall Green), but in 1939, a change of scenery saw him link with Bristol, where he proved to be both a useful scorer and popular crowd-pleaser, with his efforts recognized internationally when he was capped by England against the Dominions. After the war, Jeff joined Northen League Newcastle, where he developed into their leading rider and a big star, scoring 176 points. Being far too good for that particular sphere of racing, a move in June the following year saw him transferred to New Cross, with Ken Le Breton travelling in the opposite direction as part of the transaction.

Jeff remained with the Rangers for a little over three years, but was on the move again in July 1950, across London to Harringay. When Vic Duggan retired at the end of that season, Jeff was made captain and he remained with the Racers until retiring himself when they closed down at the end of the 1954 campaign. He qualified for the British Riders' Championship final on two occasions (1946 and 1948) and graced three World Finals (1951-53), his best performance being an 8-point tally in the latter. On the Test match front, several more caps came his way in the post-war period, as Jeff raced against Australia (1947-48 and 1952), Scotland (1952-53) and New Zealand (1953), as well as appearing for England 'C' in Sweden (1951). Following his retirement, Jeff was a hard worker on behalf of the Veteran Speedway Riders' Association.

Birmingham-born **Wally Lloyd** was another one of the sport's pioneer riders in 1928. The following year saw him have stints with both his local tracks, beginning at Hall Green; however, upon their premature closure, he switched to the Perry Barr-based outfit. He began the 1930 campaign where he had finished the previous one, but when the side resigned from the Southern League after just four meetings, he moved on to Crystal Palace. Further moves happened frequently, with Wally representing Lea Bridge (1931), Southampton/Clapton (1932) and Clapton (1933), before returning to Hall Green in 1934. He subsequently linked with Hackney Wick in 1935, before a dream move that saw him spend two seasons at Wembley. One final pre-war change of base occurred in 1938, when Wally joined Wimbledon and he was to stay with the Dons until the outbreak of war.

He made his debut for England in the fifth Test match at Sydney in the 1937/38 series, prior to again journeying Down Under in 1938/39, when he appeared in all five matches. Later in 1939, he made one further appearance for his country in the second Test against Australia at his Plough Lane base. In 1946, Wally joined Belle Vue and enjoyed a good season, netting 159 league points. His one appearance in the British Riders' Championship occurred that year, when he recorded a 5-point tally. He remained with the Manchester outfit in 1947, and once again proved to be a solid scorer with 177 points to his name. After just one more season with the Aces, however, Wally announced his retirement from racing and was later identified as speedway manager at the re-opened Walthamstow in 1949. As far as Test match appearances are concerned, he raced in two further series versus the Australians in the post-war period in 1947 and 1948.

Having been crowned American Champion in both 1934 and 1935, **Cordy Milne** made his British bow with Hackney Wick in 1936, and remained in place with the Waterden Road club the following season. In 1938, having taken over the licence of

Highly-skilled American Cordy Milne, who was favourite to win the ill-fated 1939 World Final.

Hackney Wick, First Division newcomers Bristol acquired the services of the man who rode the heaviest machine in the sport. The popular track ace subsequently joined Southampton for the 1939 campaign, a season which also saw him switch to a lighter bike. This led to him be even more successful as he topped the league averages on a huge figure of 11.29, having accumulated 191 points from 17 matches prior to the outbreak of war. Cordy qualified for all four of the pre-war World Finals, his best finish being third place in 1937, while the 1939 event never took place of course. Indeed, the Second World War probably robbed him of the sport's ultimate prize that year, for he headed the list of qualifiers for the final. On the international front, he represented both the Overseas and USA sides versus England in 1937, prior to racing for the combined USA/Canada team against England/Australia in 1938, and USA/Canada versus England in 1939. Cordy later completed a hat-trick of American titles, when he again lifted the Championship in 1947.

Fresh from winning the Australian Championship in his first season Down Under, Buffalo (New York) born **Jack Milne** invaded England in 1936, accompanied by his brother Cordy. He quickly linked up with New Cross, where he was to remain for the four seasons leading up to the war. Just a few weeks after his English debut, the American lost a thumb on the West Ham track, but quickly readjusted his starting technique to cope with the missing digit. He was to go on and qualify for the first four World Finals, the highlights being crowned as Champion in 1937, and finishing as runner-up the following year. In Test matches, Jack appeared for the Overseas and USA sides against England in 1937, as well as the combined USA/Canada team versus England/Australia in 1938. Together with Wilbur Lamoreaux, who joined them in Britain in 1937, the Milne brothers revitalized the sport, which sorely needed new faces.

As Jack Parker later wrote, 'Just before the war, English riders seemed to be eclipsed by our Yankee friends. Some of the "old gentlemen" like Eric Langton, Tommy Croombs, Frank Varey and myself, who had been hard at it since 1928, were feeling the strain. On the other hand, Jack and Cordy Milne, and Wilbur Lamoreaux, who had started riding in the early 1930s, had never had such a tough path in their own country, and were just bursting to go – and they did!' Jack headed the league averages in 1937 (11.09) and 1938 (10.96), as well as landing the London Riders' Championship in both 1937 and 1939. Reflecting on Jack Parker's comments, both Jack and Cordy had separate tours to Australia after the war, with disappointing results. Meanwhile, Wilbur Lamoreaux stayed in better shape; however, Jack Parker was back on top with a renewed appetite for racing and success, so perhaps the Americans came just at the right time to fulfil their ambitions.

George Newton was born in Aldershot on 27 January 1913, and as a teenage novice he equalled Vic Huxley's track record on his very first appearance at West Ham in 1932 – an astonishing achievement. Having joined Crystal Palace that year, he was to remain on board the following season, before linking with New Cross when the whole operation moved in 1934. Despite the whirlwind start to his career, his progress was slow as a reserve and second-string, until Tom Farndon's fatal ride in 1935. After that, Tom's ace mechanic Alf Cole took over 'Wee Georgie', transforming him into the sport's most exciting rider. He became a breathtaking broadsider and record-breaker, who added thousands to the crowds wherever he rode. George was at the top from 1936 until late 1938, when he began to tire and tuberculosis was diagnosed. That seemingly brought the curtain down on his career, but amazingly, he was to return to the saddle some ten years later.

As well as racing in the final of the Star Championship in 1934, he also made it through to three successive World Finals from 1936-38. George was chosen to represent England in two Test series versus the Australians in 1936 and 1938, as well as riding for his country versus the Overseas in 1937. With his on-going health problems, it was indeed a wonder that George was able to ride at all, but in 1948, minus a lung and with no left-side ribs, he made a comeback with his former club New Cross. Sadly, no sooner had he restarted than he was in hospital again for an abdominal complaint, described by the medics as very rare. Showing great determination, George returned to the track the following year at Second Division Fleetwood, where he showed all his old spectacular leg-trailing form to accumulate 327 league points.

In 1950, he returned to London and joined Walthamstow, where he found the points harder to come by and could only muster a total of 107, although that didn't stop him being recognized internationally when he appeared for Britain against the Overseas side. He again moved north in 1951, joining Liverpool, but he was seldom able to display his best form. Although George began the next year with the Chads, he was soon on the move to Southern League side St Austell. There, he enjoyed life and the Cornish climate, settling down to score 109 points as only he could, with his exciting leg-trailing style. George retired for good at the end of that season, but took over the role as team manager of the Gulls in 1953.

Born on 30 October 1909, **Jack Ormston**, whose real name was John, quickly rose to fame after joining Wembley in 1929, becoming the first London Riders' Champion at Crystal Palace the following year. He remained with the famous London side until 1932, before completely missing the 1933 campaign through being involved in Johnnie Hoskins' aborted tour of the USA and Canada. Returning to regular league racing, Jack spent 1934 with Hall Green (Birmingham), prior to linking with Harringay, where he was to stay for four seasons (1935-38). He twice rode in the Star Championship final, first appearing in 1930, although an undoubted career high spot was finishing as runner-up to Frank Charles in 1935. Jack also made two appearances in the World Final (1936 and 1938), as well as representing England in six Test series versus the Australians (1930-32 and 1935-37 inclusive) and the one and only series against the Overseas (1937). He also toured Australia with England in the two Test series of 1936/37 and 1937/38. Jack retired early and turned to horse racing, which was his first love, becoming a very successful owner/trainer. Like several other riders, he was also an enthusiastic aviator and competed in the famous King's Cup air race.

SPEEDWAY – THE PRE-WAR YEARS

Jack Ormston, who now enjoys his retirement in Darlington, Co. Durham.

The legendary Jack Parker, thought by many to be one of England's very best riders of all time.

Jack Parker was one of the earliest stars and an automatic choice for England. Having begun in the sport in 1928, he first raced in league competition for Coventry in 1930, prior to riding for Southampton (1931), Southampton/Clapton (1932), Clapton (1933) and Harringay (1934-39). Jack won the so-called World Championship by defeating holder Vic Huxley in 1931, but the ACU subsequently refused to recognize the 'World' title, and renamed the competition as the British Individual Championship. However, Jack always said he was the World Champion, and had an inscribed cup to prove it! He really was the outstanding rider in 1931, but injury forced him to retire from the British Individual Championship the following season, with Eric Langton taking over as holder. Jack, of course, was to go on and become synonymous with the prestigious title in the early post-war period, when it was again renamed as the British Match Race Championship. He made five appearances in the Star Championship final (1929, 1931-32 and 1934-35) winning it in 1934, as well as finishing as runner-up in the home section of 1929. Jack qualified for the first four World Finals (1936-39), although he was forced to miss the first through injury, while the latter never took place because of the war. He also represented England versus Australia from 1930-33 and 1935-39, as well as racing for his country against both the Overseas and USA in 1937. Still on the international front, he travelled to Australia for three series (1936/37, 1937/38 and 1938/39), as well as riding for the combined England/Australia side versus USA/Canada in 1938, and England versus USA/Canada in 1939. On top of all his other accolades, he also topped the entire league averages on two occasions, in 1933 and 1936.

In the post-war years, Jack was a Belle Vue rider (1946-54), and for some time he was England's best. Indeed, the British Match Race Championship became known as 'Parker's Pension' as he was so dominant in the event. After defeating Bill Kitchen in June 1946, Jack was a regular holder of the title until 1951, beating off a further 20 challengers and only losing out on three occasions to Vic Duggan (July 1947), Aub Lawson (August 1950) and Split Waterman (August 1951). He also appeared in the three stagings of the British Riders' Championship (1946-48), and having finished third in 1946, he was a worthy Champion the following year after defeating Bill Kitchen in a title run-off. Jack also rode in three further World Finals (1949-51), the highlight being a runner-up finish to Tommy Price in 1949. He was reported as considering an offer from Swindon in 1954, although nothing came of it. Nobody was quite sure whether the story was true or just some publicity generated by his brother Norman, who was the Swindon team manager at the time. After a career spanning twenty-seven years, he retired at the closure of the 1954 season and will always be remembered as one of this country's greatest ever riders. After the war, Jack made many more appearances for England, riding in five home Test series against Australia (1947-51), as well as another five Down Under (1947/48, 1949/50-1952/53). Concluding a brief look at what was a glittering career, he also represented his country against the Overseas (1948) and Scotland (1951-53).

Norman Parker, brother of Jack and a fine rider, known in particular for his wonderful team-riding.

Lancashire-born Tommy Price, a sound rider who represented several northern sides with distinction.

Norman Parker originally rode for Coventry (1929-30), but later represented Southampton (1931), Southampton/Clapton (1932), Clapton (1933) and Harringay (1934-36). Injury kept him out of the saddle throughout 1937, before he returned to the Harringay side for the two seasons leading up to the war. Norman made it to the Star Championship finals of 1932, 1933 and 1935, while also appearing as reserve in the 1936 World Final. He also gained several England caps, racing for his country against the Aussies in both 1935 and 1939, as well as completing two series Down Under in 1936/37 and 1938/39. Often overshadowed by his brother, Norman was nevertheless a brilliant team-rider and skipper of Wimbledon, a side he joined in 1946, and rode for until his retirement in 1953. He also represented his country in many more Test series against Australia (1947-52), Overseas (1948) and Scotland (1951), as well as one further tour Down Under to face the Aussies in 1947/48. Norman appeared in all three British Riders' Championship finals (1946-48), his best showing being 10 points in the first. He also rode in the World Finals of 1949 and 1951, with the highlight again being a 10-point tally in the former and fourth place overall.

In 1953, Wimbledon won the National Trophy, beating Wembley in the final and it was Norman's finest hour. He was far from fully fit at the time, and despite being very tired, he came out to ride the race of his life and keep the ever-pressing Trevor Redmond at bay to ensure victory for the Dons. It was terrific stuff, but some hours later, he collapsed and was told by doctors to quit racing. In 1954, Bert Hearse stepped in to offer Norman the speedway managership of Swindon, which he was pleased to accept and he was to stay until the end of April 1955, when pressure of business caused him to relinquish the post. When the British League was formed in 1965, Norman was persuaded to return to Swindon, where he built up a side that went on to win the British League title in 1967. Only after the Championship was safely in the hands of the Wiltshire side did he retire from speedway to concentrate on running his pub in Towcester. During his racing days, few riders were as good as Norman when it came to team-riding, as he had the supreme ability to slow down a race to his pace and bring his partner through.

Pioneer man **Wal Phillips** was born in Tottenham on 17 October 1908 and, like Gus Kuhn, also found fame at Stamford Bridge (1929-32). He was enjoying an excellent 1931 season, actually outscoring his illustrious team captain Frank Arthur, until crashing in the second Test match at Leicester Super. He returned the following year, which turned out to be his best-ever in the sport, as he became the leading scorer in the newly-formed National League. Wal subsequently linked with Wimbledon in 1933, when a further injury took him out of the top-flight, although he was to remain with the Plough Lane side until 1936. His career highlights included an appearance in the Star Championship final of 1932, riding in the first World Championship final of 1936, and representing England against Australia from 1930-34 and 1936 inclusive. Aside from that, Wal also travelled with the English tourists to Australia for three series (1934/35, 1935/36 and 1936/37). During his racing days, he rode the first machine with a JAP engine, which incorporated many of his own ideas.

Lancashire-born **Tommy Price** first rode for Liverpool in 1929, and gained quite a reputation prior to linking with Preston later that year. He subsequently appeared at both Liverpool and Preston in 1930, and Leicester Super in 1931, before having two years away from the sport. He then returned with Hall Green (Birmingham) in 1934, prior to taking another year out in 1935. Again returning to the saddle, he appeared in the Provincial League with Liverpool in 1936, while also 'doubling-up' at National League level with Belle Vue. He continued with the Stanley Stadium outfit on a full-time basis the following year, but upon their mid-season move up to Manchester, he was to represent the renamed Belle Vue Merseysiders for the rest of the campaign. In what turned out to be his final year in the saddle, he made just two appearances for the main Belle Vue side in the National League Division One. Meanwhile, on the international front, he represented the Provincial League in two international matches against Australia in 1937. Tommy had quite a speedway family, with brothers Ernie and Norman also enjoying careers in the sport. Ernie rode for Liverpool (1936); Liverpool/Belle Vue II and Belle Vue I (1937); Belle Vue (1938); Belle Vue and Belle Vue Reserves (1939) and Odsal (1946-50), whereas Norman appeared solely for Odsal (1947-50).

The other rider called **Tommy Price** was born in Cambridge in 1911, and started riding later than his namesake, first appearing on a grass-track circuit in St Ives. He then applied, and was given trials at Greenford, prior to riding at the grass-cum-speedway circuit at Barnet. This was to open the door and Frank Arthur then arranged for Tommy to have a trial at Harringay in 1934, where he rode on the cinders in a junior event. He unfortunately took a fall and was thanked for his efforts, subsequently returning to grass-track racing. In 1935, a track at Luton was being run primarily as a schooling centre for Wembley, with Jim Kempster and Don Durant on hand to do the coaching. Tommy began to develop at the Skimpot Lane venue and was subsequently offered rides in the Wembley Juniors side, who raced their home matches at the Bedfordshire track. Later that year, Wembley manager Alec Jackson gave Tommy his first outing at the famous Empire Stadium in the junior scratch event or the 'Mugs Race' as it was affectionately known.

The following season, he was sent on loan to Cardiff, for whom he made his Provincial League debut. That same year also saw him ride for Nottingham, before he finally made some late season appearances for parent club Wembley in the National League. Tommy then spent the early part of 1937 occupying the reserve berth at Wembley, but later progressed to a second-string role and ended the year with a creditable 80 points to his name in league matches. That total increased to 114 points in 1938, and he had accumulated 125 points before the war brought the 1939 campaign to a premature end. Tommy made his World Final debut in 1938, while his international career got underway the following season when he rode in two matches against the Aussies. After the war, he continued with Wembley from 1946-56, giving fabulous service to the club.

On the individual front, Tommy twice rode in the British Riders' Championship final in 1946 and 1947, winning it at his first attempt with a stunning 15-point full-house. He then went on to make a further three World Final appearances in 1949, 1950 and 1954, taking victory in the first post-war staging of the event with maximum points. Internationally, Tommy appeared in seven successive post-war Test series versus Australia (1947-53), while he also represented his country against New Zealand (1953), Australasia (1955) and Sweden (1956). In 1964, when West Ham was re-opened by a consortium of National League promoters, Tommy was duly installed as promoter at the London track, and he remained in place at Custom House Stadium the following year, prior to emigrating to the sunnier climes of Australia.

Geoff Pymar made his Wimbledon debut in 1933, and was to remain loyal to the London side right up to the beginning of hostilities in 1939. He made his international debut for England against Australia at Wimbledon in 1934, and went on to represent his country in a further three home series (1935, 1938 and 1939). In addition to that, he twice toured Down Under with England (1934/35 and 1938/39), as well as racing against the USA (1937). Aside from making a solitary appearance in the Star Championship final (1935), Geoff also made it through to just one World Final in 1938. After the war, Geoff resumed his speedway career with New Cross in 1946, but in 1949, he moved across London to link with Harringay. He qualified for the final of the British Riders' Championship as a New Cross rider in 1947, but on the night, he enjoyed no luck and scored but 4 points. In 1950, Bristol were promoted to the First Division and Geoff was quite happy to leave the capital, joining the West Country side in a June transfer deal. He did help strengthen the Bulldogs and in 1951, top-scored for the team with 271 league points. Geoff remained with the Knowle-based outfit until they closed mid-way through 1955, during which time he was again recognized by England, being named as reserve for a Test match against New Zealand at Bristol on 25 September 1953, although in the event he didn't get a ride.

In 1956, he was next to be found racing for Norwich, and a further season was spent at the Firs, after which he was thought to have retired. However, the formation of the Provincial League in 1960 saw Geoff line-up for Yarmouth, and when they closed to league racing after just one season, he moved on to Middlesbrough in 1961. Geoff was to only appear in a handful of meetings for the Bears, the excessive travelling understandably not being to his liking. As a result, a longish spell out of the saddle followed, before he linked with Wolverhampton in July. Another change in 1962, saw him ride for Bradford at the Greenfield Autodrome, but when the Yorkshire venue finished at the end of the year, Geoff finally brought the curtain down on a career that had incredibly spanned thirty years. He returned to the sport as co-promoter of Exeter, working alongside Cyril Roger in 1957/58, and was later identified as a caddy in the world of golf, being spotted on courses the world over accompanying 1969 Open Championship victor Tony Jacklin.

Claude Rye started at Preston in 1929, but after missing the following season, he established himself with with Wimbledon from 1931-37, where he was a prolific team scorer. Indeed, a sensational start to 1933 saw Claude reach 100 league points before any other rider. The year also saw him win through the preliminary rounds to face Ron Johnson in the final of the British Individual Championship, but having lost the first leg, he then broke a leg in his first Test appearance for England, giving Johnson victory by default. He rode in the 1934 Star Championship final and also represented England versus Australia (1933-34 and 1936), the Overseas (1937) and USA (1937). Poor Claude actually won three England Test caps against the Aussies, but never scored a point. In 1933, the previously mentioned broken leg came in his opening race, then he failed to score in his only Test in 1934, and as a reserve in his one match of 1936, he wasn't called upon to ride. Sadly, injuries prevented him from being the star he should have been. Claude had two brothers, namely Percy and Horace, both of whom raced briefly at league level, the former with Preston in 1929, while the latter appeared for Wimbledon in 1934.

Having originally raced in the 1928 season, **Triss Sharp** became the league's youngest skipper when he was handed the job at Crystal Palace the following year. When the star riders were subsequently allowed into league racing the following year, he handed the club captaincy over to Roger Frogley, but was to remain loyal to the Palace cause until joining Coventry in mid-July 1933. In a further move, he was to join New Cross in 1934, but he never quite got to grips with the tightness of the affectionately nicknamed 'Frying Pan' circuit, retiring at the end of the season. The one and only time he qualified for the Star Championship final in 1930, he was unfortunate to be ruled out through injury. Sadly, that was to be the story of his career, and as with so many other riders, injury marred Triss's progress in the sport.

Harry Shepherd was born in London on 5 May 1903, and began his league career with Crystal Palace in 1930, remaining with the club until the end of 1933. He then moved across London to join New Cross, where he stayed for three years until 1936, also helping out at Provincial League Bristol in the latter season. In 1937, Harry became a full-time Bristol rider, scoring 167 points from their 20-match league programme, while also appearing in a couple of National League meetings for Wimbledon. Following their elevation to the First Division, Harry continued with the Bulldogs in 1938, and he stayed on board the following year, despite the side reverting to Second Division racing after enduring a difficult campaign in the top-flight. The individual highlight of his career was just one appearance in the Star Championship final of 1931. On the international front, he represented the Provincial League against Australia in 1937, prior to racing for England versus the Dominions two years later in 1939. During his riding days, Harry helped to change the face of the sport, when, in 1933, he worked alongside Fred Mockford, his promoter at Crystal Palace, to develop an electric hand-operated set of tapes which stretched across the start line. Similar to the starting tapes employed at horse racing, the new system replaced rolling starts, which had seen few races begin with all the competitors actually level.

Although he only appeared in league racing with Leicester (Stadium) for one season in 1929, **Slider Shuttleworth** is worthy of mention. He was a great showman and leg-puller, with his favourite trick being to fill a small balloon with red ink and place it inside his crash helmet, so that if he fell and banged his head, the ink would run all over his face. Slider derived a lot of public sympathy from this and was clearly quite a character.

Bert Spencer (full name: Albert David Spencer) was actually born in London on 13 May 1908, but was taken to Brisbane, Queensland, Australia as a baby. He returned to these shores in 1928 when he proved to be a spectacular rider as he did the rounds of the London circuits, prior to being associated with non-league Exeter the following year. He subsequently linked with Leicester Super in 1930, when he appeared in 10 Northern League matches. Bert returned south the following year, joining Plymouth and he was based with the Pennycross Stadium outfit for four seasons. The exciting leg-trailer then took a break before returning with Bristol in 1936. A move to Wimbledon followed in 1937, a year which also saw Bert assist at Provincial League Norwich. He remained with Wimbledon in 1938, while again helping out at Norwich, with a full-time move to the Firs following for the final season of pre-war racing in 1939. Bert raced in the Star Championship final of 1932, and represented Australia in three Test match series versus England (1934, 1938 and 1939), as well as two more in his home country (1934/35 and 1936/37).

Continuing with the international theme, he raced for his country against the Provincial League (1937), before being identified in a Dominions race-jacket in two series versus England (1938-39). Bert was back at Norwich immediately following the war, having turned down a posting to Glasgow (White City), with Wal Morton making the long trek to Scotland instead. The 1946 season saw him sweep all before him to score 200 league points, which was not only sufficient to head the Stars' scoring, but also the entire Northern League. That year also saw him compete in the British Riders' Championship final at Wembley, where he recorded a 5-point tally. He continued to represent Norwich until 1949, after which he returned home to Australia. His leg-trailing style was ideally suited to the sweeping bends of the Norwich bowl and there were few more exciting scenes in British speedway. Remaining in his homeland, he later represented Australia in two more series against England in 1949/50 and 1952/53.

Alec Statham arrived on the scene at his local Coventry circuit in 1933, when appearing in second-half events. He subsequently moved across the Midlands to link with Hall Green (Birmingham) the following season, appearing in their second side in the Reserve League. He eventually made his National League debut with Harringay in 1935, before spending a year in the Provincial League at Southampton. Alec was back at Harringay in 1937, however, and was to remain with the Tigers until the outbreak of war. On the individual front, he qualified for three World Finals (1937-39), although the first was as a reserve and he only took one ride. In 1938, he did well to notch 8 points in the big event, while the 1939 staging was scrapped. Alec made his England debut in the first Test match against the Aussies in 1938, later going Down Under to represent his country in the 1938/39 series. He again raced for England versus Australia in 1939,

Alec Statham – a wonderful speedway stylist and a great competitor who represented his country on many occasions.

while further international calls saw him appear for the combined England/Australia side against USA/Canada (1938) and for England versus USA/Canada (1939).

A wonderful speedway stylist, Alec was based at Odsal for the first two seasons of post-war racing (1946-47), prior to moving south to race for Wimbledon in 1948. He remained with the Dons until 1950, when he retired due to indifferent health. Alec headed the Wimbledon scoring with 314 league points in 1949, having been top man at Odsal in 1947, with a tally of 197 points. In the British Riders' Championship, he was a two-time qualifier for the finals of 1946 and 1948, but he suffered bad luck in the former and was forced to retire after two races with a foot injury. Alec fared much better on the second occasion, however, and in fact was the only rider on the night to head the formidable Vic Duggan. He eventually tied on 13 points with Ron Johnson, necessitating a run-off for second place, only to find himself outpaced by the speedy New Cross star. Alec subsequently made it through to the 1949 World Final as reserve, but didn't get an outing on the night. He again represented England on several occasions following the war, racing in four successive series versus Australia (1947-50), and as well as completing one tour Down Under (1947/48), he was also capped against the Overseas (1948).

Harold 'Tiger' Stevenson, skipper of West Ham and an England regular.

Having been another of the first-season starters in 1928, **Harold 'Tiger' Stevenson**, who was born on 1 November 1907, became a staunch West Ham regular, being based with the club right the way through from 1929-39. One of the early English stars, he captained the London side for several seasons and also rode in the Star Championship finals of 1930 and 1935. Tiger was an England representative against Australia throughout 1930, 1932-35 and 1938, while also appearing for the national side versus the Overseas in 1937. He also took part in three Australian series for England in 1934/35, 1935/36 and 1937/38. The 1933 season was phenomenal for Tiger, as he captured the British Individual Championship from Ron Johnson (only to lose out to Vic Huxley in his first defence in 1934), while he also skippered England in four Tests, and broke several track records. He then journeyed to Australia for the 1933/34 winter, where he incredibly tasted defeat just once in more than 50 starts! Following the war, and at the close of the 1946 season, he ran a successful series of training schools at both Bristol and Birmingham (Alexander Sports Stadium).

American **Ray Tauser** hailed from Portland, Oregon, and enjoyed a brief career in Britain, starting with a season of Southern League activity for Wembley in 1929. His other three seasons in this country were spent at Wimbledon (1930-32), during which time he was victorious in the 1931 Star Championship final, taking glory from Vic Huxley and Tommy Croombs.

Lionel Van Praag was from Sydney, New South Wales and first arrived on these shores to ride for Wembley in 1931. He was to remain based at the Empire Stadium right the way through to the outbreak of war, during which time he became a real legend of the sport. He made his Test match debut for Australia against England at Leicester Super in 1931, before going on to represent his country in a further eight series between the two sides (1932-39 inclusive). Lionel also rode against England for the Overseas (1937) and the Dominions (1938), as well as representing the combined England/Australia side versus USA/Canada (also in 1938). Continuing with the international theme, Lionel raced for Australia in three series on his home soil (1934/35, 1937/38 and 1938/39).

On the individual front, he made it through to one Star Championship final (1935), but the thing he will always be remembered for occurred in 1936, when he took victory in the initial World Final at Wembley. He subsequently went on to qualify for the other three pre-war World Finals (1937-39), although the third one never took

Lionel Van Praag, who returned to race here for New Cross following the war.

place of course. It came as something of a surprise when Lionel decided to give British speedway another go after the hostilities, but that is what happened and the Control Board allocated him to New Cross, who were having a torrid time at the start of the 1947 campaign. He didn't do too badly either, knocking up 89 league points and qualifying for the British Riders' Championship final, in which he totted up 8 points. It turned out to be his 'final fling' in this country, after which Lionel retired and left for his native Australia. Concluding his Test career, he rode for his country in the English series of 1947, prior to reappearing in the series of 1950/51 in Australia.

Yorkshire-born **Frank Varey** had a meteoric rise to fame on his Scott machinery, spending all the pre-war years (1929-39) with Belle Vue. 1935 was his nadir, when he endured an indifferent season, but he then made the sport's most astonishing comeback in 1938, when he raced into the top ten list, plundering 197 points from twenty-three league matches. Frank made two appearances in the Star Championship final (1932 and 1933), prior to a couple of showings in the World Finals of 1937 and 1938, as well as qualifying for the cancelled event of 1939. He was a regular England international, appearing in the Test match series versus Australia from 1930-33 and 1938-39, as well as the away series of 1934/35. He also

Frank Varey, who raced at Buenos Aires and Montevideo among other places in the winter of 1929/30, acquiring the nickname 'El Diablo Rojo' (The Red Devil) from the enthusiastic South American fans.

represented England against the Overseas in 1937, in addition to riding for the combined England/Australia side versus USA/Canada in 1938. Frank continued to ride during the war years at Belle Vue, the highlight being victory in the 1944 British Individual Championship, having previously filled the runner-up spot in 1942. He later became a promoter of repute, amazingly running Sheffield in four different spells (1945-49, 1951, 1952 and 1960-72), as well as being part of the management team at Edinburgh (1948-54). Finally, one last job in the sport saw him spend a year as speedway manager at Belle Vue in 1974.

Yet another of the pioneer men in 1928 was **Colin Watson**, who went on to represent London's White City in the following season's inaugural Southern League competition, before really making his reputation with Wembley (1930-34). All told, he made five appearances in the Star Championship final (1929-31 and 1933-34), as well as regularly representing England in Test match series against Australia between 1930-34, captaining the side on five occasions. In 1931, he was nominated to be Vic Huxley's first challenger for the 'World' Individual Championship, but having forced a decider, he went down to a 2-0 defeat at Wembley Stadium. A fractured leg sustained in West Ham's opening pairs meeting in 1935, was to keep him out of the saddle until he returned to the Wembley line-up for just one league match in 1937. The following season, Colin started the campaign with Wembley, but after appearing in just two league matches for them, he was to have spells with both West Ham and Division Two side Sheffield. The final season of pre-war activity saw Colin back at the Custom House Stadium with West Ham, and he often struggled, particularly away from home, his 1935 crash obviously still affecting his riding. After the war, he recommenced his career with West Ham in 1946, and astounded everyone by revealing brilliant form, only for his career to unfortunately end abruptly, following a crash at Odsal on 13 July that year. The accident happened in a second-half scratch race, immediately after he had notched 12 points for the Hammers in an ACU Cup match. He was 47 years old at the time and had suffered a fractured skull, as well as a punctured lung. Thankfully, despite a period on the critical list, he made a full recovery from his injuries, but his racing days were over.

Arthur 'Westy' Westwood was a great crowd-pleaser and after first representing Sheffield in 1929, he moved to Hall Green (Birmingham) later in the season. In 1930, he joined West Ham, prior to stints with Wimbledon (1931), Southampton/Clapton (1932) and Clapton (1933). During his riding days, Arthur was named as the organizer of meetings at Wolverhampton towards the end of 1929. Having got a taste of life on the other side of the fence, after retiring from active racing, he promoted at a number of tracks, including no less than four in 1938, namely Birmingham (at Hall Green, a venue which he had reopened the previous year), Leeds, Sheffield and Nottingham, becoming known by some as 'The Woolworth of Speedways'. After the war, he was identified as promoter at Tamworth (Deer Park, Fazeley) for two years in 1947 and 1948.

Born in Bathurst, New South Wales in 1911, **Arthur 'Bluey' Wilkinson** spent his entire British racing career with West Ham (1929-38), prior to becoming promoter at Sheffield (1939). His domestic record was nothing short of sensational, for he scored more points in the National League (which started in 1932) than any other rider, being one of only two track aces to top 1,500 points. Jack Parker was just a few points behind Bluey, but took eight seasons to garner his tally, whereas the great Australian did it in seven seasons. He qualified for the Star Championship final on five consecutive occasions (1931-35), although injury forced him on to the sidelines in 1932, with his best performance being a third place finish in 1933. His much-chronicled loss of the first-ever World Championship final in 1936, due to the bonus point system must have been heart-rending, but he bounced back brilliantly to scoop the ultimate prize in 1938. The popular Aussie also represented his country in the nine Test match series against England from 1930-38, as well as five successive series in his home country (1934/35-1938/39). He also rode for the Overseas side against England (1937), as well as appearing for England/Australia versus USA/Canada (1938). Completing his tremendous international record, Bluey was a member of the Australian side which took on the Provincial League in 1937, while the following year he donned a Dominions bib to race against England. Tragically, Bluey was killed in a road accident in his homeland on 27 July 1940.

Archie Windmill initially began riding at Barnet, prior to making his league bow with Hackney Wick in 1937; he remained with the then nicknamed Wolves until the war took effect. In 1938, he also assisted at Smallford, representing the Hertfordshire side in the Sunday Dirt-track League. He was recognized internationally in 1939, when he represented England in the Test series versus the Dominions. After the war years, tall Archie joined Wimbledon in 1946, and he is probably best remembered for his performance at Wembley the following year, when the Dons beat the Lions by a single point (42-41) and he rode out of his skin to notch 11 points. Archie remained at Wimbledon until the start of 1949, before switching to the re-opened Walthamstow in Division Two, having completed just one league match for the Dons. He stayed with the side, also known as the Wolves, until their closure at the end of the 1951 season, subsequently linking with Southern League Aldershot for what turned out to be his last year in the saddle (1952). Today, Archie is still an active worker for the Veteran Speedway Riders' Association, and has admirably fulfilled the role of President, as well as still taking a keen and active interest in present-day speedway.

Adelaide-born **Dick Wise** first appeared in Britain for Sheffield in 1930, prior to representing no fewer than three teams the following season, namely Harringay, Southampton and Stamford Bridge. In 1932, he spent the whole of the season based with the latter of those sides, prior to switching to Nottingham in 1933. Hall Green (Birmingham) was his next port of call in 1934, before he sat out the entire 1935 campaign. Dick then returned with Plymouth in 1936, with his final pre-war move taking him to Norwich for three years (1937-39). On the international front, he appeared for Australia versus England in two Test series (1930-31), and later represented the Dominions also against England (1938). After retiring form racing, Dick later worked on the other side of the fence, beginning with a job as speedway manager of Norwich in 1945, while similar positions followed at Yarmouth (1948-49) and Cradley Heath (1950).

Les 'Smiler' Wotton was born in Bristol and actually appeared in the first-ever meeting at Knowle Stadium on 25 August 1928. He subsequently went on to ride for Liverpool (1930) and Preston (1931), prior joining West Ham in 1932. Further moves then saw him race for Nottingham in 1933, and Hall Green (Birmingham) in 1934, before Harringay beckoned in 1935. Having represented six different sides, a period of stability followed as he was to remain with the Tigers right up to the outbreak of the Second World War. Les was a Star Championship finalist three times from 1932-34, and represented England at Test match level versus Australia in both 1934 and 1938, as well as touring Down Under in 1936/37 and 1937/38. He also raced for the England/Australia combination against USA/Canada in 1938. After the war, Les became a member of the New Cross side in 1946, scoring 136 league points.

The following year, he was part of a three-way transfer, which saw him join Wimbledon, with Oliver Hart going to Odsal, whilst Bill Longley linked with New Cross. Les was a success for the Dons too, netting 195 league points to finish as second top scorer behind Norman Parker. He remained at Wimbledon until late June 1949, when he signed for Second Division Coventry, where his experience was most useful to his younger team-mates. In 1950, Les was on the move again, this time to Southampton, where he stayed until retiring when the track prematurely closed in July 1951. His only appearance in the British Riders' Championship final occurred in 1947, when he gleaned a 4-point tally, while that same year also saw him represent England for one last time in the Test series versus Australia.